THE LONGEST
FLIGHT of YOUR LIFE

Confessions of a 1980s Air Stewardess

Natasha J. Rosewood

The Longest Flight of Your Life © Copyright 2023 by Natasha J. Rosewood

First edition.

All rights reserved. Except for brief quotations in reviews, no part of this publication may be reproduced, stored in a retrieval system, or transmitted in any form or by any means without the prior written consent of the author or a license from the Canadian copyright licensing agency access copyright. For an access copyright license, visit www.accesscopyright.ca or call toll-free 1-800-893-5777.

Disclaimer: Limit of Liability: Please note that much of this publication is based on personal experience and anecdotal evidence. Although the author and publisher have made every reasonable attempt to achieve complete accuracy of the content in this book, they make no representations or warranties with respect to the accuracy or completeness of the contents of this book and specifically disclaim any implied warranties for a particular purpose. This book is presented solely for educational and entertainment purposes. You should use the information in this book at your own risk.

Any trademarks, service marks, product names or named features are assumed to be the property of their respective owners and are used only for reference. There is no implied endorsement if we use one of these terms.

Nothing in this book is intended to replace common sense, legal, accounting, or professional advice, and only is meant to entertain.

Queries regarding rights and permission should be addressed to:
Natasha J. Rosewood
PO Box 22080, RPO Capri Center, Kelowna, BC. Canada V1Y 9N9

Website: www. natasharosewood.com
Cover design: Prominence Publishing
Typesetting: Prominence Publishing
Substantive Editing: Betty Keller
Copy editing/proofreading: Betty Keller/ Natasha Rosewood
Book concept and design: Natasha J. Rosewood
Photograph: Meredith Rose Photography

Note for librarians: a cataloguing record for this book that includes Dewey classification and US library of Congress numbers is available from the National Library of Canada. The complete catalogue record can be obtained from the national libraries online database at: www.nlc.bnc.ca/amicus/index-e.html

ISBN: 978-1-990830-36-5

THE LONGEST FLIGHT of YOUR LIFE
Confessions of a 1980s Air Stewardess

By Natasha J. Rosewood

In *The Longest Flight of Your Life* Natasha, a British air stewardess flying in the 70s and 80s, finally leaves her short haul days behind (*Flight of Your Life*) and joins the long-haul pioneering Laker Airways. Instead of drunken, exit-removing hoodlums, she is now faced with disappearing Bajan stewardesses, rioting German passengers, unruly celebrities and unpredictable hijackers as well as her colleagues' dramas in the air and on the ground. Despite her own up-and-down love life, Natasha continues to show us that while humanity is imperfect, we are still loveable and highly entertaining!

Table of Contents

WHY I WROTE THE BOOK 1
ACKNOWLEDGMENTS 3
1. WHAT ARE WE IN FOR? 4
2. SO, THIS IS AMERICA? 15
3. DAYLIGHT ROBBERY 33
4. CRASH! 41
5. PEOPLE BEHAVING BADLY 54
6. GROUNDED! 72
7. NOT FULLY LOADED 92
8. WOOF! WOOF! 118
9. LOVE YOU TO DEATH 135
10. BARBADOS, MON 146
11. POSITIVE THINKING? 172
12. FAMOUS PEOPLE DAY 191
13. AND THE INFAMOUS NIGHT 208
14. SURPRISE! 222
15. DOUBLE WHAMMY IN MIAMI 240
16. RUDE AWAKENINGS 271
17. HIJACKED! 287
18. DESPERATE MEASURES 313
19. AND NOW FOR SOMETHING COMPLETELY DIFFERENT 331
20. IT'S TOO LATE NOW! 349
ABOUT THE AUTHOR 360
MORE BOOKS BY NATASHA J. ROSEWOOD 361

NOTE TO READERS:

Throughout the book, you may encounter what you think are typos or misspelled words but as these stories were experienced with a UK airline, I have used English spelling, hence the double consonants etc. In addition, as an Air Stewardess, we encountered many different nationalities with various accents and dialects. To give the situations and the characters authenticity, I have written in those accents and dialects.

WHY I WROTE THE BOOK

If some of you have already read the first book in this series, *Flight of Your Life,* you may recall the words that follow. The reason for the repetition is that the same sentiment still applies. However, the only motivation I would add to the second book in this series, *The Longest Flight of Your Life,* is that I hope it inspires readers never to give up on their dream, which in my case, was to fly long-haul. I did it and I'm so happy to be able to share these adventures with you!

Writing a book for any writer is not an easy undertaking so writers often have at least one motivation. They want to share. I wanted to share, too—but there was more. Friends and family who have listened to me regale my adventures often *begged* me to write this book. Recounting my flying adventures and recalling the memories of the amazingly brave, funny characters I flew with was a wonderful flight over memory lane.

Despite the rumor that stewardesses were on board just to serve tea and coffee—and to look good—we were actually only there—and still are—to ensure the onboard safety of passengers. Our intensive emergency training prepared us, as well as for many other situations, to evacuate people out of a crashed aircraft within 90 seconds.

From a historical perspective, the first passenger flight took off in July 1949. But twenty-five years later in 1974, when I began my fun flying career, aviation was still evolving—and was often precarious. Unbeknownst to the general public at that time, the young "girls" who I flew with were often faced with great responsibilities and potentially dangerous situations, while having to remain calm and keep a smile on their faces. They also had to gracefully tolerate the male chauvinistic attitudes of the era. So I wanted to pay tribute to all the women who flew then and offer a "good luck" wish for all the men and women who fly today, albeit in safer aircraft but perhaps with a different breed of passenger.

In these interesting times in which we live, people seem to have forgotten their sense of humor and are taking themselves so-o-o-o-o seriously! Perhaps for us "hosties," who sometimes faced potential death, we decided that if time was going to be short-lived, then we may as well make it fun. And maybe it was suppressed hysteria? You will find in this book how we laughed at everything and everybody without judgement including people of all nationalities, sizes, shapes and skin colors, but we especially laughed at ourselves.

From working with the public, I learned that none of us are perfect, thank heavens, and it is our imperfections that make us the most interesting and lovable. Through these outrageous tales and irreverent humor, I hope you will see that underneath our idiosyncratic fears and egocentric behaviors, that we are funny, loveable, vulnerable beings just doing everything—like children—for the first time.

As the song goes, "We are only human after all." In this age of divisiveness, and distrust of each other, I also wanted to nudge readers to remember that our collective humanity is beautiful and, if we let go of judgment, together we humans can achieve anything.

Finally, I hope the stories will entertain you, make you smile, and help you love yourself more just for being human after all.

Acknowledgments

Gratitude and thanks go to:

All the characters in this book and all flight crew everywhere.
    For being who you are.

Betty Keller, Editor and Mentor
    Without Betty, I would not be the writer I am and the one that I will become.

Betty's Sunshine Coast Writing Group
    For their valued input.

Suzanne Doyle-Ingram, Publisher @ Prominence Publishing and her editing and graphics team.
    Who help me manifest great books.

Emilia Hodson, Screenwriter
    Who suggested the title: *The Longest Flight of Your Life*

All those who listened to my flying stories and who inspire me to keep writing.

And last but not least . . .

Lorne A. Lyons
    My dear husband, who always loves my stories, and while writing, brings me copious cups of tea.

1

WHAT ARE WE IN FOR?

London
Dec 1978 – Feb 1979

"Eee, chuck. I think the postman just came," my flatmate, Samantha, exclaimed as we were hanging a selection of sparkling baubles on our Christmas tree. Outside our living room window, the grey light of the December afternoon was already segueing into darkness.

I had also heard the slapping sound of the second post of the day hitting the hallway's tiled floor, but a pre-Christmas funk had hijacked my cheery spirit. I wasn't really in the mood to decorate a tree—let alone rush to open mail that could bring me more bad news.

After returning from Barbados in October, inspired to change my life—in part because of Jose—I had applied to three long-haul airlines: British Airways, British Caledonian and Laker Airways. While acquiring headshots and filling out longwinded application forms was tedious—BA stopped short of asking for the colour of my grandmothers' eyes—there was also a flicker of hope for a new life. So I had provided them with all the successes and train wrecks of my checkered career path, including my four years with the notoriously dangerous Dan Air—or 'Dan Dare' as we were commonly known. After I had slipped all the envelopes into the red post box in front of my maisonette, my success or failure, I had decided, was now in the laps of the airline Gods.

But by December British Airways and British Caledonian had already turned me down. I reasoned their rejections were founded on my disastrous interviews with them years earlier, which—big mistake—I had attended with my irreverent Dan Air friend Emma. After both of us had been accepted by BA at our first interview and invited back for a second that afternoon, we had unwisely celebrated over a pub lunch. The wine might have loosened our tongues because at our second interview, when asked why we wanted to leave Dan Air, we might have been a little too flippant about our many in-flight emergencies and what we'd had to do to survive, including imbibing post-traumatic potent landing drinks. Their looks of horror had been sobering. After being rejected, we were miffed that they didn't appreciate our resourcefulness to survive disasters, so Emma and I had rationalized that they preferred virginal hosties. With our combined years of experience, as well as—sin of sins—my early promotion within Dan Air—we knew that we did not present as remotely virginal. Probably more. . . corrupted.

So now it was all up to Laker.

Samantha placed the last red ball on a lower branch. When I still didn't make any move to get the post, she urged, "There might be summat from the airline, chuck."

"I know. That's what I'm afraid of," I said. What will I do if they turn me down, too? I asked myself. As Emma had done before me, would I have to apply to some mid-east airline and hope that I didn't get caught up in a revolution?

Since my parents' divorce, Christmas had always sent me into a funk. I envied my two flat-mates who would be leaving me to cozy up to their ever-so-close families for the season. With a ranting psycho mother, my father in a new relationship, two siblings in England who, since the break-up of the family, had gone AWOL, and the remaining two brothers I was closest to now living 10,000 miles away in Canada, I did not have anywhere to go. Volunteering to fly over the holiday might be my best option.

"Ooh, yer daft bugger," Samantha said, as she stepped over boxes of tinsel and moved toward the hallway. "*I'll* get the post!"

When she returned to the living room, she was flipping through a bundle of mail which included early Christmas cards, a magazine and some flyers.

"Told yer," she said, holding up a white envelope with Laker's black and red logo on the outside.

I gulped, still hesitating. This was like Russian Roulette, but with an envelope, instead of a gun, determining the next hit or miss of my life.

"Do you want me to open it?" she offered.

"No, it's okay." I took it from her, slit open the seal with my nail and pulled out the single page. "Oh, my God!" I cried after I read the first two lines. "Oh, my God!"

"What is it?" Samantha was holding her breath.

"I'm in!" Tears welled up in my eyes. "*I'm in!*"

"Go on then." Samantha urged, beaming, happy for my joy. "Read it out loud!"

"We are pleased to inform you," I announced, my hand shaking, "that Laker Airways welcomes you to our airline. You are required to commence training Monday, February 5, 1979. Please report at 09.00 hours to . . ."

I collapsed onto the settee. At last, I would be flying long-haul! Now, instead of doing "doubles"—four sectors a day with four take-offs, four landings and four lots of passengers—and often flying ten days in a row, I would be operating just one long flight every few days and seeing the sights of New York, LA, Barbados and soon, rumor had it, Miami. The curse of having worked for another airline and being "tainted" by them had finally been erased. And the thought of spending more time on the same continent as my new love Jose—seeing him again—was also delicious. Ever since our meeting in Barbados, he hadn't been out of my mind for a minute.

"Ee, that's grand, chuck!" Samantha was smiling, happy for me. "I think this calls for a celebration, don't you?" she said, heading for our ample bar supply of miniature spirits.

As we sat on the couch, sipping on our brandy and cokes, Samantha commented, "Yer know, I think it's a brave thing you're doin'."

"What do you mean—brave?"

"Changin' airlines . . . yer know . . . after all this time."

"You mean at the grand old age of 27?"

Like me, Samantha had only worked for one airline, but with her employer, British Airtours, she was well-paid to fly all over the world. She had no need to switch. But I didn't think my change required courage. True, I would have to go through another six weeks of flight training, this time on DC-10s and the familiar BAC 1-11s, but that would be a minor challenge compared to all the gains. There was no fear, just excitement. "Sometimes," I told her, "the benefits outweigh the risk."

Two days later another piece of good news came.

"Why don't you come here for Christmas, Natasha?" my older brother, Jack asked, no trace of an English accent in his Canadian drawl. "You can fly standby, right?" For the last ten years he had lived in Calgary, Alberta, where he had found his niche in the oil and gas business and was now sharing his success with a wife and two daughters. "At least we can guarantee you a white one," he added.

"Oh, that would be great!" I responded, happy to avoid the dreaded alternatives of previous years—flying lonely and miserable passengers to somewhere, being retraumatized by a dysfunctional family or sitting home all alone. Then another happy thought occurred to me. If I flew to Canada through New York, maybe—just maybe—I could meet up with Jose. The Big Apple was just a short flight away from Boston.

After I registered for some standby flights, I wrote to Jose suggesting we might see each other in New York on December 19. Aware that his marketing job for a large corporation took him all over North and South America, I knew a meeting might be a challenge. Then just in case we missed each other, I included my brother's phone number in Calgary. Still, I couldn't help but wonder, what if he has already forgotten me?

As I packed my suitcase the day before my trip, I felt deflated. Jose had not responded. The writing was on the wall. He was not interested. But just as I placed my suitcase in the hallway late that afternoon, there was a knock at the front door. A weary, parcel-laden postman handed me a white envelope. When I saw *Special Delivery* and the US postmark, my heart raced. I tore it open. His words, which appeared as if printed in a hurry, brought both elation and disappointment.

IT WAS SO GOOD TO HEAR FROM YOU! I RECENTLY RETURNED FROM SAO PAULA AND GOT YOUR NOTE TODAY. I WILL BE FLYING FROM DENVER THROUGH JFK ON DECEMBER 19TH AND LANDING AROUND THE TIME OF YOUR ARRIVAL. I WILL TRY TO MEET YOU BUT IT MIGHT BE TIGHT. IF WE DO MISS EACH OTHER, I'LL SEE YOU IN ENGLAND NEXT YEAR. JOSE.

So he *does* want to see me again! My heart thumped almost out of my chest at the possibility of being with him again soon, even though a brief encounter in New York sounded tentative.

On the London Heathrow to JFK flight, the Boeing 707 was half empty—surprising for an almost-Christmas flight. I was grateful to my neighbouring passengers who kept me engaged in interesting conversations on the six-hour sector and distracted me from the question that was bouncing around in my brain: Would I or wouldn't I be seeing Jose in just a few hours? If I didn't, I thought, my consolation prize would be that my new long-haul career would begin in March and would surely bring us together then.

Once settled into Jack and Jean's spacious home in Calgary and enjoying a decadent Canadian breakfast of fluffy pancakes, maple syrup and bacon, my brother and I discussed my love life. "So, who is this Jose you were hoping to meet at JFK?" he demanded, feigning older brother protectiveness. "He sounds like a Colombian drug dealer!"

"Just because he's South American?" I responded, my hackles rising in defense of my new love. "Actually, he has a very responsible job." But it suddenly occurred to me that there *was* something secretive about Jose, and that he *did* spend even more time in airplanes than I did, travelling all over North and South America. Hmm? I banished my brother's nefarious suspicions from my mind.

Then the quiet trill of a phone sounded in their living room. "For you," Jack said, holding out the receiver. "It's your drug dealer." He grinned.

Hi," Jose said, a smile in his voice. "Where are jyou?"

Just hearing his sultry South American accent again took my breath away. "Calgary."

"Where ees Calgary?"

"Alberta, Canada," I told him. For someone who flew all over the Americas, I was surprised that he didn't know anything about the country to the north. (Later in my new job I would come to realize that many Americans considered Canada just an uninteresting slab of ice on the top of their cake.)

"Brrr! It sounds cold," he teased.

I peered through Jack's large living room windows and saw nothing but white. The low-lying snow-covered hills blended into a pale grey horizonless sky, preparing for yet another snowfall. "Yes, it's cold outside, a mere minus 40, but we—"

"I'm so sorry that we couldn't meet," he blurted, sounding sad and melting my heart. "My Denver plane was delayed."

"Oh." He had warned me, of course, but I had endured a torturous few hours in JFK waiting and hoping.

"Will jyou be coming to the US again soon?"

Should I tell him that Laker Airways had accepted me and that I would be flying regularly to America? But what if I didn't pass the training course? "Nothing planned yet," I told him. But when *will* we see each other again? I wondered.

As if responding to my thought, he announced, "I am definitely coming to England this jyear."

"When?" I breathed.

"I'm not sure jyet. April or May."

So long to wait. "Oh."

"But we will stay in touch," he affirmed, his last word sounding like "toch." Adorable.

"Yes," I muttered, wondering how. Phone, letter, psychic communication?

We both fell silent. I held the receiver close to my ear as if a million thoughts were being exchanged, transmitted in our breath down the line. I didn't want to hang up.

Finally, he spoke. "I guess I should go."

"Okay." How I hated saying goodbye. "See you in England. . . whenever you get there."

"*Feliz Navidad,*" he whispered.

"Merry Christmas."

Click.

I replaced the phone in its cradle. At least, I thought, I had April to look forward to.

When February 5 rolled around and I reported for my Laker training to a classroom filled with chattering, excited women, I was delighted to see in the crowd the familiar face of one of my Dan Air friends. Ellen Hopkins beamed and waved at me, then came over to join me.

"Natasha! I'm so glad you got in!"

"You, too!" I paused. "I would have rung you, but . . . you know . . . I wasn't sure if you'd made it. Praise the Lord! We've both broken the Dan Air curse."

"Oh, I kno-o-ow. I kno-ow," Ellen said, doing our usual joke, an imitation of Sybil on *Faulty Towers*. "Seriously, though, I can't wait to do long haul. Just think! No more double Zurich-Milans!"

"Well, not three a week, anyway."

Just then a female instructor entered the room, and we were asked to take our seats. This class of trainees was already different from Dan Air. Two of the 30-strong group were stewards. Apparently leery of unions and their potential demands, Freddie Laker had only recently acceded to employing male cabin crew.

"Do you want to sit together?" I asked Ellen, pointing to the first row.

"Oooh, the two reprobates at the front of the class?" She giggled. "Do you think that's a good idea?"

"Terrible, but now that we are with a *professional* airline," I mockingly admonished her, "we *must* be on our best behaviour."

"After two years with Dan, I may have forgotten how." Ellen giggled again and took her seat.

"Me, too, but let's hope we're still trainable, or that they have a good sense of humour."

Despite the new wide-bodied aircraft to familiarize ourselves with, advances in First Aid training to adapt to, more emergency equipment in various locations to remember, new US customs and regulations to absorb, triple the amount of evacuation drills to memorize and extensive airline policies to learn, the training was not really that different from Dan Air's.

What *was* different was the two-hour lecture on how to stay alive in New York.

"Do not ride in an elevator by yourself or get in a cab or go on the subway alone," Val, the blonde instructor began. "When you arrive at the Doral Inn, our New York hotel, *do not*, I repeat, *do not* shout out your room number to a crowded lobby or talk about how much flight pay you're getting. When you arrive at your hotel room, unlock your door, open it so it's just ajar, and then prop your suitcase against the door so, if you need to, you can make a quick escape. Then enter the room. Before you close it, look under the beds, in the closets and check behind the shower curtain to make sure you are alone."

I shuddered. Memories of the stabbing scene during the film *Psycho* popped into my head. What if someone got in while I was *in* the shower?

One of the stewards sitting in the row behind me snickered. I noticed how, after spending time with "the girls," he was becoming more effeminate by the day. "Oooh," he teased, "what if you *do* find a man in your room? Tie him to the bed?"

Val wasn't amused. "You may think this is funny, but one girl *did* find a dead body under her bed last year. The victim, a murdered hooker, had been there for a week. In fact," she added, "believe it or not, there are three rooms on the eighth floor that are reputed to be haunted, mainly by hookers. So, if you are ever given room number

819, 821 or 823, you may want to request a room change." She shrugged. "Your choice."

I gulped and looked over at Ellen. Her already-large brown eyes were dilating into even bigger orbs. "Bloody hell!" I whispered. "What are we in for?"

"When you are sure that no one else is in your room," Val continued, now having our full attention, and enjoying our shocked expressions, "bring in your suitcase, and put all four locks on the door. New York has an extremely high crime rate. Also always check the peephole before letting anyone into your room, even if that person claims to be hotel staff or one of us. Being airline crew and wearing red uniforms, we tend to attract unwanted and sometimes dangerous attention. The other warning about our New York hotel is . . ."

I inhaled. There's more?

". . .when you are in the bar and want to go to the bathroom, never, never go to the downstairs loo. Although it's inconvenient, go back up to your room. Nine years ago, one of our girls was . . . raped and badly beaten in that washroom. So, if you want to stay safe, use your own room. Understood?"

A sombre muttering of agreement rustled around the classroom.

"Good. Now about LA . . ."

Toward the end of our training, we began to understand that for Freddie Laker, the pioneer of the Skytrain, safety was a priority. His low-budget daily service to New York was just 99 pounds sterling one way—a tenth of what other airlines charged, but while he offered cheap fares, he was not going to be accused of cutting corners and endangering peoples' lives. After several near-death experiences with Dan Air—and their *un*-safety record of three crashes in eight years—I was grateful for and respected his philosophy.

Six weeks later, with the exception of one very skinny girl who, as part of an emergency drill, had not been physically strong enough to pull herself up out of the DC-10's lift when it was deliberately halted between the lower galley and the main cabin, our class had all passed with flying colours. While I felt sad for her, I also knew that flying demanded all kinds of strengths—and not just physical ones.

On the final day of our training, our class of 27 women and two men were awarded our Laker golden-winged bird brooches, which we pinned to our standard issue winter uniforms—black coats over polyester red tunics and black trousers, accessorized with white scarf, black leather gloves and black bowler hats. Then, on a not-so-sunny day, clutching our certificates in our hot little hands, we posed in a long, single row on the tarmac for photographs while the shadows of a Laker Airways DC10 loomed over us and our happy faces.

We were now ready for the most anticipated event—receiving our first long haul monthly roster. We were each handed a large sheet of white paper covered in scratchy black writing, as if a spider dipped in black ink had crawled all over the page. When I saw all the new and far away destinations—LAX, JFK, BGR, YYZ and BGI—scribbled alongside my name, a thrill shot through me. At last. . .long haul! And when I deciphered my first duty, I gasped. Bangor for two days, then on to LA for three days and back to Bangor for five. Ten whole days! Had Laker Crewing or the gods known how long I had been waiting to do long haul and were now bestowing this prize trip on me?

How far is Bangor from Boston? I wondered. Will I be able to see Jose?

Ecstatic at the myriad of possibilities, I didn't sleep that night. I may be 27, I thought, but my life is just beginning.

2

SO, THIS IS AMERICA?

March 1979

"As you are brand new to the airline, Miss Rosewood, we are just calling to confirm that you're doing a 10-day Bangor-LAX-Bangor reporting at 13.00 hours today?" the male voice from Laker Crewing stated.

"Thank you!" I gushed full of gratitude though this young man was not solely responsible for my new-found happiness. This would be my first operating flight with a long-haul airline, and I couldn't have been more excited. Now instead of seeing just airport buildings and tarmacs in between short-haul European flights, I was going to be seeing the world. . . well, America, Canada and Barbados at least. And who knew where else?

The night before, I had gone through my kit twice, repeated my drills and inspected my uniform. Even though I had four years of flying under my belt and had also been a senior with Dan Air, the "new girl" jitters were still wreaking havoc on my stomach—as if I had never flown before.

Would there be any downside to this airline? One great thing about the "Dan Dare" cabin crews had been our close camaraderie, an "us against them" attitude. We had made fun of the airline, the passengers and each other, perhaps as a stress release from our suppressed hysteria triggered by the dangers we had often been exposed to. With a larger crew and Laker's more professional approach, would these crews be as much fun?

Just before 1.00 p.m. that day, dragging my large suitcase behind me, I walked into the Laker crew room to check in for my flight.

A very aristocratic-looking redhead now addressed me, "I say, are you on the Bangor-LA?"

"Yes, I am," I said, happy to have found a friendly face. "This is my first flight," I confessed. Then, seeing the subtle rolling of her eyes, I added quickly, "But I'm not really a new girl. I flew for Dan Air for four years."

"Good Lord!" she exclaimed. "And you're still alive!"

"Oh, I kno-o-ow, I kno-ow!" I responded.

Deirdre recognized my Sybil imitation and we both giggled. An instant friendship took root.

"I'm Deirdre, by the way."

"Natasha."

The flight to Bangor, Maine, was only six hours. Once the dreaded pre-flight emergency drill testing was over, and the emergency equipment was checked, passengers began to board. As a junior, I was positioned at Two Door Right, and from the starboard side of the aisle I directed passengers as they entered Two Door Left and came through the galley. Unlike the European mixture of touristy "punters" who made up Dan Air's passenger list, I saw that these people—though predominantly British and American—were a combination of all races.

Four hours into the flight, after headsets, drinks, meals, teas, coffees, wine and liqueurs had all been served, I was instructed to go "downstairs" for my dinner break.

"So how do you think you'll like long haul, Natasha?" Deirdre asked as we descended together in the galley lift to the aircraft's underbelly. In her position as Number Four or "galley slave," she was returning from the flight deck carrying trays of picked-over meals.

"Eee ba gum, lass," I joked, "after 'aving to do a full service on a 45-minute Dan Air flight, this is bloody luxury."

"Oh, I kno-o-o-w," she said, laughing. "Freddie's a bit of a chauvinist, but he runs a good airline."

As I sank onto a jump seat and watched as Deirdre coordinated hot meals for the cabin crew, then pulled out mineral boxes for another bar service and hauled the heavy carts in and out of stowages, I rubbed my stomach. Recently I had felt some niggling pains.

"Are you okay, darling?" Deirdre asked. "You look a little pale."

"I'm fine. I think I've got something going on with my digestion."

She stopped mid-motion and stared at me. "Oh, God! It's not appendicitis, is it?"

"Don't think so," I said, considering the possibility.

"Because you know, I had it," she exclaimed, "and I ignored it. Then I got peritonitis and nearly died. It was absolutely awful, darling. And if you're halfway across the Atlantic, that's three hours either way, and it's too late to get to a hospital. Then you're hooped."

"Maybe it's just nerves," I offered, not really believing my own diagnosis. God forbid that I should be sick on my first trip. To change the subject, I asked, "Do you know how far Bangor is from Boston?"

"To drive? About five hours, I think," she answered absently as she opened an oven and checked on a meal. "Why?"

That would be too far for Jose to come to see me. I would have to be content with a phone call. But maybe he wasn't even in the office since he travelled 90% of the time.

She saw my disappointment.

"Oh, God," she exclaimed, hand on hip. "What's his name?"

"Jose." I beamed. "How did you know?"

"Da-h-ling, it's always about a man." She grinned. "It always is."

Four hours later, when we arrived at The Stable in Bangor, the verging-on-seedy single-storey motel was not quite the glamorous accommodation I had imagined the airline would provide. What it lacked in luxury, though, it made up for in friendliness. Unlike many hotels where the staff dreaded accommodating airline crews and their frantic antics, the receptionists here seemed genuinely happy to see us.

Before and during my early flying years, I had hitchhiked, driven and flown all over Europe sleeping in hostels, a VW camper, farmhouses and strangers' homes. On those adventures, I had met many travelling Americans, but this would be my first time on U.S. soil meeting "down home" locals. I was already struck by how *big* everything was here, especially the warmth of the people.

After we checked in, Deirdre and Joan, another Laker "new girl," and I agreed to meet in the bar for drinks. But even before I got out of my new polyester uniform, already smelling of the aircraft, I retrieved Jose's business card and dialled the number. Having learned my roster just two days before my flight, there hadn't been time to let him know I was coming.

"Good afternoon, Carrington Corporation," a woman's voice drawled.

With pounding heart, I asked, "Could I please speak with Jose Ramirez?"

"Putting you through."

He was *there!* I inhaled. There was a click.

"Jose Ramirez."

How I loved that voice! "Hi," I said, exhaling.

Even though we hadn't spoken in three months, the psychic sense that existed between us made introducing myself seem redundant.

"Hi!" He sounded delighted. Then he paused as if catching his breath before speaking. "Where are jyou?"

"Banger," I said proudly, elated that now there wasn't an ocean between us.

"Isn't banger a sausage?" he teased.

"Okay. Bang-o-o-or." I laughed. "It's my first trip with Laker, my new long-haul airline."

"Oh!" He sounded delighted.

"Where are jyou staying?"

"The Stable Inn."

"How long are jyou staying there?"

"We leave tomorrow for LA, but we'll be back on Thursday for five days." Why was he asking?

"Jyou'll be there on Friday?"

"Yes."

"I'm coming to see jyou," he stated firmly, as if making the decision in that minute.

You *will?* My stomach flip-flopped.

"I'll be there at five, okay?"

"Yes." I breathed. "That would be lovely." Just four sleeps away.

He exhaled as if emitting a huge sigh of relief. "Hasta lluego," he whispered, before hanging up.

I entered the bar and, in the semi-darkness, found Deirdre and Joan sitting at a small round table. The only light in the room was from dull yellow orbs above the bar where tattooed veteran soldiers were exchanging stories. Even in the shadowy atmosphere, Deirdre could see I was radiating joy.

"You look like the cat who just ate the cream," Deirdre commented.

"Jose's driving up from Boston to see me on Friday!" I blurted.

"Gosh. How super!" Deirdre fumbled for her cocktail and in the shadows nearly stabbed herself in the nose with her paper umbrella.

Why don't they turn on the lights? I wondered.

"This *must* be love!" Deirdre teased.

"When did you last see him?" Joan asked.

"Five months ago, in Barbados." I gave them an abbreviated version of our fated meeting and then our almost-rendezvous at Christmas.

"Five months is a long time after meeting so briefly," Joan commented. "Aren't you afraid you won't feel the same?"

"No." The thought had never occurred to me. Jose and I were connected on some deeper soul level. His spell over me was still a mystery.

Due to the excitement of our first flight and a little jet lag, the three of us opted to stay in the hotel bar for dinner. We ordered what appeared to be the safest thing on the menu: burgers accompanied by Wild Duck pink champagne. Later we slunk off to our respective rooms where, despite the noise outside from drunken veterans singing, I fell into a deep and happy sleep.

The next morning five of us assembled in the lobby to go for an all-American breakfast. Gingerly we negotiated a busy main road to get to a large diner where the formica tables seemed to go on forever. Bangor, Maine, was—from what I had seen on the drive from the airport and looking around the motel's immediate vicinity—a homey, friendly place where most Americans appeared to dress casually, eat massive meals in shadowy bars and drive very big cars down very wide roads.

As I pored over the gigantic, laminated menu and delighted at the many new-to-me choices, I couldn't help but notice the proprietors in their chef's uniforms behind the counter. Both the man and the woman must have weighed over 20 stone each, and as they waddled over to sit at their corner table, I tried not to gawk at their disproportionately tiny heads atop their heavy bodies. Always battling my extra nine pounds of excess body weight, I empathized with how uncomfortable and unhealthy they must feel. Yes, everything in America was definitely bigger.

"You're lucky to get this ten-day trip on your first flight, Natasha," Pat, who was ultra-slim, commented as she dug into the fried onion rings atop her jacket potato drenched in sour cream.

With Jose coming to see me in a few days, and my new long-haul career just beginning, I *was* feeling lucky. And later that afternoon, we would be winging our way to Los Angeles for three whole days. Another first. "Yes, I am," I said, "Very lucky."

After an uneventful four-and-half hour sector from Bangor, we landed at LAX airport around 5.00 p.m. West Coast time. The trek through the sprawling airport down faded red carpeted hallways seemed to go on for miles. Outside the terminal, and on the other side of the wide road, I recognized the circular white alien-like restaurant structure that I had seen in many a TV show and film. I was in LA!

I took my seat at the back of the crew transport that would take us to Santa Monica and the Ramada Inn on Pico. While the driver negotiated rush hour traffic, I thought how the massive cars, wide highways and sporadic palm trees were a world away from my home in Horsham with its big old elms sheltering narrow country lanes that were barely wide enough to accommodate one mini let alone two cars. But here I was in California, and I loved it.

On my first night in LA, the whole crew, all thirteen of us, agreed to go to a favorite eatery. "The Great American Food and Beverage Disaster is great fun," Deirdre shared as she linked arms with me, and we followed the rest of the crew up Pico Boulevard. "The servers are only hired if they can sing or dance so every time they dish up a course, they have to perform."

Seated around a large oval table, while devouring delicious steaks and salads, we joined the waiters and waitresses in their entertainment. These talented Hollywood-hopefuls in their bright red and white striped outfits and overdone make-up got us all singing and even dancing. My earlier fears about the larger Laker crews not being as friendly or fun as Dan Air crews were officially quashed.

The following morning under a cloudless blue California sky, a group of us ambled four blocks down Pico to the beach where we marked our territory with our towels on a spot overlooking the famous Santa Monica pier on our right and Venice beach on our left. While basking in warm sunshine—such a treat for English girls in March—our small group was infiltrated by a long-haired man who plonked himself on the edge of our group. He stretched out a hairy, tattooed arm and offered me a short butt. It looked like pot. "No, thanks," I said, shaking my head.

"Hey man, you gotta have some fun," this ragged specimen intoned, urging me to take a toke.

My parents had never needed to give me the drug lecture. As a teenager, I had watched the spaced-out youths sitting in clusters on the streets in my small northern hometown on God-knows-what-drugs, their eyes closed as they twitched and grunted in a mixture of pain and bliss. Losing control over their minds and bodies hadn't looked like fun or even pleasant. Just a year later the ringleader had, while on some hallucinogen, attacked his mother with an axe. The rest of his young life was spent in the local lunatic asylum. Lesson learned.

Restless, I got up and walked away from the man down to the water's edge. I knew that the ocean was definitely too cold to swim in, but just so I could say that I'd been in the Pacific, I dipped my big toe in the frigid waters. By the time I returned to my towel, more waifs had appeared. A little antsy and suddenly wanting to be alone, I told the girls I was going back to our hotel for a swim in the pool.

I had only walked two blocks up the gentle incline of Pico when I noticed a large blue Thunderbird driving very slowly up the road beside me. I peeked over my shoulder. A blond-haired man with one hand on the steering wheel and the other casually slung across the back of the passenger seat, was staring back at me. Was he trailing me? He looked more like a surfer-dude than a criminal and I suddenly remembered that the training instructor had warned us that the wider roads and fewer pedestrians in LA could be more dangerous than New York. Walking alone on the wide-open streets now with only isolated offices and uninhabited industrial buildings on either side, I suddenly felt vulnerable.

Just ahead was a liquor store, and I stepped casually inside. Once in the interior shadows of the shop and not caring that the man behind the counter was giving me curious looks, I peered out from behind a stack of Budweisers to see what my stalker was doing. He had stopped the car and was staring at the store, watching and waiting. Would he come inside and try to kidnap me? Pretending to inspect a wine label, I looked up. The car was gone! Gingerly I walked to the front and peeked through the dusty glass windows. The car was nowhere in sight. Was it a trick? Even if it was, I couldn't stay here all day.

Before leaving, I muttered a "Thank You" to the confused clerk and stepped outside. I turned up the hill just in time to see the blue car revving up and burning rubber as he turned right and disappeared. Worried that he might be just going around the block, I hurried the remaining hundred yards up the hill and was relieved when I stepped into the cool, air-conditioned lobby of the Ramada. Never walk alone, I thought. For the rest of our stay in LA, as we toured Beverly Hills, Venice Beach and Hollywood, I stuck close to my colleagues.

Finally, it was Friday, the day I would see Jose! We were back at The Stable and I was in my motel room, touching up my make-up and viewing my reflection in the mirror. At least, while in California I had acquired a golden tan, not like the darker tan of Barbados I had when Jose last saw me, but I also wasn't boasting the pasty-white complexion most English people presented after a long, cold winter.

At 4:20 p.m. the phone rang. Could it be him already?

"I'm early," was all he said.

"Um . . . um . . ." Oh my God. "Do you want to come to my room. I'm in #13."

A minute later there was a gentle tap on the door. My heart racing, I opened up. And there he was, grinning that irresistible smile. He stepped from the shadows into my brightly lit room. We stood, surveying each other and beaming, my stomach doing flip flops.

"Is it really you?" he said.

I could only smile, not believing that after five months, he was also right in front of me.

That evening as we went first for drinks in The Stable's bar, full of more dubious miscreants, then to dinner in an eatery across the street, followed by dancing on the fake Spanish galleon in the center of the restaurant, I was in a stupefied daze. Unable to tear my eyes away from his soulful brown eyes and with an inane grin on my face that wouldn't go away, I was the proverbial giggly schoolgirl.

Afterwards, and perhaps not wanting our time together to be over, Jose suggested we go for a short drive, teasing me about how the English would be a liability driving on the right side of the road. I rose to the challenge. Grinning nervously, he let me get into the driver's seat. He might have been terrified for his life—or his car— but he just crossed himself and made jokes about dying at the hands of an English woman.

In his still-intact vehicle, we finally came to a halt outside my motel room door. We sat in silence, each of us reluctant to say goodnight. I had been in love before, but this was like a tidal wave of overwhelming joy, and I was drowning in happiness. Whatever the ending of this story would be, I was already lost and out of control in a glorious and terrifying maelstrom of emotion.

"Do jyou want to meet for breakfast in the morning?" he asked, signalling our final parting for the night.

Oh. Do I have to wait till breakfast to be with you? I thought. Jose was staying on the second floor at The Stable, just above me, mere yards from my room. Even if it meant sleeping in a chair beside him while he slept on the bed, or just to lie fully clothed by his side while he dreamt, I did not want to waste a minute being away from him. But he was being a gentleman, dammit, and I could not, would not push.

"Yes, I'd love to," I managed with grace.

He opened my car door, gave me his customary kiss on both cheeks and watched as I unlocked my hotel room and entered, alone. What he didn't see was me sinking onto the bed and asking myself the question: If he likes me, why doesn't he want to touch me? Aren't Latin men supposed to be romantic, passionate? He must not be attracted to me, I decided.

I didn't sleep.

Jose was already waiting in the lobby for me the next morning. Another Laker crew was clustered around the front desk in the process of checking out.

"They look like a funeral party," he joked, as we watched the women swarm out of the door and into transport. He was right. Our winter uniform was all black: coat, hat, gloves, trousers, except for the red tunic underneath and the white scarf with black and red birds adorning it. "Our summer uniform is a bit cheerier," I told him. "All red."

"Thank heavens," he said, smiling. "I don't want jyou to get depressed."

As we sat on high stools at the breakfast bar, tackling another novelty for me—a massive stack of pancakes—the sun shone through the large windows of the restaurant. For someone who was on a permanent diet, I thought, I would have to watch my food intake when in the US.

Jose was in high spirits, teasing me. He talked about South America while I told him stories of travelling around Europe. "But I really loved LA," I told him. "I think I'd like to live there for a while."

"Let's go there together." He leaned into me, smiling.

What did he mean by that? For a holiday, to live, as a couple?

Not sure how to respond, I just laughed nervously. With this man, I was at sea, overwhelmed. While I wanted this insane joy to last forever, I was also terrified of scaring him away.

He looked up at the massive clock on the wall above the breakfast counter. "Oh, I jhave to get back to Boston," he said, dismayed. Then lightening up, he added, "Jyou see, this English lady dragged me away from the office jyesterday and caused a diversion."

I smiled, but my heart was sinking. But I don't want you to leave, I thought. "Okay," I muttered as we slid off our stools.

"By the way," he mentioned as he pulled open the heavy restaurant door for me, "our trip to London has been postponed until June."

Boo, hiss. Another three months! "Do you know what date?"

"The twelfth, I theenk."

Just thirty minutes later, while I stood in my hotel room doorway, I watched Jose retreat, still facing me, his eyes fixed on me. I liked to think that, as I was imprinting the image of his boyish features in my mind and committing them to memory, he was doing the same with my face. "See you in June," I called, before he climbed into his car, put it into reverse and drove away, leaving me bereft.

In my sombre motel room, I slumped against the closed door. Each time Jose left, it felt as if someone had switched off the sunlight and the world had gone cold and flat again. Last night had been unbearable knowing he was so near, yet so far. But I wouldn't think about that now. Suddenly tired, I decided a nap would be a good idea. After removing my outer clothes, I threw my Marks and Sparks pink housecoat over my underwear and lay on the bed. Before long I had drifted into dreamland.

What was that banging noise? My eyes snapped open. Where the hell was I? I surveyed the cheap furnishings and remembered. Oh yes. Bangor. Jose just left.

And someone's knocking.

I leapt up quickly, clutching my housecoat to me, and went to the door. When I pulled it open, daylight flooded in. Deirdre was standing there, grinning. Then a frown creased her forehead. I suddenly felt faint . . .

When I opened my eyes, I was sitting in the armchair. Deirdre was crouching in front of me. "Darling, are you all right?"

"Did I pass out?" I asked, still feeling woozy.

She faltered. "Natasha, . . .I don't know whether to ask you this but . . . are you epileptic?"

What? I laughed. "No . . . why? Did I have a fit or something?" Maybe I was and didn't know it.

"No . . . well . . . but just before you passed out, your eyes rolled up in your head and . . ."

"I think I'm just tired, you know, jet lag. I got up too quickly. And my stomach's been bothering me again."

"We need you to see a doctor!" Deirdre stood up and launched into action. "I'm going to call an ambulance. . ." Before I could object, she strode over to the phone and was giving urgent instructions to someone on the other end. Still groggy and feeling as if I might faint again, I was vaguely aware of her putting socks on my feet. There was a knock at the door and then chaos broke out.

Two men, Joan and others were talking around me, about me. I was half carried, half-walked in my flimsy pink housecoat into a vehicle that was like a massive jeep. Was it the American version of an ambulance? They lay me across the back seat, as Deirdre cradled my head and shoulders in her lap. She gave more urgent instructions to the male driver, saying something about appendicitis.

What was the matter with me? All I could think of was Jose, and how he might still be en route back to Boston. Maybe he was already home. "If anything happens to me," I mumbled to Deirdre, "would you please let Jose know? His card's in my handbag." Could she understand my slurred speech?

"Of course, darling!" she said. "Now just relax. The hospital's not far now."

The car braked, someone was giving orders, and suddenly I found myself in a wheelchair going down a long, yellow-painted hallway. A nurse took me into a small room and assisted me onto an examination table where, thankfully, I was allowed to lie down. She stood over me clutching a clipboard and asked a myriad of questions. What's your name? What's your address? What's your date of birth? What's your social insurance number? Who is your employer? What's their address? What's their zip code? Are you allergic to anything? When was your last period? On the questions went.

"I . . . I don't know . . . I can't . . ." I couldn't think. My mind was so foggy. "Can you ask my friend?" I asked her, limply pointing to the hallway where I hoped Deirdre was waiting. She would know what to do. Finally giving up on any coherent answers, she left.

I remained there and waited. And waited. Alone, for an eternity, I looked around the sterile room, the shelves of medications and alien medical equipment. Had they forgotten about me? Should I call out?

The door burst open and a tall, dark, gorgeous man in a white coat arrived. Dr. Handsome. With a nurse standing by, he proceeded to prod and poke my body, asking more questions I couldn't answer. Couldn't he see that it was hard for me to recall anything? Then they left.

The nurse returned almost immediately with a wheelchair and told me to get in. Slowly, I raised myself up and gingerly climbed off the table and into the chair. She adjusted the footrests and wheeled me out of that torture chamber, down a long hallway into a ward full of beds behind curtains, some occupied, some empty. The nurse supported me as I flopped onto a bed and was grateful as she pulled the covers over me. She snapped the curtain closed around my bed and left me, still wondering what was wrong with me and how long I would be there.

On the other side of the curtain, in the next bed, I heard the grunting of an older man as he too was climbing into bed. Then I heard Dr. Handsome's voice.

"So, Joe, you're back. What is it this time?"

"Hey Doc. Well, you know me. I've taken them all. PCB, DHB, GMT, E. You know I even killed a man once. Stabbed him right in the gut."

Wha-a-at? So, this is America, I thought. The land of stalkers, drugs, murderers and scary hospitals.

"Well, Joe, what's it gonna be?" The doctor sounded weary. "The drugs or your life?"

"I know, Doc. I can't help it."

"Then you know I can't help you either, Joe. Now just get some rest. I'll check in on you later."

No! Don't leave me! Not next to this loony!

I heard the curtain being pulled back and closed again as the doctor left. Except for the man's raspy breathing, it was deathly quiet. I held my breath. If I kept still, maybe he wouldn't be able to sense my presence in the bed next to him . . . and he wouldn't kill me.

The silence was broken by some far-off wailing. A woman in reception sounded as if she was in mental anguish, while others began shouting. Had I landed in a lunatic asylum or a hospital? Whatever it was, I didn't want to be left here.

Suddenly, my curtain was yanked back with a whoosh, and a slim, dark-haired girl entered. She pulled the chair from the wall and sat down next to my bed.

"How are you doing, Natasha?"

"Er . . . sorry, I'm still a bit groggy. Have we met?"

"I'm Sandra. I'm on another crew, but I'm an ex-nurse so I thought I'd keep you company. These places are horrible, aren't they? Are you okay?"

"I-I don't know. Where's Deirdre?" A familiar, friendly face would have been just what the doctor ordered.

"She's talking to the nurses. She's convinced you've got appendicitis." She laughed.

Beckoning Sandra to lean in and listen closer, I whispered, "I'm so glad you're here. The man next door is a druggie and a murderer."

Sandra sat up in her chair, huffed and then announced in a loud, disapproving voice. "Oh, I've got no time for those people!" Then turning and addressing him through his curtain, she added, "They should get their act together."

"Ssssh! Ssssh!" I hissed, alarmed that he might just get up off his bed and come crashing through the curtain and sink a knife into her back or my gut.

As suddenly as Sandra had come, she got up. "I'll go and find out what's happening." Before I could beg her not to leave me alone, she was gone.

The next person to arrive was another nurse, this one more compassionate than the last. Gently she helped me out of the bed and into a wheelchair. "You can go now," she said, as she ensured my housecoat was decently covering me. "The doctor has a prescription for you."

Thank God I was leaving this looney bin.

"And next time you come to hospital, try and get dressed first," she added as she wheeled me away from Murdering-Drug-man.

"If I'm conscious," I muttered, "I'll try to remember to put some clothes on."

In the reception area, which was full of nefarious characters awaiting their turn, a relieved Deirdre, clutching a prescription, greeted me. "Oh, thank God, Natasha," she exclaimed. "It's just a bladder infection," she announced, her haughty voice loud enough to be audible to the whole reception area. Lost in their own misery, they probably didn't care about my minor medical issue.

Later, grateful to be back in my hotel room, I invited Deirdre to join me for a snack.

"God, I don't know which was worse," I admitted. "Being sick or being in there with the loonies. I never want to go to another American hospital ever again. I was so afraid you'd have to leave me there, Deirdre." Then I remembered. "Oh, you didn't call Jose, did you?" Now my emergency was over, I did not want to cause him any concern.

"No, don't worry, darling." She gave me an inquiring look. "By the way, how did that go? Are you still in love?"

"Oh, God yes." I sighed. "But Deirdre, I just don't get it. I feel he likes me, but we don't kiss or touch. I mean, am I imagining that he likes me, or am I kidding myself?"

"Oh, Natasha. Don't be daft." Deirdre scoffed. "Tell me, what man in his right mind would drive for five hours just to see you for an evening, *not* sleep with you, and then drive five hours back. And anyway, I saw the way he looked at you. No, he's absolutely *gaga* about you."

I smiled, happy to hear those words. "When did you see us together?"

"In the lobby this morning. You didn't see us. You were too engrossed. He's very handsome. No, he just respects you, that's all. I think it's sweet."

Sweet. Yes. "Maybe you're right."

"Well, I must say, darling, that for your first long-haul trip, you've had quite a lot of excitement! Are you still sure you've made the right decision joining Laker?"

"Oh, God, yes. Apart from being in the house of horrors, I've loved every minute of it. I can't wait for more adventures."

"Steady on, old girl," Deirdre said. "Be careful what you wish for!"

3

DAYLIGHT ROBBERY

New York, New York
April 1979

"Hello-o-o," I called out as I wearily rolled my loaded Samsonite over the doorsill into the hallway. "Anyone home?"

A muffled response came from the living room. Wondering which of my flat-mates might be home—or if they had been bound and gagged—I moved warily toward the door and opened it.

Ellen glanced up from the couch. Her large brown eyes looked surprised, and her cheeks bulged with what I presumed to be food. She was still in her bright red summer uniform, her Laker Airways' scarf hanging loosely undone, stray strands of her reddish hair framing her face. She was in the middle of eating her breakfast, but when she saw me, her fork halted in mid-air.

"Hello," I said, happy that she was awake. "You're back from New York!"

Unable to speak, she nodded.

"I'm just going to make myself a cuppa." I told her, resting my suitcase in the hallway. "That Miami was hell!" We could then share, as we always did, our war stories. "Be right back."

For us to fall asleep, both Ellen and I needed to unload the highlights of our trips—exciting, scary or miserable—on each other.

Once debriefed, we were then able to retire to our rooms and descend into a place somewhere between sleep and comatose.

Ellen was scraping the remnants of crispy bacon and egg yolk onto her toast when I sat down on the facing armchair with my coffee and cereal. Though envious of her cooked breakfast, I was too tired to make myself anything more complicated.

"So, how was your New York?" I asked as she swallowed her last mouthful and took a swig of coffee.

She slammed her cup down on the glass coffee table. "Horrendous!"

At first, I thought she was joking, but tears had filled her eyes.

"What happened?"

"More like what *didn't* happen!" she snapped.

As I sat back and sipped on my coffee, waiting, Ellen stared into her cup.

"The plane was all set to taxi at Gatwick when we got instructions from the IFD that we had a tech problem, so we returned to the gate. Once we arrived and were on chocks, the IFD instructed us, of course, to disarm the doors."

When the door control on the DC-10 showed *Disarmed*, the handle would open the door manually, slowly and quietly. But when the door was *Armed*, the control was in pneumatic mode, which in the event of an emergency, caused the heavy door to shoot up rapidly into its upper recess, hissing loudly and triggering the 80-foot chute to explode outward with a colossal whoosh.

Ellen put down her coffee. "Guess where I am?"

"Oh no. Not the dreaded one door right!"

"Ex-a-ctly!"

Each of the main exit doors on the DC-10 was numbered and identified by its location. One door right–as one might surmise–was situated at the very front of the cabin on the right-hand side in full view of passengers.

"I *hate* that door," she moaned. "I can never tell whether it's really disarmed or not, even when I pull the handle all the way down."

"Ex-a-ctly," I said. "The mechanism is set so high in the bulkhead that when you look up, it's hard to see if the handle is properly out of the red zone."

Ellen nodded, grateful for my validation.

"And it doesn't look good in front of a cabin full of passengers if you're standing there staring at the lever in the forward bulkhead scratching your head," I added.

Ellen took another sip of coffee before continuing. "So, when we were told to disarm the doors, I pulled the lever down."

"As one does." I smiled, but Ellen was not in the mood for humor.

"But it didn't look right," she said. "The handle still seemed as if it was a little bit in the red zone. Still armed. I yanked on it again. But that's as far as it would go."

"Uh-oh."

"Yes. So, there I am, standing at my door . . ."

"As one does."

". . .when the face of a ground engineer peers in at me through my door's porthole."

"Why did he come to One Door Right?" I asked. "The engineer always goes to Two Door Left."

"I know!" Her eyes were wide with confusion. She shrugged. "I've no idea why they pulled the stairs up there. But he was waving at me through that tiny little window, you know, to open the door."

I nodded. That porthole was all of nine inches wide.

"So I went to the control, grabbed the handle and yanked it down to open the door." At that point Ellen's features collapsed and she put her head in her hands. "Oh my God, Natasha! It was awful . . ." she moaned.

"What? What was awful?"

She raised her head. "The door . . . shot up . . . in pneumatic mode!"

I gasped.

"And . . . the chute came out."

"Oh my God!"

I envisioned the horrified engineer seeing his life flash before him as he heard the loud hiss of that door as it shot rapidly up into its recess and instantly knowing what was coming next. He knew that the nylon pouch would drop from the sill of the door and rip apart, and the chute would then explode into full inflation, sending him flying off the top of the stairs through the air and splattering like a blob of ketchup on the unforgiving tarmac twenty feet below.

I waited.

Ellen looked up. "But the chute didn't inflate."

"Ah-h-h," I exhaled. "Thank God! . . . So, all was well then?"

Ellen covered her face with her hands again and shook her head.

"We both stood there," she continued, "gazing in horror. . . and relief at the uninflated chute, realizing how close I came to killing the poor man."

"He must have been preparing himself for the pearly gates."

Ellen's eyes drifted to the fireplace behind me, remembering it all but still in disbelief.

"Well, be happy he's okay," I offered attempting to cheer up the shaken Ellen. "And it was far better to find out while still on the ground that the chute was defective. Passengers might have been a tad upset if they needed to exit a fiery aircraft from that door and there was no chute, just a 20-foot drop to the ground."

Ellen was still staring at the fireplace. "But that's not the end of it." She picked up her warm coffee mug and hugged it to her. "By that time the IFD was standing behind me, screaming at me, right in front of all the passengers, 'You're so stupid!' she yelled. She went on and on. 'I told you to disarm the doors. You're not fit to fly. Get down the back and out of my sight!'"

"Nasty," I commented through a mouth-full of cereal. "Who was the IFD?"

"Jane Mullins."

"Figures." Jane was not known for her patience—or her humor.

"So then there was a delay while they fixed the chute. And, of course, according to the crew, that was all *my* fault, too!" Ellen glanced out of the window to the still grey dawn as if she hoped to see something out there to make her feel better. Tears made their way down her cheeks, and she swiped them away. "To-o-o-tally humiliating! So," she continued, "I retreated to the rear and switched positions with another girl. At least I didn't have to serve those passengers at the front and hear all the teasing and bad jokes."

"Yes, you might have wanted to *really* kill someone."

"And then . . ."

"There's more?"

"Lots." She sighed. "Can you bear to hear it, or do you need to go to sleep?"

"Keep going." I gulped back a yawn.

"We landed at JFK after this awful flight and guess what?"

I shook my head. Anything was possible.

"They'd lost my bloody suitcase! Said it would be on the next flight out of Gatwick three hours later."

When flying, a lost suitcase was an occupational hazard, so I wasn't clueing into why Ellen was so distressed. "Couldn't they have just sent it on with the next crew?"

"Well, they could have. But the IFD insisted that instead of going to the hotel and waiting for my case there, I had to stay at JFK until it arrived."

I shuddered. JFK Airport in 1979 was not a good place for a single, white female, especially one in a luminous red flight attendant's uniform. "My God. She really doesn't like you!"

"I was there *three hours* by myself waiting for the next flight to come in. That place is scary. Druggies, Mafia and other shady dudes everywhere. People kept asking me for flight information for every bloody airline. What did they think I was? An arrivals and departures information board?"

"Probably. Anyone in a uniform is supposed to know everything, don't you know?" I placed my cereal bowl on the coffee table. My eyelids were becoming heavy. Fatigue was setting in. I would need to sleep soon.

"And then . . ." Ellen added.

"No! Not more?"

"The plane finally arrived with my suitcase. Thank God. And I got a ride to the Doral Inn with that crew. But then, of course, I needed my flight pay."

"Of course." Once a flight crew arrived at their hotel, at the post-flight crew gathering, the captain doled out flight pay of so much per hour of duty, this money being used to cover expenses while down route at our destinations. So, stewardesses didn't bother taking American dollars with them on flights to the U.S.

"By the time I got to the hotel," Ellen continued, "my captain and crew were all out on the town or in bed. I didn't have my credit card, so no American dollars for Ellen. I just went to bed hungry and exhausted."

"Couldn't you order room service?" I asked.

"Kitchen was closed!"

"You poor thing." With a transatlantic time-change, hunger pangs always set in with a vengeance. After a New York long haul, with just time for a paltry airline meal on board, crews usually went for something hot to eat in one of the city's cornucopia of restaurants.

"Next day," she continued, taking a long gulp of her now lukewarm coffee, "when I got up, it was too late to join my crew for breakfast."

"So, you missed seeing your captain *again*?"

"Yes, but fortunately, I bumped into him in the lobby when he was on the way back from *his* breakfast. That's when he gave me my flight pay."

"Well, that was good," I offered cheerily.

Ellen huffed. "Kind of. But you know how busy the lobby of the Doral Inn is and . . . I think someone was watching our transaction."

"Maybe they just wondered why an older man was giving a beautiful young woman cash? Hmm?"

Ellen grimaced, remembering how many hookers lingered outside the Doral's front doors. And she was right. Apart from airline crews, all kinds of nefarious characters came through that hotel lobby. The two-hour lecture we had been given during training on how to survive the dangers of New York still hadn't prepared us for even the worst reality.

"So now I've got my money, off I go down Lexington Avenue," she continued, "minding my own business, looking in all the shop windows and thinking about the huge breakfast I'm going to eat . . ."

"As one does." I smiled.

". . . when suddenly I feel this yank on my shoulder. I turn around and this huge, tall black man is grabbing my handbag strap and trying to pull it off me!"

"What!"

"Yes! By that time, I'd just had enough. I turned on him and gave him what for. 'What the hell do you think you're doing?' I screamed up at him. He stepped back, surprised. 'Well,' he stuttered. 'I-I just want your purse.'" Ellen's face reddened at the memory. "'Do you know,' I yelled and shook my finger in his face, 'the hell of a weekend I've had? I nearly killed a man—accidentally of course—and then my suitcase got lost. I've had no dinner and no breakfast, and I can't find my crew and now you want to steal my handbag!' He stepped back even further. 'Whoa, lady,' he said splaying his large palms. 'Chill out, I was just trying to mug you.' 'Well . . .well . . .don't!' I told him. 'Now . . . piss off!'"

"Oh my god, Ellen. What did he do?"

"He pissed off."

"That was so brave of you . . . Or stupid."

"I know. Once he was gone, I began to shake and realized he could have just as easily shot . . . or . . . or stabbed me."

"Yes, he could have."

Silence fell between us, imagining the alternative outcome.

"But he didn't," I reminded her. "And you are home safe now. And nobody died."

She took the last gulp of her coffee.

"So-o," she asked as she put her cup down, "how was *your* Miami?"

"Oh . . . I'll tell you later." My story of the sleepy passenger who dropped a lit cigarette under his seat and nearly caused the aircraft to catch on fire could wait for another day.

4

CRASH!

May 1979
Los Angeles

"Turn on the news!" the female on the other end of the phone line commanded. Even without a preamble, I instantly recognized the aristocratic voice of my friend Victoria.

"What . . .?" I started.

"BBC. Quickly," she urged. "There's been a terrible crash at O'Hare. Don't worry, old girl. It's not one of ours. Hurry! Phone me back." Chicago's O'Hare was at the time the world's second busiest airport with flights taking off every three minutes.

I dropped the receiver and turned on the television set.

The image that instantly filled the screen was that of a great beast of a plane, its nose pointing skyward, not more than a hundred feet above the ground, violently turning onto its left side and plummeting the short distance onto the runway. A massive ball of fire instantly erupted from the plane into the mist of a Chicago winter's morning. Whoever had filmed the scene had kept a steady hand. And now the American news channel was showing us the reel again and again as if viewers hadn't quite comprehended the horror the first time.

Oh God. I sank down into my armchair.

"The port engine," the reporter's voice enunciated from the corner of my living room, "simply fell off the wing of this American

Airlines DC-10." In the foggy greyness of the thirty-second event, it was hard to decipher which parts had dropped from what part of the plane.

I gulped. Instantly an image came to mind of flight attendants belted into their jump seats for take-off, expecting to do just another flight, thinking about their boyfriends or dinner, or picking up dry cleaning and then experiencing . . . the unholy grating of metal on metal. . . the explosion of noise . . .or . . .what? Passengers would have been looking forward to what they were going to do—or loved ones they were going to meet—at their destinations and then . . . the screams and terror when the aircraft rolled onto its side. I hoped, for their sakes, the plane fell so fast there was no time for them to register the horror of their imminent fate.

But why did it have to be a DC-10?

The broadcaster's voice droned on as once again they showed the aircraft lifting off, turning and dropping. "Losing an engine right after take-off," he proclaimed, "is always fatal. The flight crew would not have known what hit them, let alone have time to recover."

Thirteen crew and 258 passengers on their way to LA and suddenly their lives were over. Hopefully, the person taking that footage had not been the parent, spouse or child of one of those passengers or crew members. But unless the videographer had been a plane watcher, why else would he or she be filming that specific American Airlines flight? Mercifully, death would have been instantaneous for all 271 souls on board.

And then another horrific thought struck me. Jose flew all over North America. What if he had been on that plane? And then I comforted myself with the thought that he rarely flew out west.

When the phone rang again, Reginald Bosinquet, the starchy six o'clock news presenter, had already moved on to other disasters in

Belfast and the Middle East. Now fear was laying heavily in my stomach like a bad meal.

"Did you see it?" Victoria's usually stoic tone was uncharacteristically unnerved.

"Yes," was all I could muster in response.

"Bloody hell!" she muttered. "Those poor people. And it would have to be a bloody DC-10, don't you know? When's your next flight, Natasha?"

I gulped. "Tomorrow. Saturday. LA. How about you, Victoria?"

"Tuesday. Bangor."

"What does this mean?" I asked, as if my friend would know.

"Not sure, old girl. It's awful, though. Those poor people," she repeated, still in shock.

"Yes . . . but it would have been instant. No time . . ."

"God!" she blurted. "I hope they sort out the problem. I don't want to be up there flying one of those planes and wondering if one of its fucking engines is just going to pop awff." Victoria was the only person I knew who could say the "f" word and make it sound elegant. Her eerily accurate similarity to Princess Anne, right down to her trademark "fuck awff" expression, always made me smile.

"No," I agreed, still stunned. Airline crashes were always horrendous occurrences, so why was this one more disturbing than most? Because it was another McDonnell Douglas DC-10? "I better call Laker and see if I'm still going."

"Good idea." In the background at her end, a female voice muttered something. "Sorry, old girl," Victoria said. "Mother's here. Must go."

After I put the receiver down, I suddenly felt bereft, but the phone's loud ring reverberated again immediately.

"Miss Rosewood?" the mechanical male voice of one of Laker's crewing personnel inquired.

"Yes?"

"Not sure whether you know this but all DC-10s have been grounded . . . worldwide. There's been a . . ."

"I know . . . I just saw." The crash, I reminded myself, must have happened in the States in the early morning, Chicago time and five hours behind the UK.

"Your LA tomorrow has been cancelled until further notice. Please remain on standby."

Happy for the brief reprieve from getting on a plane, I asked, "Why have they all been grounded?" Aircraft were usually only taken out of service if it was suspected that a common fault existed on all the planes. And maybe it was a stupid question.

"Not sure," he responded in a damned-if-I-know tone, unwilling to get into a conversation.

The memory of my near-death experience on a Dan Air Comet re-surfaced. With sickening clarity, I remembered the white-faced captain pointing out that for the whole flight, including take-off and landing, the plane's main steerage, the tail plane, had been fluttering loosely like a sheet in the wind. Only God knew how the plane had been able to fly. All Comets worldwide had been grounded immediately afterwards. On investigation, it was discovered that at least five planes would have crashed had they done one more flight because they also had a metal-fatigued tail mechanism.

"Just be ready to go," the man from Laker crewing added. "The plane is in the hangar now and they're not sure how long it will take."

Do they even know what they're looking for? I wondered.

Replacing the receiver, I sank down into my armchair. How I wished one of my flatmates was home, but Ellen had gone to stay with her boyfriend, Greg, and Derek was away on business. Attempting to take my mind off the disaster, I opted for a little light-hearted comedy and watched The Two Ronnies. A very stiff scotch and coke on ice also helped to melt away some of my initial tension.

The following morning as I sat on the settee sipping hot tea and wondering about my immediate future, Ellen burst through the front door clutching a Daily Mail. She stomped into the living room and without so much as a "how's-your-father" waved the newspaper at me, her brown eyes even bigger than usual. "Look at this!" She flung the paper at me and turned to go into the kitchen.

The same image I had seen on television was now frozen in one large grey and white grainy photograph on the newspaper's front page. The headline screamed, JUST ONE BOLT!

As she returned to the lounge with a cup of coffee, she huffed. "It's stupid! Just stupid!"

Ellen and I had both experienced short haul with Dan Air and had survived our fair share of near emergencies on that airline. During Laker training we had agreed that we felt so much safer on Laker's DC-10s. But now this.

We sat together on the settee, poring over the paper, trying to make sense of the horror and the reporter's version of the problem.

"And look!" Ellen added, snatching the paper from me and opening it to the third page. She pointed to a large sketch of a DC-10 wing, below that an undersized bolt and underneath that a massive engine. *Initial investigation of yet another DC-10 crash points to the erosion of just one bolt which caused the engine to detach from the port wing on take-off,* the journalist speculated.

"Oh, my God!" Ellen suddenly sat up. "Don't you have an LA today?"

"I did," I said, passing the paper back to her. I had seen enough. "Thirteen hundred hours. But you know they're all grounded internationally, don't you?"

"Yes!" Ellen nodded, tapping the offensive newsprint.

We both sat back into the sofa cushions, clutching our warm drinks, absorbing the implications. No flights meant no flight pay, no bar commissions and maybe because we were at the bottom of the totem pole, no jobs. But at least we were alive.

"Those poor people," Ellen murmured, staring into her coffee. "Can you imagine what that was like? Sitting on your jump seat one moment and then . . ."

She was repeating my imagined scenario exactly. I shuddered. "Crewing told me to stay on standby. The plane is still in the hangar . . . What about you, Ellen? When's your next flight?"

"Oh, not till Wednesday. But that's another. . . five days," she added cheerily as if that made it all okay. She swatted me on the arm in a meant-to-be-comforting gesture. "They'll be flying again by then."

"Do you think so?" Half of me hoped she was right, but my intuition told me this was no quick fix.

We sat in silence, mulling over the information in the paper and what we knew about stress fatigue. One thing was certain: that engine must have been attached to the fuselage by more than one bolt. It had to be.

"Weren't you going to look up Muj in LA?" Ellen asked, breaking the spell.

"I was but. . ."

Muj was an old friend of my ex, Julian. We had only met recently at one of my infamous parties and talked a total of three times before he had moved to LA. When he discovered I would be flying there on a regular basis, he had suggested I call him.

"What does Muj do in LA anyway?"

"No idea." I smiled. "I still can't get past his name."

At noon the phone rang. A mixture of relief and dread were doing battle inside me, fighting for supremacy.

"Your plane just came out of the hangar," the man from crewing announced. "Your flight's the very first DC-10 back in the air," he added as if that should make me proud.

"Oh," I responded. Dread was winning the battle.

"I'm going," I yelled up to Ellen from the bottom of the stairs, uniform on, faithful Samsonite at my heels and war paint masking my fears.

She appeared on the landing; a towel wrapped around her head. "Good luck," she said and stared at me as if memorizing the sight of me for the last time.

"We'll need more than luck." I smiled. "Just hope we have strong bolts."

The press was touting the crash as the worst in airline history, but for the relatives and friends of those lost passengers and crew, wasn't any crash the worst in their history?

The passenger terminal at Gatwick Airport was crowded, and an adrenaline-fuelled buzz permeated the clusters of people crowding the brightly lit departure lounge. In my vibrant red summer uniform, and with eyes straight ahead, I hoped to glide unaccosted through the crowds of passengers who had been delayed and were now finally getting news of their DC-10 flight arrivals and departures. Lights flashed somewhere to my left, and when I glanced over, I saw a crowd of journalists with cameras perched on their shoulders labelled CBS and NBC. A dazzling white light was shining down on a clearly terrified young woman with two tired kindergarten-aged children clinging to her legs as she was being interviewed. Why did they have to harangue a young mother? I thought, annoyed.

The crew room, usually noisy with the chatter of excited stewardesses, was half empty today. And sombre. No one spoke of the crash, the worldwide grounding, the potential loss of jobs or fears of our Laker DC-10s being potential death traps. But those thoughts were no doubt on everyone's minds.

Once on the plane, our IFD, Janet, suggested in her pre-flight briefing that passengers might be a little more tense than usual so to give any difficult people more leeway for bad behaviour. Apparently one reporter had commented to an already scared passenger, "After all, haven't there been four DC-10 crashes in the last three years?" He neglected to mention, of course, that at least two of those crashes had been the result of human error and not technical failure.

With heavy hearts we began our pre-flight duties. Eventually the passengers dribbled down the finger, and as I stood close to the entrance ready to greet them, I saw that the NBC cameraman was standing right outside the aircraft door pointing his camera at another thirty-something woman with three children in tow. For a moment I wondered why ground security had let him through to airside without a boarding pass, but security was not tight. Two months earlier, to test the system, one extremely attractive flight attendant had put a photo of a monkey in her airport pass. She went back and forth for three months before a security agent noticed that she bore no resemblance to the animal.

The cameraman now leaned into the woman and demanded, "Ma'am, do you think you are being a responsible mother taking your children on a Deee Ceee Te-e-en?" enunciating the last words as if the aircraft was a bomb about to explode.

The woman blanched, glared back at him, and mutely shepherded her children into the plane. I wanted to give her a scotch, but she didn't look like a drinker, just a caring mother.

For take-off, I sat at Two Door Right, to the side of the forward galley and faced passengers seated starboard in the middle cabin. As the plane barrelled down the runway, making its usual mechanical noises and picking up speed to reach 190 miles per hour for take-off, all the passengers, it seemed, inhaled, and then held their breath. As the wheels left the ground, there was another collective intake of breath, and as if orchestrated, they all made a quiet gasp. Ten minutes later when the undercarriage noisily clunked back into its stowage in the plane's underbelly, passengers jumped. When the plane reached cruising altitude, then and only then did all three cabins full of passengers finally exhale in unison.

Once in the air the cabin crew went into automatic service mode. Two hours later, all of us, while still more subdued than usual, had begun to relax. When the flight attendants relaxed, so did the passengers. Contrary to the warning by the IFD of people behaving badly or having hysterics, everyone was quiet. Perhaps they believed if they moved too much or made too much noise, the bolts on our DC-10's three engines might just become detached.

On landing in LAX, I saw pesky reporters harassing more passengers in the airport. "Sir, did you fly on a Dee Cee-10? was the standard question or "Weren't you scared?" Why weren't they asking us, the crew? On the other hand, stewardesses admitting on TV to being terrified of flying on Laker's planes might have cost us our jobs.

Why was this plane crash such big news? Was it because yet another DC-10 had crashed or because it was an American plane and that garnered more importance? Or were they just exploiting the drama of the "one bolt" theory?

Once in my hotel room and happy to be in the dry California heat again, I climbed out of my polyester dress and showered, then donned jeans and a top. Maggie, a tall, curly-haired redhead I had worked with in-flight called me. "What are you doing tonight, Natasha? Any plans?"

Although we were eight hours behind the UK and any sensible person would have eaten and gone straight to bed, that was not my style. "I'm just going to call someone I know here and maybe go for dinner," I replied, thinking of Muj. Though he had given me his phone number, I was not sure that we had anything to talk about except the fact that we had both lived in Horsham and that both of us knew Julian. "Would you like to come with us, Maggie?"

Thirty minutes later in the brightly lit lobby of the Ramada Inn on Pico Boulevard, Maggie and I waited for Muj. When he appeared, I remembered his stocky frame, hunched shoulders and fine blonde hair and was reminded again of an unkempt college professor. But the black bags under his eyes were even darker now. Despite his obvious pleasure at seeing us, he seemed tired. His slightly dishevelled appearance cried out for a woman's touch, I thought, so when he spotted Maggie and his eyes lit up, and she also warmed to him, I wondered, Hmm? Could I be playing cupid here?

In his brief time in LA, Muj had apparently found his way around Santa Monica and now recommended a fish restaurant just a few blocks from the hotel. When I suggested we walk there, he laughed. "This is not Horsham, Natasha. You don't walk anywhere in LA. Especially at night."

"Not even with you as our protector?" I smiled.

Muj just shook his head and ushered us out of the hotel to where his car was parked. The California night air felt so good on the skin that it saddened me that we had to drive everywhere out of fear of being mugged.

Once the salads and the herbed red snapper had arrived, Muj asked, "So what did you girls fly over on?"

"The Deee Ceee t-e-e-e-n," I answered, mimicking the dramatic drawl of the reporters.

"Really?" Muj's pale face seemed to drain of any remaining colour, and his knife paused in midair. "You ladies are brave," he added, shaking his head.

I didn't like the way he said that and changed the subject. "What are you doing here in LA anyway, Muj? I never did ask you."

He dropped his salad-laden fork onto his plate and turned to face me. "Don't you know?"

I frowned. "No," I responded a tad defensively. "Should I?"

"I design aircraft engines. . ." he paused, "for McDonnell Douglas aircraft."

Maggie and I both stared at him.

"You m-mean," I stammered, "the people who make the DC-10s? Our DC-10s?"

Muj suppressed a wry grin. "That's right." He cast a glance over at Maggie, afraid of a negative reaction.

She had stopped eating and leaned forward. "Then . . . do you know anything about . . .?" She didn't want to say the word "crash" out loud.

"Yes." Muj nodded grimly. A new heaviness made his posture slump even lower.

"Oh my God," I muttered.

Maggie and I exchanged glances. What should we ask first?

"In the UK, they're saying it was just a bolt," she whispered, looking around the crowded, noisy restaurant, "that was holding the engine onto the wing, and it . . ."

Muj shook his head and stared into his water glass. "There are about fifty of us that have been locked in a room for the last twenty-four hours trying to figure out why that engine behaved the way it did."

"What do you mean?" I was puzzled. "The pilot had just rotated. He was no more than 100 feet off the ground. Any time an engine fails on take-off at that low altitude, it doesn't allow any recovery time. The pilot didn't have a hope in hell of righting that plane. . ."

"Yes, but . . ." Muj twirled his glass as he considered his answer. "That engine was designed, if it became detached, to simply fall, or if it did go over the wing, that it would clear the ailerons. But this one didn't. It took the ailerons and part of the tail plane with it. That's why it crashed."

I shuddered, imagining again the deafening sounds of metal on metal.

"It shouldn't have done that," he said, almost as if blaming himself.

"Did you help design that engine?" Maggie wasn't accusing him. She seemed more concerned for his soul.

Muj shook his head. "Not that particular one. No."

"So, is it safe to fly on the DC-10 then?" I asked. "I mean, they checked it out in the hangar before we left Gatwick." Then I added facetiously, "So the bolt must still be in place."

"Oh yes." Muj gave Maggie a weak smile. "They're safe."

"Then why are the press making such a bloody fuss?" Maggie asked, dabbing her mouth with her napkin. "Our poor passengers were terrified by all the hullabaloo."

"The problem with the DC-10 and why it gets so much flack is that it's a cheap version of the Jumbo," Muj explained. "On the DC-10 there are only three systems, engines, hydraulics and so forth, but on the Jumbo, you have four. That's why the DC-10 gets a bad reputation."

"And let's not forget they've had a few crashes in the last ten years," I added.

"They weren't all the result of technical issues, though," he said, reminding me and finally taking a bite of his fish.

"But it is safe?" I asked, studying Muj's expression carefully as he responded.

"Oh yes," he muttered, staring down at his unfinished meal. "They're safe."

Then he turned to me and patted me on the back as though it had been nice knowing me, but this would be the last time we would meet. "My God, you girls are brave!"

After arriving back at our hotel, all subdued, Muj handed Maggie his business card. "Lovely to see you ladies," he said looking at Maggie, and smiling for the first time that evening, "I hope I will see you on your next trip."

She beamed at him. "Try and get some sleep."

Maybe, I thought, something good could come out of this tragedy after all. That's if we survived to tell the story.

5

PEOPLE BEHAVING BADLY

Toronto
June 1979

"What's your favourite destination?" The dark-haired teen sitting in 15C gazed up at me with something like admiration in her eyes.

Well, not Toronto, I thought, as I handed her a coke with ice and lemon. And Toronto is exactly where my crew and I would be staying for the next seven days. "Every place has its own charms," I responded, "though it's not always the place itself." I was remembering a strange Barbados trip in April with an assortment of odd and antisocial crew members who had made even a week in paradise feel lonely. "It's more about the people."

"When I'm old enough, I want to be an air stewardess," she gushed, visions of exotic travels in her young eyes. "Do you have any advice?"

"Just be aware it's not all glamour," I warned. "Sometimes it's more like labouring as a navvy on a construction site," I added, placing a breakfast snack on her lap tray. "It's *very* hard work, the hours are long, and you *really* have to love people because some of them can behave very badly. And make sure that you get other qualifications before you fly, so you have something else to fall back on. Otherwise, *you* might start to behave very badly, too."

While I didn't want to dampen the girl's fervour for what she thought was a dream job, I had seen this kind of enthusiasm before. Once the joy of flying faded, the young women without qualifications for an alternative career where they could maintain the lifestyle they had become accustomed to often found themselves trapped in work they had begun to hate. Frustrated, they inflicted their misery on passengers and crew. More than once I had begged one of these individuals to "do us all a favour and l-e-a-ve."

My crew on this Toronto flight, however, seemed like a great bunch. I knew that fun was on the agenda with our captain, Sexy Lexy, and our co-pilot, Ben Atkins, leading the team as well as our cabin crew, Deirdre Scott, my saviour on my first Laker trip, Margo, my funny colleague who was often willing to indulge me in goofy Monty Python repartee, and my delightful Irish friend, Amy O'Connor. The other aspect of our Toronto destination was our luxurious hotel where we would be staying, the Hilton Harbor Castle, a 34-storey property located downtown on Lake Ontario. The deluxe rooms with their shag-pile carpets offered amazing views over the city, and on a clear day, I was told, you could see into the United States.

Yes, we would have a fun trip.

On our first day in Toronto the rain came down in sheets non-stop all day. We couldn't see anything clearly—not from any height.

The next day the rain continued.

And the next.

There was plenty of time to think and I had two things on my mind. Jose would be arriving in England just three days after I returned from Toronto, and already I was tingling with anticipation. Just the thought of being close to him made me feel alive again.

The other topic was something I was trying *not* to think about: the safety of the DC-10. Most passengers were unaware that our primary job as flight attendants was to be safety marshals. As such we *always* had to be on alert for potential emergencies. After many international aviation accidents—crashes and ditchings—we were sent the accident reports to study. They detailed the circumstances of the crashed plane, the behaviours of the passengers in the emergency, how the aircraft landed, which exits had been available for evacuation, where the fires were and more. We would then discuss these findings amongst ourselves to expand our awareness.

But on the subject of the recent American Airlines DC-10 crash, our crew was strangely quiet. While it had only been two weeks since that fateful flight, investigators and my new friend, Muj, were still mystified as to why the engine on that plane had become detached and destroyed the other essential flying mechanisms. Was this a one-off occurrence or a fatal design flaw? Our silence seemed to confirm the unconscious agreement between cabin crew members that if we didn't talk about the danger, the danger did not exist.

On day six of perpetual rain, I sat in the hotel restaurant eating a fruit salad and yogurt breakfast and drinking bottomless cups of black coffee while my friend Amy scarfed down a pile of pancakes and bacon. Having exhausted our tourist options—getting soaked at Niagara Falls and shopping at the Yorkdale Mall—another long and restless day stretched before us. She peered out of the window at the endless downpour cascading into the lake. "Jesus, Mary and Joseph!" She shook her head. "Will it ever stop? Anyone would tink dat dey're hosin' down heaven."

She was right. The rain, like Niagara Falls, continued to pour down in sheets like I'd never seen before. As the Americans claimed, everything on this side of the Atlantic *was* bigger but not necessarily better.

"And the Canadians have the nerve to tease us about rainy England!" I scoffed as I watched Amy cleaning her plate with gusto. She was so tiny. Where did she put all that food?

"Ach, deir questions about whether we have central heatin', now dat irritates de hell out o' me." She smiled and whispered conspiratorially, "But don't tell anybody dat *I've* just installed it in me own flat."

"Any ideas of what we can do today?" I asked.

"Well . . ." Amy smiled. "We could do de gym again or we could start drinkin'." She grinned mischievously. "Oh...," she said, delving into her black Laker handbag. "I nearly forgot. Look at de photos!" She lay the signature yellow and blue Kodak folder on the table. "I got doubles so if you like any of dem, help yerself."

Several of the blurry images showed our group posing in front of Niagara Falls two days earlier. Through the grey mist, you could see us huddled together while behind us gushing, frothing waters fell into the chasm below. Despite shivering with the damp and cold, we were beaming into the camera.

"I like this one," I said, picking one of Sexy Lexy, Ben, Margo, Hannah and Amy laughing in the rain. "Thank you," I said, tucking it into my handbag.

After the gym, a swim and then a sauna, we had by early afternoon run out of things to do. Amy invited Margo and me to her room where she proposed a game of Scrabble, borrowed from the front desk. I soon regretted challenging Amy, remembering that for every English word, the Irish have five. She slaughtered both of us.

As I tipped the wooden tiles back into the green Scrabble box, Amy got up and peered out of the twenty-fourth-storey window into the greyness. "For the love of God, will dis rain never stop? It's crazy!" Even though she was complaining, her soft Irish lilt still sounded like music to my ears.

"Speaking of crazy, did you hear that one about—" Margo began but the phone rang and interrupted her.

Amy picked up, listened and nodded. "To be sure! Come on over." After she hung up, she explained, "Some of de crew are comin' here fer happy hour. Natasha, help me move de furniture, would yer? Margo would yer mind gettin' some ice?"

"It's only three in the afternoon, you alkies!" Margo chided.

"Ach, we can choose to be happy anytime, can't we? And wid dis rain, do yer tink I care?" she grinned. "If dis doesn't drive you ter drink, nuttin' will."

Five minutes later there was a light tap on the door. Amy opened up as nine of our crew, including our flight deck, burst into the room, laughing, talking and clutching bottles, glass tooth mugs, plastic glasses, ice buckets and bags of crisps. After we had poured ourselves our own personal poison and found a spot to sit—on a chair, a sofa, the edge of the bed and even on the floor—a litany of jokes and airline stories started to flow.

Ben began. "Did you hear about the new girl who had a sense of humor failure?"

"And what trick did you play on her?" Cathy, our IFD asked, smiling like an indulgent mother of naughty boys.

Ben shrugged and grinned from ear to ear. "Chicken soup."

A few people groaned knowingly, but I frowned. "What's that?"

"The new girl is sent up to the flight deck," Alex supplied. "While Ben clutches his stomach and groans, he hands her a full, warm sick bag and says, "Can you please take this away?"

"Ew!" Margo muttered.

"The girl grimaces and reaches out for it, but before she can take it, I snatch the bag back and say, 'No, don't waste it. I like to eat the chunky bits.'"

We all groaned.

"It's *just* Campbells chicken vegetable soup," Alex added, grinning. "But she ran out of the flight deck crying. Sadly, she never flew again."

"That's awfully mean," Deirdre commented.

"But if you can't laugh, you'll go daft," Cathy commented, "especially in this job."

"Don't you find," I asked, "it's always the ones that dream about being an air stewardess as little girls that can't even handle breaking a fingernail. On this flight over I had another dewy-eyed teenager asking me about flying."

"I hope you told her, *don't do it!*" Hannah said, chuckling.

"I did warn her about people behaving badly, present company excepted, of course. In fact," I raised my glass, "if I had to be stuck in rainy Toronto with anybody for this week of rain, I'm *so* happy it's been with all of you."

"Hear, hear," Ben agreed and beamed at everyone in the room.

"Yes, you always remember your good crews, don't you?" George, the ruddy-faced engineer, sat forward in his chair. "I had a fun bunch on a night-stop in Moscow once. We had quite the event."

"Moscow?" Alex enquired. "With Laker?"

"No. This is a few years back when I was with British Midland," George explained.

"It was some ad hoc flight."

"Ooh, Moscow!" Deirdre piped up. "Do tell!"

"Well," George began in a cockney-tainted twang, "you know what it's like goin' into those communist countries with the KGB an' all and the feeling that you're always being watched. Everything feels grey and ominous some'ow. It's a bit bloody scary."

We all nodded. Most Laker crews had only seen communism, specifically the East German variety, over the wall from the safety of West Berlin, but in 1976 my boyfriend, Julian, and I had driven the

150 miles from West Berlin over a still bombed-out *autobahn* through East Germany. We were greeted at the Berlin Wall and West Berlin by *Stazi* police, gun-toting soldiers, ferocious-looking Alsatian dogs and twelve-foot-high walls crowned with strings of barbed wire. At that time Maggie Thatcher was also criticizing Brezhnev's communism, so he had retaliated by calling her *Iron Knickers* and then revoked all British and American visas. Despite that, Julian and I were travelling through Finland by then and had managed to get a special visa to get into Leningrad. George was right. Their communism was scary.

"Anyway," he continued, "we were driven to this big hotel in the centre of Moscow. Then yer know, we gathered in the captain's room for our crew party. We're all sittin' around, havin' a good time chattin' and getting a bit squiffy when I suddenly get this idea that the room is bugged. You know, we're in Moscow." George surveyed our faces, looking for agreement. "Brezhnev's got a tight rein on everything. We're westerners. Made sense."

Westerners in Russia in the '70s, I knew from experience, stuck out like coal on snow, and because they were suspected of tempting Russians to defect or to sell them western goods, they were constantly watched.

"Well anyway," George said, getting into his story, "the whole crew agreed that we should look for the bug. So we pulled the room apart, felt behind the bedhead, pulled out drawers, scoured the wardrobe, looked underneath the lamps. Nothing. We gave up, put everything back and carried on talking. Then suddenly the captain, who was more than two sheets to the wind by then, pointed to the centre of the room where there was a slight bulge underneath the carpet. 'There it is!' he said. 'George, you go and get your bag of tricks while we move the furniture so we can look underneath.' I was a bit dubious, but I think most of the crew had lost their roubles by then.

I snuck back to me room, past the KGB bloke in the corridor, and got me tools.

"By the time I returned to the captain's room, the bed, the chairs and the desk 'ad all been moved off to the side and the frayed carpet was rolled back. Right there in the middle of the room was a metal plate attached to the wooden boards by four screws. No problem, I thought. While the others watched, I got out me screwdriver, took out the screws and slid the 'eavy metal piece across the floor. Somewhere off in the distance we thought we 'eard a big cheer and decided they must be having a hell of a party somewhere. Underneath the metal plate was just a pile of wires. 'Nah, that's not it, either,' I told them, 'unless it's KBG central for the hotel's whole bugging system.' So, we slid the metal plate back and I put the screws back in. We were just rollin' back the carpet when there was a bang on our door."

"Uh-oh!" Hannah sat forward, cramming crisps into her mouth as if she was at the cinema watching a suspenseful film.

"Of course, we all froze," George said. "While behind me my drunken crew clumsily pulled the furniture back into place, I opened the door just a sliver. Sounds a bit cliché, but the man at the door was a tall, dark Russian with a pock-marked face. 'E was dressed in a drab dark suit. Reminded me of Lurch. Typical KGB. In my best British accent, I said, 'Yes, sir? Can I help you?' He sounded like bloody Dracula when 'e spoke. 'By any chance,' he said, 'have you been interferingk wiz ze metal plate in ze center of ze floorrr?'

'Er . . . no,' I told him, lying to his face, and stepping into the corridor so he couldn't see what the banging behind me in the room was all about. 'Why? Is something wrong?'

'Yez,' he droned. 'Forr yourrr inforrrmation, ze chandelier in ze rroom below has just crrashed to ze floorrr!'"

Our crew emitted a collective gasp.

"Good lord!" Deirdre exclaimed in her aristocratic voice. "Was anyone hurt?"

George shook his head and sat back in his chair, smiling, his story done.

"Were there any . . . repercussions?" Alex asked. From time to time the airline received hotel bills for damages incurred by crews' naughty antics.

George shrugged. "Never 'eard a thing."

"But they must have known *you* did it?" I stated rather than asked.

George just shrugged.

"Ach, you're lucky you didn't all get sent off to a gulag, never to be seen again."

Amy who had been perched on the edge of her queen-sized bed, climbed on top of it and was now leaning back against the quilted headboard.

"Deirdre?" Margo addressed my friend who was just getting up to refill her glass. "Remember that awful Barbados we did?"

"O-o-h," Deirdre groaned as she plonked herself back into her chair, the ice clinking in her tooth mug filled with gin and tonic. "Of course, darling! How could I possibly forget?" She touched the side of her face, just under her right cheekbone. "I've still got the scar to prove it!"

"What happened?" Amy enquired as she shuffled off the bed to turn on some bedside lamps. Outside the rain continued as grey light faded into blackness. Airline crews, I noted, were suckers for stories. And we all had plenty of them. What better way to fill the time?

"Oh, it was gha-a-a-astly!" Deirdre sat up in her chair. "We had just taxied away from the terminal when the captain told us there was a fuel leak in the port engine. So they brought out a kerosene truck. Pax weren't allowed to smoke, of course. The poor things had to sit there with no air conditioning while the engineers did their thing. And you know how awfully humid Barbados is," she said, addressing the whole room. "I felt badly for the passengers, though fortunately most of them were in shorts and t-shirts. We were stuck on the ground for *hours*. Of course, it was much worse for us with our polyester dresses clinging to our hot, perspiring bodies."

"Anyway, there I was serving rum punches to the punters in A when I looked down the aisle, and just at the front of B I saw this *very* tall Bajan man with dreadlocks standing in the aisle. He looked like he was dancing, you know how they do, moving back and forth." Deirdre moved her shoulders to demonstrate. "Then I saw him light up a cigarette!"

A few of us gasped, aware of the dangers of any kind of flame within fifty feet of a kerosene truck.

"So, of course, I approached him. He had his eyes closed and was humming as he held the cigarette in his fingers, just puffing away, oblivious to the fact that he could blow us all up any second. 'Excuse me, sir,' I said. At first, he didn't seem to hear me, or didn't want to, anyway. 'Ahem, excuse me, *sir,*' I repeated a bit more loudly. He finally opened his eyes, looked down at me and sneered, 'Yeah, mon?' as if I had just woken him up from a nice dream. 'I'm *awfully* sorry, sir,' I repeated, 'but would you please extinguish your cigarette? We have a fuel leak and there is a tanker full of kerosene just a few feet away.'"

I imagined the somewhat haughty, but she-who- expected-to-be-obeyed, red-headed Deirdre being extremely polite, staring up at him.

"Well!" she continued. "He stared down at me defiantly and said, 'Yeah, mon. I'll put my cigarette out.' And then . . .," Deirdre paused and touched her cheek, her eyes watering. "At first, I thought he was going to put it in one of the rum punches on my tray, but he . . . he leaned forward, and when I realized what he was about to do. . . I turned my head to the left to avoid him, the tray fell out of my hands and the rum punches went flying all over passengers on the window side, and... he stubbed the cigarette into my right cheek!" she exclaimed, still traumatized.

"You poor thing," "Bastard!" and "Good lord!" and other commiserating comments circulated around the room.

"I screamed with pain, of course, and ran up to the galley," Deirdre said, her voice quivering and struggling to keep a stiff upper lip, "leaving the poor passengers covered in that awful sticky concoction. Behind me, I could hear some of the male passengers yelling at the black man, some in my defense, and some because I'm sure they were angry at being covered in rum punch. I reported it to the IFD, of course, hoping she would get him awff the plane."

"Who was the IFD?" Cathy, our IFD, wanted to know.

"Mary-Beth Clarke."

Knowing smiles lit up faces in the room. Mary-Beth was a beloved and respected Bajan known for her entertaining irreverence for passengers, flight deck and all professional airline protocols.

"Who was the captain?" Alex asked. "I hope he had the bastard thrown off!"

"David Wilson," Deirdre replied, pulling a face. "And no," she added, "he didn't arrest him or unload him. I know it would have meant finding his luggage and security etcetera, but we had plenty of time just sitting on that tarmac. The captain couldn't even be bothered to fill out the paperwork."

Amy huffed. "Ach, David's as useful as a lighthouse on a bog!"

"Tits on a bull," George added.

"A chocolate teapot," Amy retorted.

"While one of the girls put ice on my cheek," Deirdre continued, "passengers were getting ugly in the middle cabin. One man at the front of B who saw the whole thing was standing shaking his fist and yelling at the local man. Another man covered in rum punch and a cherry in his hair was berating him, too. The last thing we needed was a melee with a bunch of sweaty macho white passengers beating up a black local and starting an international incident. And he was so-o-o tall. I think he's known locally as Bamboo . . . for obvious reasons. And he could have had a knife for all we knew. But you know, Mary-Beth?" Deirde looked around the room. "She went right up to him, and gesticulating wildly, gave him hell in that dialect of theirs. We all watched from the galley and were amazed when he just slunk back to his seat and sat quietly for the rest of the delay."

"But that wasn't the end of it, was it, Deirdre?" Margo said, sitting down on the sofa again after refreshing her drink.

"Good lord, no! I'd forgotten about that." Deirdre shook her head.

Margo picked up the story. "Just as I carried a full tray of rum punch into the rear cabin on the starboard side, I suddenly tripped and went lurching forward, face-planting on the floor while the tray went on its own trajectory. When I picked myself up, feeling lucky I hadn't landed on an armrest and done some real damage to my face, I saw that the German passengers were laughing. I realized then that one of the men had deliberately tripped me up! But *my* revenge was seeing them all sitting there coated in the stuff, cherries and orange garnishes stuck in their hair for the next ten hours or more. And I wasn't about to offer them any assistance."

"Serves them bloody well right!" Ben muttered.

"Mary-Beth is so funny." Hannah chuckled. "She was on a flight I did when we had a short delay at Gatwick. This older man sitting in B stuck his bony hand up in the air and started clicking his fingers, trying to get Mary-Beth's attention. So rude! Finally feeling irritated, Mary-Beth went over to him, leaned over and said, "I'm so sorry, Sah. But we dawn't allow flamenco dancin' on dis aircraft."

"Well, if you really want to know about people misbehavin'" Hannah piped up, "you *have* to do a Haj."

"Dat's roight!" Amy began laughing and sat up on the edge of the bed. "Oh my God, Hannah. Remember Lagos?"

She nodded "The decompression!" Both women began laughing.

Everyone turned toward Hannah as she explained, "We were inbound from Jeddah and about two hours from Lagos when suddenly all the overhead oxygen masks dropped down. We thought, of course, that we must be going through a decompression, but there was no blue mist or rapid descent."

"The two of us were at de front," Amy chimed in, "and everythin' seemed otherwise normal in de cabin, so we couldn't understand it. Of course, I checked with de captain to see what was happenin', but he couldn't figure it out either. Mind you, he was just another undertrained African pilot who didn't know his ass from his elbow and with not enough hours to be a stewie, let alone a pilot, so who de hell knows if he knew what he was talkin' about. Accordin' to him, der was no decompression and nuttin' was wrong."

"Nothing can go wrong, go wrong, go wrong," Ben droned the old airline joke of a captain playing a taped PA recording just before he parachutes out of the plane.

"Ach," Amy continued, "we figured it was just another antiquated 707 with all its idiosyncrasies, but when I came out of the flight deck to do a no-smoking PA and looked down the cabin, all the Hajis were sitting there holding the oxygen masks over their ears and looking confused. Dey were probably wondering why there was just hissing and no music!"

"But what about de toilets!" Amy added.

"Ugh!" Hannah groaned. "We used to strap sanitary napkins over our mouths for masks and wear rubber gloves to deal with the mess. Let's just say most of these people had never been on a plane, let alone seen a real toilet before so they didn't know, shall we say, where to put it . . . . They couldn't even seem to aim at the can. . . and so there was . . .you know . . . stuff ... everywhere . . . even on the ceiling."

A loud groan of disgust went around the room.

"We had a few scares, too," Amy added, "because dey tried to light fires down de back to cook der meals."

"And they doused themselves in water all the time and so we were constantly mopping it up and worrying about the electrics!" Hannah shook her head.

"Sounds so interesting!" I said. "I *really* want to go on a Haj!"

"Ach, yer probably don't, Natasha," Amy advised. "I can tink of nicer destinations. Maybe Freddie will get his route to Hong Kong and Australia."

"Oooh, I thought that was just a rumour," Margo said, her eyes wide with excitement.

"Freddie's working on it," Alex announced. "And we'd be flying jumbos."

"That's if the DC-10s don't get grounded again." Ben muttered, bringing up the elephant in the room. "Then we can forget the jumbos. We might all be out of a job."

"I thought that was all sorted." Cathy frowned.

Alex shook his head. "The FAA still haven't really resolved why that engine became separated from the fuselage."

I decided not to mention the gloomy conversation I had shared in LA with my friend Muj, a McDonnell Douglas engine designer, just 36 hours after the DC-10 crash in Chicago.

Suddenly the room went quiet.

"Is anyone hungry?" Ben asked, standing up. "I could eat a horse."

"Horse?" I smiled. "That reminds of when I was in Tenerife . . ."

He put up a hand to stop me. "Natasha, not before dinner . . ."

Ben suggested we dine at the Sutton Place Hotel, a popular place in downtown Toronto with restaurants and roof-top dancing. When we arrived in our hotel lobby, we saw that miraculously the rain had finally stopped, so in groups of twos and threes, we walked the illuminated downtown streets. Grateful to be outside, I inhaled the after-the-rain smell of fresh air.

The waitress sat us at a long table at the back of the restaurant where we perused the massive menus. Though it was great to be having dinner with our entire group, cabin crew were all aware that flight deck crews—much to our chagrin—often suggested splitting the bill equally. While the girls would eat smaller portions of fish and salad with a single glass of wine—because they were not hungry, were on diets or trying to save money—the men would often indulge in starters, expensive Filet Mignons and desserts plus liqueurs—and expect us to pay their share. Considering that flight deck crew earned at least three times our salary, we resented this exploitation, and most of us made sure it didn't happen twice. But before I could request a separate bill from our server, Alex—true to his gentlemanly style—was already asking our waitress for individual receipts.

Ben was making us all laugh when two middle-aged diners passed by our table. One of the men stopped and stared. Seeing the three males with ten younger attractive women having fun, he shook his head, sighed and said, "Some guys have all the luck!"

Later, after a stroll along an illuminated Yonge Street and then back to our hotel, most of the crew retired to their own rooms, but Amy, Deirdre and I accepted Alex and Ben's invitation to join them for a nightcap in the hotel bar. While I perched on a stool next to Ben, my two friends sat on either side of Alex.

"Is it just a rumour, Natasha, or do you really read palms?" Ben asked after ordering Brown Cows. He was leaning forward, his arms casually crossed on the bar.

"Yes, but it is amazingly complex and I'm just learning. Why? Do you want me to read yours?"

"Why not?" Ben's brown eyes twinkled. His reddish hair and freckled face gave him a perpetually boyish look.

I could have told him why not. A memory of reading another first officer's palm at a bar in Manchester when I was with Dan Air a few years earlier popped into my head. I had warned the embittered ex-training captain—now demoted to first officer through no fault of his own—not to resort to vengeance in his problematic marriage. His anger could cause him big trouble. "Take the high road," I had urged. Not long after that, I had learned, with horror, that he had been arrested for murdering his wife! Reading passengers—people I would never see again—was easy but delving intimately into friends' and colleagues' stories could sometimes become awkward.

I put my drink down on the bar. "Well, okay, but I'm warning you not to take anything I say *too* seriously. Remember, I'm just a beginner and I can get things wrong."

Without uncrossing his arms, he flipped his left hand up. Though he was pretending to be nonchalant, there was a tension in him that betrayed his apprehension. I peered into his left palm and saw the lined map of his life story.

"Oh," I said, a little surprised and sat back.

"What is it?" Though Ben was smiling, there was a question in his eyes.

"Well, do you mind telling me how old you are?" I asked, having learned to be careful with the delivery of potentially bad news.

"Promise not to tell?" he said, grinning.

"I promise."

"Forty-two."

"Ah, well. That's a relief!"

"Why?"

"Well, you see, this is your lifeline." I traced the line from above his thumb descending toward his wrist. "Right here," I said, pointing.

Ben peered a little closer.

"And here," I pointed to a spot on his lifeline where it stopped, and another line immediately resumed adjacent to it. "But I think this has already passed. Did something happen to you about . . . four years ago?"

He stiffened.

"It's like you died, though obviously you didn't die . . . Did you have a heart attack or a near death experience, something like that?"

He quickly withdrew his hand, and as he took a slug of his cocktail, his shoulders appeared to cave in.

"I'm sorry if I upset you," I said, feeling as if I had crossed into some forbidden territory. Ben was always so much fun that it was hard to imagine him having had any hard times.

"No . . . not a heart attack. . ." He twirled his empty glass, bracing himself, searching for the words. "You're right . . .four years ago . . . my three-year-old son . . . died."

Oh God!

"It was an accident," Ben muttered. "A drunk driver." He raised his head, looking at the wine glasses hanging upside down above the bar, perhaps searching for an answer. "It happened so quickly."

Feeling inadequate to console him and guilty at having brought up his painful past, I offered, "Would you like another drink?"

He laughed derisively. "Maybe I should buy *you* one."

Yes, I was in a state of shock. I nodded mutely, feeling an overwhelming urge to run away so he couldn't see his sorrow mirrored in my face, but at the same time not wanting to leave him alone with his painful memories.

My shock was also at how well Ben had disguised his grief. I could relate. People often assumed that I, too, had led a charmed life. 'Oh, it's all right for you,' they would say. 'You're strong'. If only they knew how I had earned that strength. And so, I had learned early on that people weren't really interested in anybody's pain except their own. Out of survival or a need to belong, I had adopted a public smile and a dark sense of humor. But that didn't mean I didn't feel pain.

As the bartender put two more drinks in front of us, Ben spoke into his glass and sighed. "We've all got our stories, haven't we, Natasha?"

"Yes, we certainly do!" I thought of all the horrendous tales I had heard from others, and all the people who had hurt me. Unfortunately, those offenders happened to be not crew, not passengers, not even drunken strangers, but people who should have been my nearest and dearest—my own family. As Ben would know, those were the ones who could hurt you the most.

The next morning, excited about our imminent departure, the entire cabin crew gathered in uniform in the hotel restaurant for breakfast. With ten females in bright red uniforms, we received the usual unabashed, curious stares from other hotel guests. I had just finished my coffee when I heard the girls behind me greeting the captain and first officer. Suddenly I felt a kiss on my right cheek and then another on my left. Surprised, I looked up and saw Alex and Ben, handsome in their uniforms, on either side, beaming down at me. I wasn't sure what I had done to deserve their affection, so I just smiled back and treasured the feeling of their warmth.

Years later, I would often take out that photo at Niagara and be reminded that even when it rains in life—and doesn't stop for a long time—we can still find joy. Yes, humans can do stupid things and behave badly, but when people behave well and stick together—when they love, respect and accept each other—we can all be happy with who we are and that is the sunniest feeling in the world.

6

GROUNDED!

June 1979
London

The yellow glow of sunrise flooded the cabin as our DC-10 flew over Greenland, heading back from Toronto to Gatwick and home base. Our passengers had been fed with skinny omelettes and miniscule too-crusty croissants that had been washed down with two teas and coffees. The in-flight entertainment, *Fawlty Towers,* had just ended, and some passengers were still chuckling, though I wasn't sure how many Canadians really understood our very British humour.

When Maggie and I pushed the breakfast cart back into the forward galley, we saw Bridget, our IFD, huddled with Deirdre and Margo in what appeared to be a serious conversation. During our seven-day-rain-bound Toronto trip, we had come to know each other well and bonded.

"What's up?" I asked. Dismay was written all over their faces.

"We've been grounded," Bridget moaned, "by the FAA, the bloody Federal Aviation Authority!"

I frowned, not quite understanding. "We?"

"Laker. And all DC-10s . . . again . . .worldwide. But this time it's for real. Not just a quick looky-loo at a bolt in the hangar. Apparently, the FAA want to do extensive tests."

"But what right do American authorities have to ground a British airline?" Deirdre asked indignantly, showing her aristocratic side. "I thought only the Civil Aviation Authority had power over us on safety matters. Laker is British, after all."

"Well, we *do* fly over their airspace and take off from their airports," Bridget pointed out. "That might have something to do with it."

"Ah, yes." Deirdre nodded.

I groaned inwardly. While an extended vacation might be nice, I would miss flying. More importantly, with a mortgage to pay, I would feel the pinch of my reduced salary. Being grounded, though, might offer another advantage. Jose was due to arrive in London within the next three days, and I would be able to spend every available minute with him. A flutter of excitement at the thought of seeing Jose softened this new blow.

"Don't mention anything to the passengers," Bridget commanded. "No need to scare the you-know-what out of them any more than necessary."

"How long will the grounding last?" I wondered out loud. "Days? Weeks?"

"Ach, who knows?" Bridget pulled our cart towards the elevator, opened the door and pushed it into the lift to send it down to the lower galley. She then banged the button a little more ferociously than usual.

Did Bridget know more than she was saying? Were the DC-10s in danger of being taken out of service completely?

"Sexy Lexy was just told," Bridget continued, "that all DC-10s must, once landed at their destinations, stay grounded. So just be grateful we're headed home. Knowing Freddie," she added, grimacing, "he might have left us stranded in rainy Toronto."

As we went about our duties, we were probably all thinking the same two things. Is the DC-10 unsafe? Will we need to look for other jobs? For the remaining three hours of the flight, passengers noticed the morose mood that had settled over the crew and a strange hush descended over the cabin.

Finally home and wearily dragging my Samsonite over the front doorsill, I called out, "Hello-o-o-o-o. Anyone home?" But my voice bounced off the walls into emptiness.

Disappointed not to be able to share my recent adventures with my flatmate, I left my suitcase at the bottom of the stairs and walked into the kitchen. A small piece of white paper lay on the counter. In large, clear writing the message in Ellen's hand read: *Jose called on Sunday! He was so disappointed when you weren't here. I told him that you were getting back Tuesday. He wants to see you. Call him on this number asap.* At the bottom of the note, she had added in brackets, *I've been called out for a Tenerife on the Airbus. Maybe see you tonight. . . or not? (Wink, wink).*

My heart leapt. Jose was in England ahead of schedule, and he was impatient to see me! As much as I had tried to analyze the joyful effect this man had on me, I could not figure it out. Was it his classy Latino way, his adorable South American accent, his gentle voice or those brown eyes that delved into my very soul? Yet I knew it was much more than a physical attraction. In his presence I was at home. More than love at first sight, our meeting had felt more like recognition and a reunion. Even though we had only spent three hours together after our first encounter in Barbados, on my return to the UK, I had ached for him every moment we were apart. I didn't understand the magnetism I felt to someone I barely knew. Whenever I was near him—even on the same continent—my heart felt like it would burst with happiness. And whenever he was away, with an ocean between us, I was only half alive. Then I would go numb, and life became flat again.

Through the kitchen hatch, I saw another note lying on the glass coffee table in the living room. This one read *Jose called. He's dying to see you. Call him as soon as you get in. He's staying at the Mayfair, Room 329.* I smiled at Ellen's diligent note-leaving. Ever since I had met him, she had witnessed me on many an evening pretending to watch TV, lost in dreamland, missing him.

Sleeping off jet lag could wait, I thought. Elated and with heart thumping, I picked up the phone and dialled the number of the hotel. Barely breathing, I waited for the hotel operator to put me through.

He picked up. "Hello?"

That voice! "Hi," was all I could muster.

Did I imagine it, or did he also take a sharp intake of breath? "Hi." There was delight in his tone.

As we sat in silence, each holding a telephone receiver, I imagined his smile. Just knowing he was at the end of the line, only an hour and a half away, rendered me speechless. In the silence between us we communicated volumes.

"When did you get back?" he finally asked.

"This morning." I let another silence be. "I didn't think you were coming until Friday."

"They changed my schedule." Another pause. "When can I see you?"

I wanted to leap in the car right then and drive like a bat out of hell and go to him. "Well . . ." Should I say 'tonight,' or play it cool? "I need to get some sleep," I said, "but–"

"How about tonight?" he blurted, perhaps just as excited to see me as I was to see him. I was never sure. "I'm sorry but I have to go out to dinner with my colleagues, but if you don't mind that, you could join us?"

When I had first met Jose, and he had not given me his home number as he said he was moving, a nagging doubt had plagued me. Was he married? But here he was inviting me to dinner with his work colleagues. He wouldn't do that if he was married . . . would he?

"I'd love to. What time?"

"Why don't you come a little early and we can have a drink before dinner? Say five?"

Do I have to wait that long? I won't be able to sleep. "Okay," I agreed, feeling elated and disappointed all at the same time.

"How far will you have to come?" he inquired.

"It's about an hour and a half, but it's a lovely drive."

"You won't be too tired?" he asked, concerned.

Wild horses wouldn't keep me away. "I'm used to driving up to London," I told him, not lying.

After I reluctantly put the phone down, my exhilaration gave me the strength to carry my heavy suitcase upstairs. In my bedroom another note from Ellen lay on my bed . . . and yet another in the bathroom. Yes, Ellen understood love.

In the late afternoon as I drove the country lanes with green fields and hedgerows bathed in a golden light, nothing—not even the uncertain protracted grounding of our planes—could dampen my spirits.

When Jose opened his hotel room door and stood there beaming at me, it was hard to breathe. I couldn't take the stupid grin from my face. Each time we reunited, my instinct was to throw myself into his arms, but as usual his only demonstration of affection was a constrained kiss on each cheek. Although he emanated love from his whole being, especially his eyes, I was confused.

After so much time of missing him, and only being able to imagine this moment, his physical presence felt surreal. We sat across from each other, me sipping on a rum and coke, him on a gin and tonic, taking each other in. We talked, but somehow the words did not seem important. I basked in his glow.

Later at the Italian restaurant, the three other stereotypical American businessmen were jovial, and though older than Jose, I gathered they were his juniors and appeared to respect him. He introduced me proudly with no explanation of whether I was a friend or a lover. While enjoying the cannelloni, Jose informed them that I flew for Laker, which spawned a discussion about the tragic DC-10 crash. The worldwide inspection of all DC-10s was once again front and center news.

"How long will you be grounded?" one of them asked.

I shrugged. "No idea. I don't think we should be grounded at all. Perhaps it's just a natural assumption on the part of the FAA that Freddie is scrimping on safety," I proposed, "because his flights are cheaper. But the opposite is true. Our boss is fanatical about safety, and we are drilled on our emergency procedures before every flight."

"Don't all airlines do that?" the oldest one asked.

I knew that all these men, especially Jose, spent a lot of time travelling in planes and I probably shouldn't scare them. "Well, on my last airline we didn't need to be tested."

"Whatddya mean?" another asked.

"We were always using our drills on *real* emergencies."

They all laughed, though a little nervously.

"Like what?" the man opposite me inquired.

"Oh, the undercarriage not coming down, hydraulics failures, air systems going u/s, landing without a rudder, that kind of thing. . ."

"Oh, my Go-o-o-d." he drawled. "You're a brave girl."

Apparently.

While Jose emanated so much warmth toward me, and an intense adoration shone out of his eyes, this was just our third meeting and we still had not kissed. Would this trip finally change things? Maybe his reticence was due to his South American culture, his sense of politesse or . . .? So when during dinner he gently stroked my back, his touch was electric, and I melted.

Later after a nightcap back at his hotel, Jose accompanied me to my car and sat in the passenger seat.

"Will you be okay driving home?" he asked, concerned.

"Oh, yes," I replied, wondering if his question was a veiled invitation to stay the night. "I'm used to the drive."

"Okay." He nodded but still didn't move.

Neither of us, it seemed, wanted to part company, but he surprised me by leaning in and oh-so-gently kissing me.

"Drive carefully," he said as he climbed out of my car, leaving me feeling like putty. "I'll see you on Thursday."

Thursday was so far away, but he had business meetings in town until the end of the week, and so we had agreed that I would make the journey up to London again.

On our next date I decided to take Jose to one of my favourite London restaurants, the *Borshtch n Tears* in Knightsbridge. Very bohemian and lively, the establishment was in an old three-storey house on Beauchamp Place, just down the road from Harrods. The menu had a Russian theme. While we were eating our *Chicken Dragemoff*, Cossack entertainers broke into Russian song and performed their leg-kicking dance in front of us while we were encouraged to knock back shots of vodka.

Over the noise of the rousing Russian music and the conversations of the other diners, Jose and I talked about our last meeting in Bangor, Maine. "I didn't tell you, but after you left, I was taken to hospital."

"Oh, no! What happened?"

"I waved goodbye to you and then went back to bed for a nap. Later, my friend, Deirdre came banging at my door. I think I was in a deep sleep and got up too quickly. I answered the door and then immediately passed out. Deirdre thought—because I had mentioned some stomach pains earlier—that I had appendicitis, so she called an ambulance immediately and had me rushed to hospital."

"Oh, that's terrible," Jose seemed stricken by this news. "Why didn't you call me?"

"I thought you would be back in Boston by then, and I didn't want to worry you."

"Oh." He hung his head as if my ordeal had been his fault. "If anything like that happens again," he said earnestly, clutching my hand, "*please* call me."

"I will," I responded, touched by his concern. Did this mean he really cared for me?

As agreed on the weekend, Jose came to my home in Horsham. Sharing a love of horses, I organized a ride for us over the Sussex Downs. When my horse, "Bullett" galloped away with me, Jose chased after us and was able to save me from a too-high leap over a wooden fence and a real "ditching." We also took a road trip to Brighton and visited some country pubs en route. Since he had been in England, I had been filled with so much happiness, I had barely wanted to eat. The pounds, which normally required stringent dieting, were melting off me.

On our last night together, I drove us through local country lanes to a favorite Tudor-style restaurant. As we sat in the cozy room at a small table, I was mesmerized by Jose as he told me about his job, flying all over North and South America. I tried to take the inane grin from my face, but I was euphoric in his company and felt like an out-of-control besotted teenager. Maybe it was a kind of subdued hysteria at the horrible thought of him leaving the next day.

Over coffees and liqueurs, he suddenly became serious. "Do you ever fly into Boston?" he asked.

My heart leapt. Was he inviting me to his home?

"No, just New York, LA, Miami and Barbados. But you never know. We do the odd ad hoc flight to Chicago. I could always jump on a plane in New York to come and see you in Boston. That's if we ever fly again," I added, reality suddenly hitting me.

"I'd love to show you Boston. It's a great city." He smiled then, and my whole world lit up. "Com'on," he said. "Let's go home."

When we walked into my living room, he faltered. Until now he had slept in my guest room. Although I wanted to be with him day and night, I had not pushed the issue. Now I sensed he was struggling with the thought, so I made it easy on him. "Where would you like to sleep tonight?"

"I'd prefer to sleep with you," he said coyly.

Praise the lord! "I'd love that, too," I said, exhaling a huge sigh of relief.

The first time we lay together, as I savored the moment of my head resting on his naked shoulder, he turned to look at me. His eyes were so full of love it took my breath away. He rolled over to take me in his arms.

Then it happened. Words unbidden suddenly blurted out of my mouth, words that I knew would hurt him or me . . . or both of us.

"Are you married?" I asked.

He froze in mid-embrace, rolled onto his back again and covered his face with his arm. As if finally caught with his hand in the cookie jar, he said, "Jyes."

I could only lie there, my head still on his shoulder. Paralyzed. Unable to move. Tears welled up and spilled onto his skin. Of course, I had suspected it all along. That nagging voice in the back of my head. But now, hearing him confirm my worst nightmare, all I could feel was anger—strangely not at Jose—but at God. Why, when I have finally found this love, does he have to be married? Thanks a lot, God! Is *everything* good going to be taken away from me?

Jose felt the damp caused by my tears and rubbed his skin. "Are jyou crying?" he asked, puzzled, as if he had merely announced that it was cold outside.

I could only nod.

"Why?"

"Oh . . . you have no idea!" I blurted, finally realizing that he had no clue how much I loved him and although I had imagined it so intensely, it was obvious now that he didn't feel the same way about me. Yes, he liked me, but he was married. And by omission, he had lied. There was no avoiding that. Talk about being brought back down to earth with a wallop. Now I was well and truly grounded.

"I can sleep in my bed?" he offered.

"Yes, I think you better," I muttered, knowing that I would probably be crying all night.

"And I can get a cab to the airport in the morning?" he said, pulling on his trousers.

"Jose!" I said, my heart breaking, knowing that after he left, I could never see him again. "No, I'll take you."

"I know," he said, as if he suddenly acknowledged the pain of our parting.

On our drive to Gatwick for his eleven o'clock flight the next morning we were both silent, but this time our silence was not shared. I had decided that as he was a married man, I could never see him again. Still, my emotions and my morals were doing battle. My father's affair had broken my mother and blown our family to pieces. But how could something so wonderful be so wrong?

In the departure lounge, and unable to turn my back on him, my final words were, "Thank you for all the wonderful memories." As I retreated, I managed a small smile. "Take care of yourself."

"You, too. And if you ever come to Boston . . ."

What? No, it was done. Then I backed away, his saddened face forever etched in my memory.

The lights had gone out. Numbness was already setting in.

I walked stiffly through the terminal, trying not to cry, then past the airport windows and seeing a still life of all the DC-10s parked in rows on the tarmac, I prayed fervently that we could be ungrounded soon and fly again. At least, work would take my mind off my heartbreak.

As it turned out, it wouldn't be flying that would provide me with a much-needed distraction, but my friend, Emma. She would go through another type of grounding which had nothing to do with mechanical issues.

The following Saturday was sunny, and I was sitting at the breakfast table, staring at the kitchen wall grappling with the mystery of why the men in my life who I loved, didn't love me, while the men I wasn't attracted to showed up in droves. Where was the disconnect? Then the phone rang.

"Are you on a day off by any remote chance?" Emma asked without preamble.

"Still grounded," I muttered. "So yes. But it's so good to hear from you." After she had begun training in January with Iran Air and then was rescued from the Iranian revolution, Emma had joined an executive airline flying corporate people out of Heathrow to destinations around Europe. Recently, our different rosters had rarely allowed us to get together.

"Amazing! We both have a Saturday off!" She chortled. "So why don't we go shopping like normal people."

"How boring," I teased, but I was also unexpectedly excited at the prospect of joining the human race in mundane Saturday rituals.

"I'll pick you up. Say, one o 'clock?" Although she accused me of driving like Stirling Moss, the famous racing driver whom I had met while working at BMW, Emma's erratic driving in her little mini often left me with *my* heart in my mouth.

"No," she countered. "Come over here. I want to show off my new car."

"Uh-oh. What kind of car is it?"

"You'll see," she said. "And there's a story to go with it."

"There's always a story with you!"

The early morning blue sky promised a gorgeous, sunny May day. When I pulled into the Cherry Tree Close courtyard in my older not-so-glam white Morris Mini, Emma was already waiting in the driver's seat of a black MGBT convertible, the roof down as she sunned her pale face. She waved happily as I approached. Though she seemed ecstatic, for some reason the black car suggested something ominous. I pushed the feeling away.

"So, what do you think?" she asked as I climbed into the passenger seat.

"It's lovely," I exclaimed, a tad envious. The MGBT's tan leather interior was sumptuous and the seat comfortable. "Is it brand new?"

"Almost."

"That airline must be paying you well."

"You could say that." She chuckled and turned her head to reverse onto the road.

When we arrived at Crawley's main shopping centre the car park was surprisingly empty. Emma turned off the engine but didn't move. "There's something I need to ask you, Natasha." She was suddenly serious, fidgeting with the keys still in the ignition. "And I haven't told anyone else, so you must swear . . ."

"Is this about seeing 11-11 again?"

Emma had asked me about six months ago whether her repeated occurrences of noticing those numbers everywhere in her environment should concern her. I had told her then I wasn't quite sure except that the numbers might be an indication of a big change in her life.

"No, this is something else," she responded, more concerned.

Uh-oh. Had she tampered with Stewart's ex-girlfriend's brakes as she had once threatened? Or mine? "Depends," I said. "Will I be accused of aiding and abetting?"

"I know you are into all this woo-woo stuff . . ."

"You mean metaphysics."

"Okay, whatever. Well, for the last . . . oh, few months, I've had this recurring dream and it's . . . a little disturbing."

"Tell me." Dream interpretation was fascinating, but I was still very new to the topic.

"Well . . ." Emma began. She looked out across the parking stalls to where a few stray shoppers loaded down with bags were going home. "In the dream I'm always driving down this same road. In the beginning it's a bright sunny day, but as I'm driving, the sky gets darker and darker, and the road gets narrower and narrower and the hedgerows crowd in on me. Then, when I brake, nothing happens, and I wake up in a panic!" Emma exhaled a large breath as if she was expelling the dream. "It's always the same dream, more or less, but it feels so real!"

I sat back in my seat, considering the possible interpretations. "Is the 11-11 thing still happening?"

"Oh . . . no." She shook her head, as if shaking off a fly. "What do you think the dream means?" She searched my face, seeking reassurance.

"Well, what I do know about dreams is that the mind sorts all the information that we take in during the day, and in the process our subconscious creates dream images that tell us how we feel about things. But you can't always take the images literally. Most dreams are symbolic. So, your dream isn't necessarily pre-cognitive."

Emma sighed and flicked her fringe of hair out of her eyes. "For God's sake, Dr. Freud, speak English!"

"Well, you're always talking about fixing Sarah's brakes. The dream might be telling you that you are going down the wrong road. Or it may just mean that your brakes need checking."

"Just did that, so that's not it."

"Or it might represent your fears about the narrowing choices in your life?"

"But things are good right now. I *love* living with Stewart."

Correcting her version of "living with Stewart" was pointless—she was living in his house while he was living elsewhere—but I had a bad feeling about the dream, too. However, I didn't want to scare my friend. "I know," I said cheerily. "It's telling us if we don't go shopping soon, all the shops will be closed."

"Ha, ha." Emma pulled the keys out of the ignition. "C'mon," she said, shaking her fine auburn bob and grinning. "You're right. It's probably nothing. Let's go and spend. Stewart's house really needs my help."

"Was that the story you were going to tell me about the car?" I asked as we walked into Marks and Sparks.

"Oh, no. That's something else. Let's go for a drink later and I'll give you the whole scoop. Now we've got shopping to do."

For the next hour I watched bemused as Emma, a woman on a mission, picked out flowery, feminine tablecloths, linen serviettes, tea towels, cushions and other matching linens apparently to give Stewart's house "the feminine touch." If only I could be a fly on the wall when Stewart arrived home from his austere Aberdeen lodgings to find his bachelor pad transformed into a rendition of Monet's

Garden at Giverny. When we eventually re-emerged into the sunshine toting bulging bags, it was five o'clock.

"Where shall we go for a drink?" she asked while cramming her spoils into the MGBT's cramped boot.

Once we were seated at the Plough with glasses of blackberry wine in front of us, she asked, "So what's the latest with you?"

I briefly thought about sharing how the FAA still hadn't finished their investigations on DC-10s so we all might be out of our jobs soon and how devastated I was at the prospect of never seeing Jose again.

"Oh, nothing much new," I said, shrugging. "Tell me the story about the car?"

"Well . . ." She glanced over to the next table where two airport workers, oblivious to our conversation, were enjoying a pint, but she still lowered her voice. "You know what it's like when you meet someone, and you know they like you and you like them?"

I felt a pang as I remembered meeting Jose for the first time. "Yes," I responded. Where was this going? Was she over Stewart and had she found real love? Praise be!

"Well, about two weeks ago, I did a Zurich on the Lear jet." She wouldn't look me in the eye as she spoke. This coyness was new.

"And . . .?"

"There was just one passenger. A man. An Arab."

"Yes?"

"Well, he took one look at me, and I took one look at him, and you might say that was it."

"What was it? You mean . . . love?"

"Suffice it to say," she continued, a mixture of defensiveness and defiance in her voice, "that when we arrived in Zurich, he asked me to join him for dinner at the Zurich Inn by the Lake. It's very expensive, you know."

I knew exactly which hotel she was referring to. When I had lived and worked in Zurich, one of my father's business colleagues had stayed at that same hotel, and over dinner he had made less-than-paternal advances to me. The most expensive hotel in Zurich seemed to lend itself to these nefarious liaisons. "So, of course, you accepted," I teased.

"Of course!" She looked me in the eyes then and took a large gulp of wine.

I waited.

"Well, you know," she continued, "how one thing leads to another and—"

"Will you see him again?" After Emma had got caught up in the Iranian revolution, we had all worried about the sanity of her choices. But maybe she was destined to live in a middle Eastern culture, just not a Persian one.

"God, no. It was purely a lust thing."

"Oh," I said, trying to keep the judgment out of my voice. Or was it jealousy? After Jose I would probably never fall for, or lust after anyone else again.

"The next morning when I got on the aircraft for the inbound flight, I discovered this big fat brown envelope in my handbag." Emma was beaming although a tiny frown creased her forehead.

"What was in it?"

"A thousand pounds!"

"What!"

"Yes. It was a thank you for the previous evening."

"Emma!" Wasn't this sinking to some forbidden level for well-brought up middle-class young ladies, let alone fuelling more rumours about loose air hostesses? "You didn't accept it, did you?"

"Of course, I did! A thousand pounds is like a bouquet of flowers from an Arab."

"I'd rather have the bouquet of flowers!" I exclaimed, not attempting to disguise my horror. Was I being a prude?

"Well, I'd rather have a new car!" She shook her fringe out of her eyes and emptied her glass.

"I wonder how the airline will view that," I mumbled as I finished my wine.

"Oh, they won't care," she responded, putting her head down so her hair fell over her eyebrows again, covering that almost imperceptible frown. "C'mon!" she nudged me. "Let's get back to #36. I can't wait to transform Stewart's place with my new things."

"Are you sure he will be okay with these changes?"

"Of course! He'll love them."

By the time we got back to Cherry Tree Close, daylight had softened to a golden glow. I held some of Emma's bags and watched as she stood on the doorstep and put her key in the lock of her new home.

Suddenly her image morphed into something else, as if she had become a black and white negative of herself. I blinked. Were my eyes playing tricks on me? I heard a voice in my head say, "She's not strong enough for this life. She'll die within six months." Then just as suddenly, the colourful, full-bodied Emma came back into focus. Happy, she turned to smile at me. "Let's make some coffee, shall we?"

"That would be lovely," I said as, shaken, I followed her into the darkened hallway.

After ooh-ing and aah-ing at the feminine transformation of Stewart's home, I drove home that night reflecting on my friend's moral choices. Although Emma and this Arab had been consenting adults, and she hadn't slept with him *for* financial gain, she obviously didn't care that she had perhaps prostituted herself.

Unfortunately, the airline did.

A week later Emma called me. She was in tears. "I've been fired!" she exclaimed.

Quelle surprise! "No! What for?"

Emma scoffed as if she was the innocent. "For getting too familiar with passengers!"

Familiar, I supposed, was one word for coitus. "How did management find out? Did he send in a compliment card?"

She didn't laugh. "I think it was that bastard captain who reported me." There was a pause. "Now what do I do?" she moaned.

"Now we're both grounded." I sighed, but I refused to let her dour mood bring me even further down. "Oh, there are lots of airlines out there, Emma. One of them will take us, except on your resume, you may want to claim the reason for your little fling was that you've been flying too long."

"What do you mean?"

"Because that's when passengers start to look attractive."

Emma laughed. "Oh yes, and you've *really* been flying too long when the flight deck begin to look good."

By Day 41 of the DC-10 grounding, I had painted my living room walls, sewn several summer tops and dresses and enjoyed copious pub lunches with friends and other restless Laker stewies. Still no verdict seemed imminent on the reason for the crash or the future of the DC-10s. So, as I watched the six o'clock news that evening in my living room, I was surprised when Reginal Bosinquet shuffled his papers and glibly announced that the Civil Aviation Authority had released its findings on the American Airlines crash at Chicago's O'Hare Airport. I jumped up and turned up the volume.

"American Airlines have now been found culpable for the crash of their own DC-10 and the death of all 258 passengers, two ground crew and 13 crew on board," the newscaster announced. "The American airline had apparently not followed aircraft maintenance procedures as stipulated by the manufacturer, McDonnell Douglas, causing metal fatigue on the wing and creating a crack in the engine housing."

So American Airlines was the culprit. But what did this mean? Did we have the green flag to fly again? As if answering my question, Reginald continued, "The CAA has just announced that the UK grounding of DC-10s has been lifted. On investigation it was found that all UK airlines adhered to the maintenance regulations and have, therefore, not incurred the same metal stress. Further investigations continue in the United States."

The phone rang.

Could this mean we are back in business?

"Am I speaking to Miss Rosewood?" The young man's voice had a smile in it.

I had never been so happy to hear the dulcet tones of a crewing member. "Yes?"

"We'd like you to do a JFK tomorrow departing at thirteen hundred hours. And can you pick up your new roster in the crew room."

"With pleasure," I breathed.

When the entire crew gathered in the captain's room at the Doral Inn in downtown Manhattan for our ritual post-flight drink, the mood was jubilant. We were all so happy to be back in the old routine.

The first question on everyone's mind was "What really happened to the American Airlines DC-10?" Reg Hammond, our middle-aged, health-nut captain provided us with more details about the cause of the crash.

"McDonnell Douglas," he explained, "had written strict instructions in their maintenance manuals on how to service their DC-10s. The engines, it stated categorically, were to be removed from the fuselage *before* any maintenance was to be carried out. American Airlines thought that they would save time and money by ignoring the manufacturer's instructions. So, their engineers did their regular servicing from a forklift with the engine still attached to the wing. This caused the stress on the engine's metal attachments to the wing—which was not just one bolt by the way—and subsequently the detachment of the engine at the point of major stress, take-off. Now American Airlines are going to have to pay out millions to those families."

"And possibly Laker," the first officer added. "Being the only airline to have such a large fleet of DC-10s in the UK, Freddie was the most affected by the shut-down. He's also talking about suing the FAA for grounding his aircraft," he added. "Apparently, they didn't even enquire into his maintenance practices. We could have been flying weeks ago, and it would have saved him millions."

"Well," Reg said, raising a glass, "let's drink to being in the air again."

As everyone cheered, all I could think of was Jose in Boston—merely one hour away by air—and now that I was back in the US again, how I must not weaken and call him just so I could hear him say, "Hi."

7

NOT FULLY LOADED

London- Miami-London
October 1979

"Dis testing of emergencies all the time is a pain in the arrrse," the Irish Rose complained. "I bet you didn't have to go t'rough dis with Dan Air."

My Irish colleague and I were sitting with the rest of the stewardesses at the front of the middle cabin on an otherwise empty DC-10 waiting to hear the briefing for our imminent London Gatwick-to-Miami flight. As per our usual Laker pre-flight routine, our IFD would also be testing us on our emergency drills.

"No. We didn't need to get tested . . . we used our drills all the time . . .."

Rose's eyes went wide. "You've got to be jokin'?"

"Wish I was. Old aircraft. We were always having emergencies. Undercarriage would not come down, fire bells going off, fuel contamination, tail planes falling off . . ."

"Oh, faith and begorra!"

Our In-Flight Director, Sarah Browning, suddenly appeared.

"Dis is her first flight back at work, you know," Rose whispered.

The whole airline knew that three months earlier in the Doral Inn, our New York hotel, Sarah had been in the wrong place at the wrong time. Ten years earlier, one of the Laker girls had been savagely beaten and raped in the bar's washroom. Since then, and as part of our what-not-to-do-in-New-York pep talk when joining the airline, every stewardess had been warned to avoid those facilities and instead use the bathroom in her own hotel room. But as time passed, the fear of the bogey man had faded and the crews who gathered in the hotel bar for post-flight drinks had ignored the warnings.

Unfortunately for Sarah, when she had opted to "just go downstairs," she had met with another vicious attacker. Rumour had it that he had broken her jawbone, one of the hardest bones in the body to break. He had also been about to sexually assault her when another woman had come into the washroom and scared him away.

"Okay, everyone," Sarah began. With her long black hair and her self-possessed posture, a young woman who glided rather than walked, Sarah had always reminded me of a Hawaiian goddess. Her supreme self-confidence had even been a little intimidating. But now as she stood in front of us, there was something fractured in her aura, and she seemed like a frightened little bird. I hoped she was truly ready to come back into the fray.

Seven and a half hours later, after a busy but blissfully uneventful flight to Miami, we climbed aboard the large bus that provided our crew transportation for the short ride to the Airport Marriott Hotel, a massive complex of four buildings with a pool at its center. Then as we waited to be checked in and handed keys, my heart leapt out of my chest every few minutes as, one after another, Jose look-alikes, Cubans, Mexicans and South Americans, came in and out of the lobby. For a moment I would hold my breath, and then release it when I realized that it wasn't Jose. There was always that possibility though—because we both flew all over America for our work—that one day, fate would bring us together again. Hope was all I had.

Suddenly Sarah grabbed my arm and pulled me out of dreamland. She showed me her room number. "Please, Natasha, can you walk with me?" Apparently, our room numbers were close together.

"Of course," I responded, still shocked at this new, very fragile Sarah but eager to have her remove the sharp fingernails she had embedded in my arm.

After the crew agreed to meet in one hour in the main lobby to go for dinner, Sarah and I began our long trek, rolling our cases behind us, up elevators, across bridges between buildings and along open corridors. As we made our way along the shadowy walkways bordered by hotel doors on one side and a railing that overlooked a courtyard below on the other, I also found them a little creepy. It would be so easy for an undesirable to open a door and drag us inside without anyone hearing a disturbance or coming to our rescue. And maybe Sarah's paranoia was catching.

At the end of the walkway on the third floor we came to a halt. Sarah's room was the first on the right, mine on the left. "I'll come and get you when I'm ready," I assured her.

Thirty minutes later I knocked on her door. There was no response. After another light tap, I heard a thump and a muffled "Aaah," from inside the room.

Oh no! Was Sarah being attacked *again*?

Silence. I peered through the narrow, curtained window adjacent to the door but couldn't see anything. Suddenly the curtain was snatched back, and Sarah's enlarged, terrified eyes stared back at me. When recognition finally dawned—as I was now in civvies and with my hair down—she quickly unlatched the chain, undid the other two locks and opened the door.

I stepped inside but she had retreated to the far end of the room as if needing lots and lots of space. Why was she shaking?

"Are you all right?" I asked, mystified.

"The light in the bathroom was out . . ." she panted, "so I called down to Housekeeping."

"Yes?"

"They said they would send someone up . . . straight away so . . . I-I began unpacking." Agitated, she swept her long black hair over one shoulder. "I came out of the bathroom and . . . this man was in my room!"

"Oh no!" Poor Sarah.

"I screamed at him. 'Get out! Get out! Get out!'" She sank down onto the bed, defeated. "But he was just the maintenance man with the new light bulb."

Poor guy.

"He should have knocked," she muttered defensively.

"Yes, yes. He should have knocked." I sat down beside her—though not too close, to give her the space she seemed to need.

"Then I calmed down," she continued, "and I stepped out of the room while he changed the bulb."

Silence fell between us. I wanted to comfort her, to ask her about what had happened in New York, but did *she* want to talk about it? I suddenly felt terribly sad that this trauma had crushed this strong and beautiful woman's spirit and had made her afraid of everything. After three months she was still traumatized by being alone with a man in a room. How long would she continue to live in fear, and would she ever regain her former serenity?

"My boyfriend got me to take karate lessons so I can at least defend myself now," she mumbled.

"Oh God! You did not give the maintenance man the death chop and throw him over the balcony, did you?" I enquired, trying to lighten the mood.

"No," she said and grinned. "But I could have. He should have knocked."

The next day at four o'clock local time we all piled into the airport transporter bus for our return Miami-Gatwick.

"The Chilean ambassador will be sitting in C at the emergency exit," Sarah announced in her briefing once we were on the aircraft. "As much as possible, please try and give him VIP treatment."

Some of us snickered. We knew full well that, unlike British Airways or Ward Air, we dished up our meals on plastic, not on Royal Doulton china. And there would be no champagne unless he had ordered a bottle.

"That's all," Sarah added. "Now let's get to work."

On this flight, Rose was positioned at Two Door Left, the main entrance to the aircraft, directing passengers to either go down the first aisle or come through the galley to where I was posted at Two Door Right starboard side. I then pointed either into the forward cabin on my right or to my left into the middle and rear cabins, B and C. I watched as people of all shapes and sizes entered the aircraft, noting how some would step across the threshold from the finger into the plane, as if in a trance, appearing as if they had crossed some mighty void and landed inside an alien spaceship.

Having practiced my rudimentary palm reading skills on willing crew members, I was already known throughout the airline as somewhat of a clairvoyant. Now I was also strengthening my intuitive abilities. Some passengers would twitch and struggle with their belongings and ask lots of questions. These were often the more demanding and neurotic passengers, while other scared-of-flying attention-seekers had the potential to become drunken troublemakers. I could usually pick out the problematic travellers, though sometimes I was wrong. Most people, however, when instructed where to sit simply nodded calmly and went to their seats.

Passengers were coming toward me now. One of them was a big man, over six foot two inches, somewhere in his early 40s. I could not help noticing his tacky-tourist shirt covered in blue, yellow and green macaws, his beige polyester slacks and straw hat with a light jacket slung over one arm. Through his finely rimmed gold glasses, his eyes glinted when he smiled. "Good afternoon," he addressed me heartily. "6A?"

Accountant going on holiday by himself, I surmised. Despite his taste in shirts, I assessed him as a frequent traveller, a quiet passenger.

"Good afternoon," I returned his cheery greeting. "There, on the right." I pointed to a window seat in the forward cabin just three rows ahead.

He nodded and, grappling with his large hold-all, moved forward. I watched as he folded his tall frame into the window seat and crammed his bag underneath the seat in front of him.

Once all passengers were on board, heads counted, paperwork signed, doors closed and armed, the aircraft "off chocks" and pushed back, we began our taxi out to the runway. Then Sarah commenced her pre-take off PA. "Good afternoon, ladies and gentlemen . . ."

On a Miami-Gatwick flight—a five- to seven-hour sector depending on winds, hurricanes or other eventualities—we provided a full service. Even though on this day when we weren't fully loaded—with forty empty seats—we would still be working our usual busy routine.

After take-off, Rose and I began working in the starboard aisle from the front of Cabin A, while our counterparts worked their way down the port aisle. The four of us continued serving toward the middle of the aircraft while the girls in the rear began the same service going forward until we met, usually in the center of Cabin B.

"Would you like a headset, sir?" I asked my friendly, tacky-tourist accountant in 6A.

He glanced at me and shook his head.

I moved on to the next row, waving headsets in the air.

The next service was drinks from the bar cart. When offered a beverage, 6A shook his head again and resumed staring out of the window as if he resented being disturbed.

He seemed sad, I thought, and was reminded that we never knew what passengers were leaving behind or what they were facing at the other end—a funeral, a reunion, a separation or an escape? Or they were just terrified of flying in a slim metal container, surrendering their precious lives to complete strangers—the flight crew—who were now responsible for their fates.

I shrugged and turned to people on the other side of the aisle.

After the bar cart was disassembled and sent down to the lower galley, we waited for carts loaded with steaming dinners to be sent up. The small aluminum containers would be delivered to our passengers on trays accompanied by an offering of red or white wine, then tea or coffee followed by liqueurs, all presented in the highest quality plastic, of course.

6A wanted nothing. No dinner, no red or white wine, no tea, coffee or liqueur.

"Would you like a glass of water, sir?" I offered. Then, sounding like his mother, I added, "You should really drink something every twenty minutes while in flight, you know. We dehydrate more rapidly up here."

He just stared back at me—or more accurately, right through me as if I didn't exist. The lights were on in his eyes, but the man who had wished me a hearty good morning less than two hours previously had disappeared. His choice, I thought, and carried on down the cabin.

Once the meal debris was cleared away, Sarah announced to the passengers that cabin lights would be dimmed, and the movie would begin. *Being There* with Peter Sellers and Shirley MacLaine was a good, long movie and would keep them entertained for a while. For anyone requiring refreshments during that time, drink trolleys would be set up in the forward and aft galleys she told them.

"Why don't you go on first meal break?" Sarah suggested to me as passengers snuggled down to sleep, donned headsets or climbed out of their constricting spaces to head for the loos.

"Rose and I can wait," I told her. "The new girls can go first." I didn't know if it was intuition, but for some reason I felt the need to stay with Sarah.

As we set up the drinks cart in the forward galley, Alexa, one of the crew, came up from the rear to get more ice. "Oh God," she moaned, "there's a man in C just two rows behind the Chilean ambassador who keeps singing 'It's a long way to Tipperary.' We've been giving him more Scotch, hoping he'll go to sleep, but he just sings louder and louder. I don't think Mr. Chile is impressed. So much for VIP treatment!"

"Well, if he wanted first class, he should have flown BCAL," I retorted.

"Not BA?" Rose asked me mockingly.

"Not if he wanted to eat or drink." We all laughed.

BA stewardesses were known for their shoddy service at that time, which was doled out, in my experience, with an unwarranted air of superiority. And maybe we were just jealous of their international routes and much higher pay.

After Alexa disappeared back into the shadowy cabin, I busied myself with slicing lemons while Rose filled the ice buckets. While the galley was brightly lit, the rest of the cabins were shrouded in darkness, with just the muted flickering from the movie screens casting shadows on passengers' faces. As I looked forward into Cabin A and then back into Cabin B, I saw that people were beginning to doze.

"Do you mind if I take a load off?" I asked Rose.

"To be sure," she replied. "You sit down. I'm just going down to get more cokes."

I sat down on my jump seat. Across the aisle at Two Door Left, Sarah was also sitting completing the flight paperwork. All was quiet.

And then it happened.

The voices were coming from the forward cabin, and at first, I thought it was just people conversing. I stood up, turned and saw that 6A was talking with the woman in 6C, and their voices were getting progressively louder. Were they arguing? I squinted into the shadows. The other passengers in the forward cabin had also heard the commotion and were peering around their seats to see what was happening.

"Why are you watching this fucking crap?" 6A yelled at the poor woman in the aisle seat.

She mumbled something in response, trying to placate him.

Then he got up on his seat, crouching on his haunches, facing the others in the cabin, his spectacles a little askew. "You're all fucking crazy!" he yelled into the shadows. "Why are they making us watch this fucking crap?"

Now he had my attention—and everyone else's. I glanced over at Sarah. With her paperwork still on her lap, she was staring at the man, terrified, her features collapsing in misery, knowing that another horror show was about to unfold in her life. In her still fragile state, this might be too much.

One man at the front of the cabin on the port side got up out of his seat and began to walk toward the galley, his eyes on 6A. Oh no, I thought. We don't need any heroics or confrontations. I stopped him before he reached the galley. "Sir," I whispered, "please return to your seat. We'll deal with this."

"Okay," he drawled, "but let me know if you need my help."

What to do? Sarah was sitting frozen to her jump seat. She was not going to be of any use. I approached row 6. The woman in 6C was huddled in her seat now, cringing at the threat of this large man gone wild.

"Madam," I whispered. "There are empty seats at the rear of the plane. I suggest you move."

Frightened, she nodded gratefully, climbed out of her seat and skittered down the aisle, clutching her handbag. In her angst she had left her hand luggage behind.

The man in 6A had slumped down into his seat again. I leaned in toward him. "Sir, can I help you?"

"I have to get to Frankfurt!" he yelled so the whole cabin could hear him. "Turn that fucking crap off!" He waved his arm at the flickering screen. He was, I noticed, now wearing his jacket as if he was ready to get off the plane.

"I'm sorry, sir, but the other passengers are enjoying the film. I can provide you with earplugs and eye shades?" Or I could put a sick bag over your head, I thought. Maybe you're hyperventilating?

Without answering me, and like an agitated ape he moved across the seats, pushing me aside, and stood in the aisle. Oh no. What was he going to do?

He walked forward, waving his arms at the faces in the shadows. The man I had asked to return to his seat stood up and was now waiting, ready to pounce.

"You people are all crazy," the man from 6A yelled. "I'm going to Frankfurt!"

Now everyone in Cabin A was staring at him, fully awake, some puzzled and bemused, others terrified.

For only the second time in my six-year flying career, was I unsure what to do with an unruly passenger. What had set him off? I could only watch and wait.

Then he turned and strutted back to 6A. For a moment I thought he was going to tackle me. Instead, he sat down on the middle arm rest and proceeded to take off his shoes and socks.

All the passengers in Cabin A were now watching, the atmosphere thick with fear. Some were out of their seats, ready to tackle him, or flee. Others were sitting staring intently.

"I've got to get to Frankfurt!" he mumbled.

In my most soothing air hostess voice, which I normally reserved for children or nervous passengers, I cooed, "Yes, sir, we can get you to Frankfurt, right after we fly to Gatwick."

He grunted, and still on his haunches, climbed into the middle seat and turned toward the window. Then with his back toward me, he shouted, "Let me o-u-t!" And without warning his right leg suddenly flew out and his bare foot made contact with the aircraft window.

Cra-a-ack!

Behind me a woman screamed.

Others gasped.

A man's voice, "What the f. . .?"

What had he done?

The man from 6A turned to me, grinning weirdly as the light from the galley shone on his skewed spectacles. In his hands he held two pieces of transparent plastic.

Oh my God! He's broken the window!

A commotion erupted behind me. One woman was crying, another man yelled, "He's broken the fucking window! Get the hell out o' here!"

I turned around. Now all the passengers in Cabin A were out of their seats, grabbing their belongings. One woman whimpered, "We're gonna get sucked out!" They were all tugging and pushing at each other to move down the aisle and into another cabin as quickly as they could, getting as far as possible away from this lunatic and the fear of dying.

If they hadn't been so frantic, I could have reassured them that he had only broken the scratch panel, the interior plastic part of the window. Even if he had been Superman, it would have been impossible for him to penetrate the other two layers of window maintaining our pressurization and our air supply. But they weren't waiting to find out, and within minutes I was alone with 6A or "Frankfurter" as I now thought of him.

Out of the corner of my eye I saw Sarah standing in the galley, her hands clasped to her cheeks, her mouth a dark oval of horror, reminding me of Edvard Munch's painting, *The Scream*. Hiding behind her, the woman from 6C, now in full panic mode, stared at us, desperately dragging on her inhaler for breath. Lady, please don't die on me, I thought.

"If you don't get me to Frankfurt," the man was now towering over me, his beady eyes manic as he yelled into my face, "I'm gonna break every window on this fucking plane!"

"I understand, sir, and I'll tell you what I'm going to do. I'm going to talk to the captain and see how we can help you get to Frankfurt. Why don't you just sit down, and I'll be right back?"

"Okay," he said, suddenly acquiescing and sounding like the Tacky-Tourist Accountant again. Normal.

I left him sitting all alone in the shadows of Cabin A, the movie screen still flickering, as I moved to go through the galley. At that moment Rose emerged from the lift, bearing a tray of cokes. She frowned, puzzled, aware that something very odd was happening.

"We've got a nutbar in 6A," I told her.

I approached our IFD who was still standing, horrified. "Sarah, why don't you go downstairs? I can handle this," I said, lying through my teeth. "Rose can keep watch, too."

Sarah nodded gratefully and hit the button on the lift to take her downstairs. Her eyes were blank, and I was afraid this trauma had brought back her previous nightmare. Was she going catatonic?

"Madam," I then addressed the asthmatic woman still hovering at the edge of the galley, "Didn't you find a seat at the rear of the aircraft? I think you would be more comfortable back there."

"I forgot... my things ...?" She was staring in terror at Frankfurter who was now draped over the back of the seat, staring in our direction but focused on something else. His glasses were even further askew on his face with the yellow light from the galley shining on the lenses. He appeared more inebriated than our Irish singer who had by now probably downed a whole bottle of Scotch. But I knew Frankfurter hadn't had a drop to drink, not even water. And if he wasn't so scary, he would be comical.

"I'll get them for you. And don't worry. I'm going to ask the captain to speak with him. Everything will be all right," I told her. Even as I spoke, I was doubtful that even though our captain was one of the good ones, he might not leave the flight deck to manage this unpredictable passenger. When incidents of this kind occurred, flight crews would often lock the flight deck door and tell the cabin crew to "just deal with it."

While the asthmatic lady, breathing a little easier and clutching her belongings, found her way down to the rear of the plane, I told Rose, "6A has broken a scratch panel. All other passengers from A are in the back. I'm going up to the flight deck. Be on alert."

Then I crossed the galley and walked up the port aisle of the now deserted forward cabin toward the cockpit. With all the extra weight now at the rear, I had cartoonish visions of the DC-10 flying along with its rear end sagging and its nose stuck up in the air.

As I entered the darkened flight deck, I saw in the shadows that the captain's and co-pilot's picked over meal trays had been left on the floor awaiting collection. My friend Brian Wilson was sitting in the supernumerary seat behind the captain and because he was training to be a first officer on the DC-10, he wasn't in uniform. He leaned over and passed the meal trays to me thinking that was my purpose for being on the flight deck, so I obliged and took them.

"Captain Webster?" I called above the noise of the aircraft. How was I going to explain this? "Er. . ."

He turned to look at me. Alan Webster was tall and strong with reddish hair and a beard, and fortunately, he had a great sense of humor, which he would need tonight.

"Captain, we have a large man in 6A who took off his shoes and socks and thrust his foot through a scratch panel and broke it. All the terrified passengers in A have moved down to C and this man is threatening to break every window in this aircraft if you don't take him to Frankfurt. I told him that I would speak with you. Can you talk to him, or do you want me to . . .?"

Even before I had finished, Alan had removed his harness and was out of his seat. "Never had a hijacker before," he said gleefully, following me out of the flight deck.

Once back in the dim cabin, I could see that Frankfurter was still in his seat, now staring out of his window. Alan approached him directly from the starboard aisle while I walked down the port side to the galley where Rose relieved me of the flight-deck trays, placed them in the lift and sent them down.

"Dis we have to see," Rose said, smiling. Observing a captain dealing with a troubled passenger was a rare occurrence, so we positioned ourselves at Two Door Right where we could watch and listen.

Alan slouched into the aisle seat of row 6, mimicking Frankfurter's body language and leaving an empty seat between them.

"I've got get to Frankfurt," 6A told him, acknowledging the captain's arrival, "and I know where we are." Frankfurter pointed out the window into the blackness. "Jupiter is over there, and Venus is up there."

Alan leaned over and peered where the man was pointing. "You know, you're right."

"So don't try and trick me," Frankfurter added, calmer.

"I wouldn't think of it," Alan answered in his deep calm voice.

At that moment I could have hugged our captain. Humoring and placating Frankfurter was working. Perhaps their similar size and height was also a factor, an equalizer.

I glanced behind me, peering all the way down the plane into Cabin C, expecting to see passengers standing in the aisles, terrified. But everyone was seated and probably belted in. The atmosphere in the cabin was tense as if they were holding their collective breath.

Alan then talked in a low voice as if he and Frankfurter were two old friends sharing a beer on a pub patio somewhere. We couldn't hear the words.

Finally, Alan stood up and said something more to Frankfurter who nodded and slumped down into his seat and out of sight.

When the captain stepped into the light of the galley, he said, "I've told him we'll take him to Frankfurt . . . after Gatwick." He shook his head, but he was grinning.

"Oo-o-kay," I said, nodding. "So how should we deal with him?"

The airline only trained us how to handle drunks, not people with nervous breakdowns, neuroses or whatever it was Frankfurter was going through, despite the fact there was a borderline case on almost every flight. Mark Twain had a point when he had written, "If we accepted that we were all quite mad, all would be revealed, and life would be much easier."

"Just leave him alone," Alan advised, "but keep an eye on him. I'll call the authorities to meet us at Gatwick."

He turned to go back to the flight deck. "Where's Sarah?" he asked, frowning, suddenly remembering that, as IFD, she should have been the one liaising with the flight deck over any in-flight incident.

"Oh . . . she's downstairs . . . not feeling very well," I responded. "She asked me to . . ." It wasn't a complete lie.

Alan nodded, understanding the words that didn't need to be spoken.

We still had another four and a half hours before we landed. Would Frankfurter remain calm? Rose and I stood in the galley, serving drinks and chatting with passengers. Intermittently we peered into the forward cabin to see what Frankfurter was up to. In the shadows, I couldn't even see the top of his head. He was sleeping.

A half hour later the intercom buzzed and the Number One stewardess at the rear requested extra cokes for her drinks cart. I scooped some cans from our trolley onto a tray and negotiated my way down through the darkened plane, being careful not to trip over stray feet. All was quiet until I reached the end of the middle cabin.

" . . . *to Tipperary*." The Irish man's singing carried through the otherwise silent rear cabins. I was surprised that no one was complaining, but apparently, the passengers preferred to put up with a loud drunk singer to being sucked out of a DC-10 window into a minus-56-degree temperature.

As I handed over the minerals, Sheila mentioned casually, "The captain just buzzed us. He wants you to search the forward toilets."

"What? Why?"

"Your window breaker has just taken that big bag of his into the starboard toilet in Cabin A and come out again very quickly. Alan thinks he might have left something in there."

"You mean . . . *a bomb?*"

"Shsssh!" She turned to serve a young girl waiting patiently for her coke on ice.

Rose and I approached the forward toilets cautiously. Other crew had already switched off and put away the movie projector in A affording us little illumination, but we could see Frankfurter was back in his seat. She whispered, "What do we look for?"

"Anything as small as a lipstick could be a bomb," I whispered, remembering my former Dan Air bomb scares and searches.

"Bluddy hell!" she exclaimed, her lovely soft Irish lilt making the curse sound like a blessing.

While I opened the starboard loo door, Rose inspected the toilet portside. Apart from the usual mess where passengers had stuffed used paper towels into the wrong stowages, I could not find any "foreign objects."

Rose emerged from the toilet and shrugged. "Can't find a ting. Maybe he had just wanted to change his knickers?"

I looked over to 6A. Frankfurter was still in his seat.

The flight deck door was locked. I knocked.

The engineer opened the door just wide enough for me to peek in. "Forward toilets are clear," I told him.

Once we were back in the galley Rose began to disassemble the drinks trolley while another stewardess prepared the pots for teas and coffees to go with the next service, a hot breakfast. "We should have air marshals on our flights," Rose complained. "How are we girrals supposed to grapple with big fellas like dat one?"

"Oh, I kno-o-ow," I said, doing a Sybil. Then I got an idea and returned to the flight deck. I could ask my friend Brian, who was in civvies, to help if we needed him.

Half an hour later, as the credits were rolling on the movie screens in B and C, passengers began sitting up and opening the blinds flooding light into the middle and aft cabins. In A, the window covers were still down. Frankfurter sat up again in his seat, allowing us to see the back of his head. His shoulders were hunched, and he was restless, twitching. The muscles in my neck felt like concrete with the tension, and I felt myself beginning to twitch, too. Would he stay calm to the end of the flight?

As the meal carts arrived from the lower galley, a still-nervous Sarah finally emerged from below and made her announcement informing passengers of the imminent breakfast service.

I had just handed an omelette to a man in row 13, just a few rows into the middle cabin, when I saw that Frankfurter was up and out of his seat, pacing up and down again between the front and middle cabins. Should we offer him a meal, something to drink? Perhaps severe hydration was causing his psychotic break? No, Alan was right. Let him be.

Rose and I wheeled our cart farther down the middle cabin. From my position, facing the front of the plane, I could now see Frankfurter, hands in pockets, standing in front of Two Door Left, staring at the controls as if trying to make sense of them.

Uh-oh.

Was he going to tamper with the exit while we were at 35,000 feet and pressurized? I knew he couldn't *open* the door with all the inside pressure to contend with, unless he was superhuman, but once we began our descent in about an hour, and at 10,000 feet he could let her fly. In pneumatic mode, this would create an explosively loud hiss as the door shot up into its recess, and then the 80-foot-long chute would inflate—if we were lucky—*outside* the aircraft. But while flying at 400 mph on the descent, the chute might blow back inside the cabin and people close to the exits could be crushed and severely injured. Lovely!

As I continued to hand out breakfasts to sleepy passengers, I threw surreptitious glances toward the front, but Frankfurter had disappeared from my line of sight. Where was he? What was he doing? Then I caught a glimpse of him pacing up and down the aisles in Cabin A, hands still in pockets. He appeared calm but he was muttering to himself. On the other side of the aisle, two more stewardesses were also dishing out breakfasts. Like me, the girl in the forward-facing position was eyeing Frankfurter. By the look on her face, I could see that her fears echoed mine.

We exchanged worried glances.

Sarah was now sitting on the Two Door Left jump seat, completing more paperwork. Was she oblivious to the roaming danger or had she completely abdicated responsibility? It suddenly occurred to me that neither she nor Frankfurter were fully loaded. But please God, do not let Frankfurter set her off again! One person going nuts on any flight is enough.

Rose and I were halfway down the middle cabin when suddenly Frankfurter loomed up behind her. "Can I get past you?" he asked politely.

Rose and I exchanged questioning looks, then psychically deciding it was better not to argue, we pushed the cart backward until he was able to slide into a vacant seat so he could then pass behind me. As he continued down the aisle, hands in pockets, all four of us on the forward carts turned to watch. As long as he was moving, he stayed calm. But he was an unknown quantity. None of us had any idea what he might do. Would the still-singing Irishman have a happy effect on him? As he passed by passengers, they either put their heads down, avoiding eye contact or with heads up, they regarded him grimly.

Breakfast service, collecting headsets and handing out immigration forms took another two hours during which Frankfurter continued to roam the aisles. In the forward galley, Rose had just cleaned and put away the last coffee pot when the engines changed tone. We had begun our descent.

Sarah made the landing PA. While passengers returned to their seats and buckled up, Frankfurter suddenly arrived at Two Door Left again, hands in pockets, studying the controls.

Now the fun begins, I thought with dread.

What would he do? He was a big man. Even with the four of us standing behind him in the galley, ready to pounce should he make a move for the door, would our combined force be enough to overpower him? Could we stop him from doing whatever he had on his disturbed mind? What *was* he thinking? Committing hari-kari by leaping out into the void? Or just opening the door while we were still airborne and jumping out?

Suddenly Brian appeared from the flight deck. "Here I am. Do you still need me, Natasha?" he asked.

Thank God! Though Brian would be missing the most crucial part of his training, landing the DC-10, everyone's safety was more important than learning landing routines right now.

"Absolutely," I said, relieved. In his navy V-neck sweater and beige pants, he looked just like another passenger, and though he wasn't as tall as Frankfurter, he was solidly built. "Thank you, Brian. I'm going to ask those two passengers sitting at Two-Door Left to move down the back for landing. Can you sit next to the door and keep an eye on him?"

The young couple were invited to the galley while the precarious situation was explained to them. Once they understood, they were only too happy to sit far away from Frankfurter and the possibility of sudden, loud, high-speed ventilation by the door being opened or death by a prematurely exploding chute. They moved quietly down to the rear of the aircraft where Tipperary was still belting out the same old song. Was he going for a Guinness record?

A *Time* magazine with Maggie Thatcher on the cover was sitting on the galley counter. Brian picked it up and carried it over to the aisle seat close to Two Door Left. As casual as could be, he took his seat. Ignoring Brian, Frankfurter continued to stand, staring at the door controls. He seemed unaware of the whispered plotting and the furtive exchanges between the people around him.

Brian pretended to be engrossed in his magazine, but every now and then he glanced up to see what the big man was doing. Should the need arise, he was ready to restrain him. Behind Frankfurter's back, four of us stood in the galley, also on alert, silent, watching, holding our breath.

Frankfurter took his hands out of his pockets.

We inhaled.

Then he moved to the seat next to Brian.

He stood debating something.

He sat down.

We exhaled.

Brian shifted slightly in his seat to make more room for the bigger man as he settled into 10D.

Sarah's voice came over the PA from the rear with No Smoking and final landing instructions.

Frankfurter obediently put on his seat belt.

Rose and I set off down the aisles to check passengers were fastened in and to clear the cabin of any extraneous debris while the other girls remained on watch in the galley, pretending to discuss the weather and keeping their eyes on the now calm man. Out of the windows we could see the patchwork of the Sussex countryside below.

As the noise of the undercarriage winding down warned us that landing was imminent, we also took our seats—Sarah on her jump seat right in front of Frankfurter and Brian—while I sat on the other side at Two Door Right. From my position across the galley, only Frankfurters' feet were now visible. The rest of him was out of my sight, hidden behind the galley bulkhead.

When I glanced over at Sarah, I wondered how she felt about sitting not three feet from her current nemesis. Was he a mirror for her? Was she looking at him and wondering, is that me? Her whole body seemed to have crumpled into itself as if she had been shredded. Flying, I reflected, was not for the faint of heart, and you could not operate if you didn't have a full load.

As the wheels touched down on the Gatwick runway, my shoulders finally released the concrete-like tension.

All stewardesses undid their seat belts. Then, as the airline's protocol demanded that we appear identical for the disembarkation process, we all donned our black winter coats, hats, scarves and gloves. From her position at Two Door Left, Sarah picked up the black phone and gave her post-landing PA. Her voice was fragile as she instructed passengers to stay seated until the aircraft came to a full and complete stop. Something in her voice made me think it might be the last announcement she would ever make.

I could see Frankfurter rubbing his hands together. He seemed antsy to get out of his seat, but after six hours of being pinned in a tight space with a threatening presence on the loose and an irrepressible Irish singer, so was everyone else. The aircraft finally came to a stop and as the engines whined down—seemingly with a sigh of relief—the big metal bird settled on its haunches. Sarah instructed cabin staff to disarm the doors as she reached up to her own Two Door Left and brought the handle down into its *Disarmed* position.

Brian stood aside, watching closely as Frankfurter got up and made his way into the empty forward cabin, clambering over seats to get to seat 6A and his belongings. From my viewpoint at Two Door Right, I observed him donning his jacket and shoes again, putting his straw hat on and retrieving his holdall from beneath the seat. Then he came forward, now ready along with everyone else to disembark, appearing to have reverted to Mr. Normal.

He smiled at me. I shivered, feeling a vague eeriness. Was it possible that he could suddenly switch back to being the tacky tourist accountant going on holiday?

Along with others, he stood at the side of the galley, waiting patiently for the doors to be opened and to be allowed to get off. The broken scratch panel lay in two pieces on the galley surface in full view.

Sarah called over to me. "Natasha, come here!"

I nudged my way through passengers.

"What is it?"

"I can't handle this." She shoved an envelope of paperwork at me. "You deplane them, would you?" She pushed people aside to get to the galley door. The lift clunked as she descended.

Before opening the passenger door, I checked again that Two-Door Left was disarmed before pulling the door handle down. The heavy panel moved silently inwards and slowly upwards into its recess. People in various uniforms were waiting on the other side: one ramp officer, two policemen and one nurse with a navy cape around her shoulders and a big red cross on her bib. Where were the men in white coats?

An unusually short policeman stepped into the plane, the other bobby and the nurse close behind him.

"Where is 'e, Miss?" the bobby asked in a clipped cockney accent. Except for his lack of height, he was the quintessential policeman portrayed in old British comedies.

I turned and pointed to the tall man standing on the other side of the galley. "There."

"And can you tell me exactly what this gentleman 'as done?" he asked.

"Yes, certainly." All around stewardesses and passengers stood silently watching the scene unfold. They were still holding their breath. "He threatened the captain with hijacking, harassed the passengers and," I pointed to the broken scratch panel, "caused destruction of the aircraft. He also wanted us to take him to Frankfurt."

"Oh, I see," said the bobby, still trying to sound posher than he was.

Followed by the taller policeman and the concerned nurse, the short bobby stepped up to Frankfurter and looked up at him. "Sah," he said as he reached up and poked him in the shoulder, "I understand, Sah, that you 'ave threatened the captain, 'arassed the passengers and caused destruction to this aircraft, so I'm afraid you will need to come wiv us. Sah."

I watched with morbid fascination, together with the surrounding passengers, the man's reaction to his accuser. Frankfurter looked down at the short bobby and laughed as if he was out of *his* tree, as if the bobby had accused him of being Jack the Ripper. "You gotta be kidding!"

I glanced over at Rose. Her expression mirrored mine. Her mouth had fallen open. I felt sick to my stomach. The man was completely oblivious to what he had done.

Then, with a policeman on each side taking him by the arms, and closely followed by the very worried-looking nurse, Frankfurter was dragged off the plane.

"But I gotta get to Frankfurt," he protested as he was forcibly hauled away.

"Yiss, we know that, sah," was the bobby's reply as they crossed into the finger and moved out of sight.

The ramp officer, who was waiting for the flight's paperwork to be handed over, looked at me and frowned as he witnessed the scene as if to ask, what happened? Too tired to supply details, I just handed him the manila envelope and said, "It's a long story." Then I stood back to allow the passengers to disembark.

As the Chilean ambassador was leaving, he nodded curtly but with a twinkle in his eye. In a charming South American accent, he commented, "Very entertaining flight." True, he hadn't received the first-class treatment he had been hoping for, but his trip hadn't been dull.

The next man in line seemed panicked and asked me in an Irish accent, "Where are all de policemen?"

I recognized Mr. Tipperary, his eyes darting nervously around the plane's entrance.

"They're gone," I answered, puzzled. Why was he so worried?

"Oh, tanks be to Jesus, Mary and Joseph. I t'ought dey'd come for me!"

"No." I smiled. "They came for another challenging passenger."

"Oh, I'm terribly sorry." He looked down, abashed. "I really didn't mean to cause a ruckus, not at all, at all."

"It's okay," I assured him. Better a singer than a Frankfurter.

"It's just that I'm terrified of flyin' and well, you know how it tis, de singing helps me get t'rough it."

I bet the scotch helped, too. "Maybe next time you could keep it down a bit, so others can sleep," I suggested as he moved out of the aircraft.

When the plane was finally empty of passengers, I called down to Sarah on the intercom. "They're all off. Safe for you to come up now."

When I caught sight of the broken scratch panel again, it made me wonder about Frankfurter. What had happened to him that caused him to snap like that, to break a window and to try to hijack a plane? Was it a brain tumour, trauma, psychotic break, nervous breakdown, dehydration or lack of oxygen causing brain damage?

And Sarah? Because of her recent trauma there was yet another person broken in two. I wondered if the man who had attacked her, this beautiful young woman, knew how much damage he had done. Would he even have cared if he had known? Not only had he hurt her with his physical assault, but he had also robbed her of confidence, her spirit, her peace of mind and her ability to cope. Her life had been hijacked, and she had landed in a place where she didn't want to be, the land of fear.

As we trudged off to the crew room to debrief, it occurred to me that despite the danger, and thanks in part to the captain and my friend, Brian, 325 passengers plus crew had arrived safely. For Sarah, though, it was still a long way to Tipperary—and home after her battle—but it would be even further for the man who needed to get to Frankfurt.

8

WOOF! WOOF!

March 1980
Chicago

"Have you read the book *Airport* yet?" I asked Sandy, my IFD and traveling companion for the day. She was sitting facing me on the upper level of an Amtrak train, her long legs stretched out. "And I'm not talking about the Arthur Hailey one," I added. Sandy and I had struck up a friendship on the flight over, but with just our job as the common denominator, what else would we talk about except books, boyfriends and the bad behaviours of passengers and flight deck?

The two of us were part of a DC-10 crew on a rare three-day trip to Chicago. While our hotel was in Ann Arbor—over 200 miles away from the windy city—we had decided to take the four-hour journey on an Amtrak train to go sightseeing. The train had left the station and we were now picking up speed so as the flat early spring scenery rushed by with traces of snow in the distance, we chatted.

"The author writes about the dangers of various airports," I continued, "nutty flight deck crew and aviation incidents. All true."

Sandy gave me a sounds-interesting look.

"There's one incident with a stewie," I continued, "just getting on a DC-10 for her flight. She's at the top of the stairs when she feels this searing pain in her right ankle. When she looks down, she sees her captain—in full uniform—grovelling on the stairs and gnawing on her leg. Shocked, she asks, 'What *the hell* do you think you're doing?' He smiles up at her and says, 'I always like to play dog before a flight.'"

"Oh my God!" Sandy exclaimed. "That was one of our captains! Tim Simons? He bit Rose, the IFD."

"Isn't he a training captain?" I asked, a little horrified.

"He's the one," she affirmed and shook her head. "Sounds like our chief stewardess should read that book!" Sandy commented sourly, watching the scenery rush by. "She might learn something."

"Why do you say that?"

"I'm guessing you didn't hear about my dog incident on my LA?"

"No. What happened? "

"It's a long story and . . ." Sandy cast her eyes down and shook her head.

"We've got time," I said, sitting back in my comfy seat, "if you want to tell it?"

"Just promise me one thing, Natasha," she said, not smiling.

I nodded.

"You won't laugh."

"Promise."

Accompanied by the steady rhythm of the train, Sandy began her story.

"The two hundred and ten passengers had boarded the DC-10 at LAX and were settling in for their ten-hour flight to Gatwick. Californians, Brits, Australians, Hasidic Jews, the Hollywood elite, the not-so-elite, Disneyland visitors, families on holidays and businesspeople—the typical eclectic mix of humanity on a Laker flight out of LA. As usual, they stood on both aisles, stuffing luggage into the overhead bins, and since the plane wasn't quite full, they quickly spread themselves and their belongings onto vacant seats throughout the three cabins.

My cabin crew were helping passengers get comfortable when Captain Bryant made his stiff welcome-on-board announcement, then added, 'With a lighter passenger load we will be flying directly to London Gatwick with an estimated arrival time of 9:20 a.m. local . . .'

I was puzzled. The passenger load wasn't *that* light—two thirds full in a 365-seat plane—and if we met with strong headwinds, we might still have to land in Bangor, Maine, to refuel. But he was the captain.

You know how it is. Three hours into the flight, after a light dinner, wine and liqueurs followed by a movie, passengers begin stretching out. Some puffed up the small, skinny pillows on unforgiving armrests to get comfortable and doze. A soft orange sunset light bathed the interior cabin and lulled most of the passengers into sleep. All was well.

When the intercom buzzed, I was sitting on my jump seat adjacent to the forward galley completing my in-flight paperwork. Captain Bryant demanded, as he does, my presence on the flight deck. At the front, a Swedish rugby team were enjoying a private drinking party. As I passed them, one of the blond-haired men gave me a flirtatious grin, but being a good Irish girl, I pretended not to notice.

Once inside the cockpit, I nodded at the engineer on my right then stood behind the captain and the first officer's seats and called over the engine noise, 'You rang?'

Without turning to face me, the captain barked, 'We have to land in Bangor.'

Uh-oh, I thought. Why had he teased them with visions of a direct flight? I knew the punters wouldn't like that.

'Pax can stay on board'" he continued. 'We'll just refuel and take off again.'

'But shouldn't they—?' I protested.

'If we unload, we'll go out of hours and then we'll all be stuck in Bangor. Do you want that?' he snapped. 'Flight attendants must arm their doors and stand guard during refuelling.'

"As you know," Sandy reminded me, "the flight deck crew are limited to a twelve-hour duty, which could be extended under mitigating circumstances—and at the captain's discretion—to fourteen hours. With unusually strong headwinds, landing at Bangor and refuelling, the delay could have indeed put us close to—or over—the limit."

Sandy sighed and peered out of the window at the desolate countryside, upset at the memory but still needing to share it.

'*You* tell the passengers,' Captain Bryant commanded.

'Thanks a lot,' I muttered under my breath. He was such a coward making me the bearer of bad news.

As I returned to the forward galley, I saw that most of the Swedish rugby team were now spread-eagled across seats, snoring as they slept off their alcohol consumption. The flirt, though, was still awake and he grinned, appraising me. This time, I returned his smile.

When I made my PA announcement advising sleepy passengers of the refuelling stop, people roused themselves from their rest positions. The three junior stewardesses, who were huddled in the forward galley enjoying a cup of tea, listened for a collective groan from the cabin—but surprisingly none came. 'I'll give them another ten minutes before I make the landing PA,' I told them.

It was then that I heard a scream.

I frowned and peered around the bulkhead and down the starboard aisle.

'What is it?' Anna, my Number Nine asked, stepping out of the galley and following my gaze.

'Sounded like a passenger yelling,' I told her. As I scrutinized the middle and rear cabins—with people standing and stretching—I could see that a cluster of people were gathered around a center row of seats in the rear.

I had a bad feeling about it. 'Anna,' I said, 'come with me,' and I strode down the aisle with her right behind me.

In the middle row, a group of passengers had vacated their seats and were standing in the starboard aisle staring at something behind them. As I neared the huddled group, I heard a man's raised voice and a growling sound. Oh God, I thought, someone's sneaked a dog on board! Passengers moved aside to let me through. But still blocking my view was a young couple looking down at the seats.

As I arrived at row 26, the young couple suddenly backed away as if there had been an explosion. The woman's expression was one of bewildered horror while the young man—who I presumed to be her husband—was frowning and watching with morbid fascination.

'Excuse me,' I asked the young man. 'What appears to be the problem?' Turning and seeing the bright red of my airline uniform, he stepped back, gently guiding his wife out of my way.

When I glanced down, I saw a fiftyish man in an expensive grey suit. He was thrashing from side to side in his seat, slamming his well-manicured hands on the armrests, muttering something unintelligible. A low deep growl emanated from his throat. The center seats in row 25 were all empty but standing in the opposite aisle was a young, hippie woman staring at the crazy passenger and holding her hands over her heart as if to protect it. She had been seated next to him and probably was the screamer.

'Madam?' I called over to the young woman. 'Why don't you take that seat at the back of the plane for now,' I said, pointing to the last row of seats.

The woman nodded, relieved, snatched up her meagre belongings and moved quickly toward the rear.

'How long has he been like this?' I addressed the young American.

'Since the announcement about refuelling in Bangor,' he drawled. 'We were sitting here having a nice conversation. He told me he's a doctor, going to London for a medical conference, but when he heard that we're going to land in Bangor, he flipped and started to foam at the mouth.' He shrugged. 'Maybe he's Doctor Jekyll.' He attempted a grin, but I could see that he was shaken.

'Why don't you take some seats further up for landing?' I suggested to the couple and the other passengers in the aisle. They didn't hesitate and moved quickly away. Dog-man was now sitting alone in the center row of four seats.

'Sir?' I leaned toward the man. 'Can I help you?' No training had been offered on how to deal with a human-dog, so I wasn't sure what to do with a growling passenger. But the sight of my face, my voice or–like a bullfighter's cape to a bull–my red dress incensed him even further. Eyes bulging with rage and with the veins on his greying temples throbbing, he leaned toward me and snapped at my cheek as if to bite me.

Startled, I pulled back. 'Sir! What are you doing?'

Then as if the plane was on fire, he began to fumble frantically with the clasp on his seatbelt, struggling to get free. Once his belt was undone, he stood up, towering over me, and growled at me again. Uh-oh. He was bigger than I had thought, and I knew he could be a real problem on landing.

'Sir, are you feeling unwell? Can I get you some water?'

Snarling, he backed away from me and stepped into the portside aisle. Then he turned to the passengers on the far side of the plane.

'Woof, woof!' he barked at the surprised people. The sound that came out of his mouth was not even remotely human.

Passengers on the other aisle gaped, pulling back into their seats and clinging to the person next to them.

Behind me, I heard Anna mutter, 'Bloody hell!'"

"Do you think he had rabies?" I interjected.

Sandy shrugged. "Possible. Or he was having a psychotic break."

Before continuing, she changed position in her seat, crossing one long leg over the other.

"Yelling across the central cabin to his back, I persisted, 'Sir, what can we do to help?'

Then he bent over a woman and did something that I couldn't see. A short piercing scream made other passengers turn. The doctor stood up and carried on up the aisle, leaving the woman sobbing and clutching her neck. 'He bit me! she cried. 'He bit me!'

I turned to Anna whose wide eyes were fixed on the doctor as he moved forward. 'Go and tell the captain we have a dangerous passenger. And make *sure* he keeps the flight deck door closed.'

Anna nodded, turned and hurried up the aisle, glancing nervously behind her to see where Dog-man was.

I marched down to the rear galley and saw that the two senior stewardesses had been watching in fascinated shock.

'See to that woman in 26 B quickly,' I instructed, shaking them out of their stupor. 'This man might have given her rabies.' One stewardess moved immediately towards the overhead compartment to locate the First Aid kit. 'Roxanne,' I addressed my number one, 'call the forward galley and tell them to block that man if he tries to get into the flight deck. Then make sure that young hippie in the last row didn't go into apoplectic shock or have a heart attack. Oh, and please do the landing PA for me in about ten minutes. Got it, Roxanne? I might be busy.'

Her response was interrupted by another yelp further up the left aisle. 'Oh god,' I said out loud. 'And people are afraid of flying because they think something will go wrong with the *plane*!'

I hurried up the cabin after the man—still not sure of my strategy except to stop him from entering the flight deck. I halted briefly by the first woman who had been bitten, still clutching her neck. 'A stewardess will attend to you right away,' I told her.

Dog-man was slowly working his way up the left aisle, snapping at shocked passengers. As I trailed behind him, people peered around the back of their seats, some clutching their children close to them as they heard the growling man coming from behind. A tense hush descended progressively up the cabin as if everyone, sensing danger, was holding their breath. Children began crying, afraid of the strange man and feeling the confused fear of the adults.

As I entered the middle cabin a few yards behind him, I realized that I couldn't tackle him. He was at least six foot two and strong. I would need a beefy male—the engineer—to help me restrain him.

Dog-man was in the forward cabin now. I paused in the galley, studying him. The two junior stewardesses, now standing behind me, stared in disbelief at the growling man. Passengers up front and closer to the flight deck were just becoming aware of Dog-man. They peered around their seats, looking back, frowning and wondering who or what was making that noise.

Think! *Think*! I told myself. The interior of an aircraft and other passengers were so vulnerable to a crazy person. What damage might he do?

On either side of the galley and at the front of the forward cabin were a total of four emergency exits. While they were pressurized, Dog-man would not be able to open the doors, but we were about to begin our descent into Bangor. In about ten minutes the plane would reach 10,000 feet and depressurize. Dog-man would be able to open a door by flipping the emergency exit handle and the pneumatically-armed exit would shoot up into its recess. Of course, the emergency chute would instantly and fully inflate with a very loud hiss and a bang. The doctor might even jump out. Passengers had tried to escape before, and despite there being eight exits, and I don't know if you know this, Natasha, passengers always instinctively choose the door through which they had boarded. If the chute inflated *outside* the aircraft, there should be no threat to passengers' safety–but it could hurt them if it got blown back inside.

'Watch the exits!' I instructed the two junior stewardesses. 'And whatever happens, don't let that man touch the door controls.' The two shocked women moved to their respective doors on either side of the galley and stood guard.

With Dog-man on the port side, I slipped through the galley to the opposite aisle. By now, the doctor was half-way up the forward cabin. People were shrinking back from him as he bent over every few rows, barking, snarling and snapping at them.

Why wasn't Anna out of the flight deck yet? I wondered. Maybe the captain was giving her a rough time? Then the plane's engines changed tone. They had begun their descent. The engineer would be busy with the pre-landing process. If Dog-man got into the flight deck now, we could all be doomed.

Attempting the impossible to conceal my red dress, I slunk toward the flight deck, cowering behind passengers in their seats. Behind me, curious people leaned out into the aisle, wondering what the hell I was doing. At 5B, portside, the doctor suddenly leaned over another poor passenger, making this inhuman noise, while I moved ever closer to the flight deck door. In the hushed cabin, he must have sensed my movement, and he spun around. I was almost at the front, but he glared at me, understanding my intention. Our eyes locked. Both of us stood frozen. He challenged me with a low growl, sounding like a real dog. Never taking my eyes off him, I edged ever closer to the front of the plane.

Finally, I reached the flight deck door."

As Sandy told her story, I let out an involuntary, "Oh my God!"

She nodded and carried on. "I stood tall and defiantly planted myself in a protective stance in front of the door. All the front cabin passengers were watching me intently, holding their collective breath. Did they understand the real threat? I wondered.

'*Grrrrrr*,' he snarled again, with his eyes flashing anger at me, not two feet from my face now.

I was nudged from behind as the flight deck door opened slightly.

'Is that you, Sandy?' Anna whispered from inside.

'Yess!' I hissed. 'Come out quickly and make sure they keep the door locked.' I moved aside slightly so that Anna could step out.

With me standing there, Dog-man couldn't get into the flight deck. As you know, the cockpit door is only made of fibreboard, and the lock is flimsy, so if he really wanted to, he could push me out of the way and kick his way in. I decided that no matter what he did, I would not allow him to take all these people down. Not on my watch.

Anna stood beside me, staring from Dog-man back to me, wondering what to do, but the doctor's rage was focused only on me.

'Call down the back and get two of the junior girls up here,' I whispered, still not taking my eyes from him. 'And tell the number one to do the landing PA *now*.'

'But will you be. . .?' Anna was afraid for my safety, but she was even more afraid to look at Dog-man.

'Just go,' I hissed, sensing that the man was about to pounce.

Anna marched quickly down the starboard side to the galley and from the intercom at Two Door Left, communicated my instructions to the rear. In the front row the flirtatious rugby player was staring at the doctor and me in a stand-off, puzzled.

Then Thank God, the number one's cheery voice over the PA broke through the frozen silence. As soon as she said, 'Ladies and gentlemen, we have now commenced our descent into Bangor. Would you please return to your seats etc.' Dog-man looked away from me and up toward the ceiling and the sound of the voice filling the cabin. Roxanne's gentle tone seemed to break his spell. I watched fascinated as the crazed Dog-man relaxed and reverted to the respectable doctor. He was now glancing around, dazed, as though wondering how he had arrived at the front of the plane. I could see my crew watching from the exit doors with mystified expressions though ready to pounce on him if need be. Anna came back up the aisle and approached him tentatively from behind.

'Sir,' she said tenderly, 'would you like to return to your seat now? We have begun our descent.'

'Yes, yes, of course,' he responded graciously and then hesitated as if he couldn't remember where his seat was.

'You can sit here if you like.' Anna indicated a vacant aisle seat in the last center row of the front cabin. The man nodded and moved gingerly into 9C, fastening his belt. He didn't have a clue that the other passengers were nervously eyeing him."

"My God!" I said, exhaling and sitting back in my seat, thinking that Sandy's story was over. But it wasn't.

"The flight deck," she continued, "was busy with the descent so I couldn't update them until we were on the ground. They would have to off-load the doctor in Bangor, of course, as he was a threat to crew and passengers. There would be paperwork to complete, and a delay, which might make the flight deck go out of hours but keeping him on board for our six-hour flight to Gatwick was too much of a danger—for everyone.

So once the tires hit the ground and the plane slowed, I made my landing PA. I informed passengers that the aircraft would be on the ground for about 45 minutes to refuel. While they would remain on board, there was to be absolutely no smoking and flight attendants would be guarding the armed exits. While I was imparting these words, I watched the doctor from behind his seat. He had slumped over slightly, as though exhausted, but he didn't appear to have regressed to his dog persona."

"I hung the intercom back in its cradle and walked up to the flight deck. 'It's me,' I called, knocking gently on the door. The engineer tentatively opened the door. I stepped in.

While the aircraft continued taxiing, I waited for the captain and first officer to finish their landing checks. Finally, when they had slowed, and with the first officer at the controls, the captain removed his headset and turned to look at me.

'What is it?' he asked.

'We have a big problem,' I began. 'One of the passengers, a doctor, had an . . . episode. When he found out we were stopping at Bangor, he started barking and biting passengers.'

'So I hear,' the captain responded drily. Both the engineer and first officer glanced up at me with suppressed grins.

'And what are you suggesting?' Captain Bryant demanded.

I was gobsmacked. The captain was supposed to make that decision. To me, there was only one thing to do. 'Well, we have to unload him . . . obviously,' I retorted. 'He's already bitten at least one woman. He is a risk to passengers and the safety of the aircraft. He might even have rabies.'

'Is that so?' He stared right back at me.

Bloody hell! I thought. Not two nutcases on one flight.

'Do you realize,' he demanded, 'how long it would take to complete the paperwork and make arrangements for him to be escorted back to wherever he's from?' He glared at me, exasperated.

'Well, yes, but . . .' I noticed that the first officer and engineer both had their heads down, appearing to be busy and determined not to laugh. This isn't funny, I thought.

'Where is he now?' Captain Bryant asked.

'He's calmed down and is sitting in 9C.'

'Good. Then we'll just carry on,' he said and turned his back on me.

I stood there for a moment, stunned. I was on my own with this maniac, and I wasn't only thinking of the doctor.

'Well, *you'd* better keep the flight door shut,' I told the captain's back. 'I won't be held responsible if he gets in and takes us all down.'

Resigned to a potential nightmare on the next sector, I turned to leave. As I grasped the handle, the door was snatched from me and flung wide. The doctor's hand reached in and grabbed me by the wrist, yanked me out of the flight deck, slamming the door behind me. With white spittle on his lips, his face was in mine, snarling. I felt a thump on my head and hands curling tightly around my throat as he pushed my head up against the flight deck door.

'*Grrrrrrrrrr*,' he snarled though gritted teeth.

With one hand, I tried to pry his fingers from my throat. With the other, I grappled for the door handle and pulled with all my might. It opened just a little.

'H-e-l-p, help me!' I tried to scream, but I could barely muster a desperate whisper. With my right foot, I banged my heel against the door.

To my horror, somebody inside the flight deck snatched the handle from the other side and pulled the door closed. 'You take care of it, Sandy,' I heard the engineer shout through the flimsy fibreboard.

So, guess what? The engineer wasn't going to help me! Now I can understand how in the air it's dangerous to be vulnerable to nutbars, but on the ground!"

"Bloody flight deck!" I muttered, horrified for poor Sandy.

She shook her head.

"Beyond the snarling man, I could see rows of passengers just staring in shock. Still holding me by the throat, the doctor banged my head against the door again and growled. I could see the foamy saliva on his lips. I couldn't breathe. Everything was going dark.

Then from somewhere far away, I heard a commotion. Men's voices in another language shouting. Suddenly the pressure was gone from my throat. I sank to the floor, coughing and gasping for breath.

Anna was by my side. 'Sandy, Sandy. Ohmigod. Are you okay? Breathe slowly.'

Then another voice. A man speaking in a lilting foreign accent. 'Let's get her to a seat.'

I allowed myself to be helped up and guided to the empty front row. I sank down gratefully, clutching my throat. Anna offered me a glass of water. Once I took a sip, though it hurt to swallow, I began to feel better. The blood was beginning to flow to my head again.

'Where is he?' I rasped nervously, looking around for the doctor.

Anna pointed behind me and smiled. 'Look.'

When I peered between the seats, I saw that the armrests had been raised, and the doctor was prostrated across the center row. Mr. Flirt and another two members of the Swedish rugby team had him in their vice-like grips, one sitting on his legs, and the others were, despite his thrashing and snarling, restraining him. They laughed, enjoying their role as heroes, and repeating, "*Ja, ja, sta stil.*" Stay still.

'Those men can't fly back to Gatwick like that,' I whispered, 'sitting on that madman.' It hurt to talk. Still feeling a little faint, I addressed my Swedish saviours. 'Thank you!'

Mr. Flirt looked at me, concern on his face. 'Are you okay?' he asked in his charming, lilted accent as Dog-man continued to squirm beneath him.

I just nodded, still shaking. No thanks to that dammed misogynist captain who refuses to offload him, I thought. Be it on his own head! I am going to crucify him and the engineer in my flight report.

'Get off me!' the doctor protested. 'What the hell do you think you're doing? Let me go!' He sounded sane again as if he had absolutely no idea why he was being subjected to this humiliation.

'Maybe we should sit him up in the seat with his belt on?' I suggested to the Swedes. 'Would you mind sitting beside him for the flight to London?' Acting us unpaid bodyguards was not their job, or even legal, but I had no choice.

'Don't you haff any hantcuffs so vee can tie him to zer armrest,' the flirt suggested.

'No, we don't,' I said, 'but that's a good idea.'

'Zen vee will haff to stay wis him.' With their muscular physiques I knew that they would be able to manage the doctor. 'Zis will be our pleasure,' he added, pulling the doctor up by his suit lapels into an upright position and placing him in a center seat. As one of the other men did up his seat belt, a third one removed the doctor's tie and secured his left arm to the armrest.

Dog-man was still confused but more compliant. 'Why are you doing this . . . ?' he whimpered. 'I'm a doctor. I'm going to London.'

'*Ja, Ja.*' I heard the flirt affirm as I went to retrieve my flight report. 'You are definitely goink to London. And *you* need to see a doctor.'

As I sipped on a hot tea in the forward galley, my shaking subsided. 'Anna,' I said, 'please go and tell our so-called captain that we will need an ambulance, the police and a straitjacket to meet the aircraft at Gatwick.' I was tempted to request two additional straightjackets—one for the captain and one for the engineer. 'I've got a very long flight report to write.'"

Sandy took a deep breath. Remembering the horror of it, she appeared to be unnerved by the trauma all over again.

"How awful!" I muttered. "You were so brave, Sandy! But you're right. I always think we should be more afraid of nutty passengers than mechanical failures."

"There's more," Sandy added. "After Jessica Parsons got my lengthy flight report, she called me up to the office. As you know, I'm the head of our new Flight Association, so I was *very* happy to state my case to our Chief Stewardess."

I nodded. The newly formed association was hardly a union—which Freddie would not allow–but at least we now had a collective voice.

"I *begged* Jessica to either install bodyguards on flights or provide us with plastic handcuffs."

"What was her response?"

"She refused and accused *me* of overreacting."

"But violence on board is getting worse!" I persisted. "I just did a Miami when a big male passenger had a meltdown, broke a window and threatened to hijack the plane. Plastic handcuffs would have saved us and our passengers a lot of fear-filled hours, terrified of what he might do."

"Yes, I heard about that one, too." Sandy gazed out of the train window at the more built-up areas passing by us now. "Ach," she retorted, "Jessica hasn't flown for years, and she flew when flying was more civil. She has no idea how much more aggressive passengers have become. That's why she needs to read that book. What did you say it was called? Airport."

I nodded. "So how did she leave it with you?"

"The usual platitudes." Sandy scoffed. "She insisted that the incident was just a one-off but that she would look into it."

"Right. And one day I'll be captain on the Concorde."

"Before I left her office, I warned our intrepid leader. 'I really hope you take action because the next time someone goes nuts on a plane—and there will be a next time—and injures a stewardess, passengers, or worse, brings the plane down, it won't be me who could have changed the outcome.'"

"Good for you!" I told Sandy. If she could survive Dog-Man, she could stand up to senior management, not that it made any difference. When I had been with Dan Air, I had also complained about our unrealistic conditions to the executive director, to no avail. "But nothing's changed, has it?"

Sandy shook her head. "No, nothing's changed."

Seeing her still unsettled by the incident made me wonder. As well as the assault by Dog-Man, was it the uncaring flight deck or the dismissive chief stewardess who had done the most damage by not validating her trauma, and her courage.

"Well, if the flight deck and management don't have your back," I said, "maybe we should request a Swedish rugby team on every flight?"

And finally, and just before we arrived in Chicago, Sandy smiled.

9

LOVE YOU TO DEATH

The West Country, England
August 1980

"Aye up, chuck." The front door of my maisonette had swung open, letting in a blast of hot August air as my room mate Samantha entered, wearing her British Airtours uniform and dragging her suitcase behind her. She was, I remembered, just returning from her Mauritius flight.

"'Ave you 'eard what 'appened to Emma?" she asked as she dumped her luggage in the hallway.

What now? I thought. "No . . . what?"

"Belly landing," Samantha said. "This mornin'."

"No-o-o! Is everyone okay?"

"Oh, aye," Samantha continued, removing hat, scarf and gloves and setting her feet free from her high-heeled shoes with an audibly relieved exhale. "You better get the details from 'er cos I'm buggered. I'm going to me bed."

I watched as she climbed the stairs, opened her bedroom door, closed it behind her and, as we all did after a long-haul flight, probably shed her clothes, collapsed into bed and descended into a comatose sleep.

Emma must be home by now, I thought, as I dialled her number. "I just heard!" I said over the phone. "Are you okay?"

She sighed as if she was tired of the question already. "Oh, ye-e-e-es. I'm fine."

"What happened?"

She chuckled. "Well, let me tell you, they only had one green so that undercarriage definitely *wasn't* coming down."

On the flight deck, three illuminated green lights would indicate that the undercarriage was down and locked for landing. As ex-Dan Air crew, Emma and I had experienced our fair share of potential belly-landing scares with just "two greens," but on those occasions, it was probably because the microswitch itself had been faulty. At the last moment, the wheels had, more often than not, come down and locked without any problems. But just one "green" meant there was a real doubt.

"Where did you land?" I knew that Gatwick wasn't equipped for belly landings.

"Stanstead."

"What was it like?"

"Well, you know how we train and train for things like this, but when it's actually happening, you think, 'Oh shit, this is the real deal.' But then you *do* find yourself going into drill mode. We had to circle for ages while they foamed the runway at Stanstead and that was a tad nerve-wracking." She paused and took a breath.

A picture of a 727 sliding along a foam-covered runway popped into my head.

"Were you scared?"

"We were too busy to be scared. The passengers were good, though. Calm. The worst thing was when we hit the runway and slid along it. All we could see outside the windows were the flames licking at the plane. Of course, I thought we were on fire, but it was just the friction of the metal hitting the runway."

Just friction! She sounded so blasé.

"But the noise was the worst," she continued. "We all went into brace position, but when we finally skidded to a stop, we opened the doors and just stepped out. No chutes required. The plane wasn't on fire or anything. We all stood around, stunned, not knowing what to do while the firemen were rushing around checking everything. It was kind of funny."

Funny? Had muted hysteria set in?

"Well, once again, Emma, I'm happy you're alive. Has it put you off flying?"

"Hell, no!" she scoffed. "I've got an 08.00 Munich tomorrow."

"What's this new airline like?" Since she had joined British Midlands, I realized that we hadn't spoken much. As I was now doing long haul, she was either withdrawing from me or I from her. We didn't quite share the same closeness as before.

"It's okay." She sounded tired. "Kind of like Dan Dare, though maybe not quite as bad."

"Nothing's as bad as Dan Air," I quipped. "But that's good. At least you're working." Part of me felt guilty that I was loving my trips to New York, LA, Miami, Barbados and weeks in Berlin. "Gives you time to look around for something else."

"Yes," she responded absently.

There was a pause. Should I mention the dream where I had suggested that her choices were closing in on her? Something told me not to.

"Let's get together soon," she said. "I'd love to see you."

"Okay. Let's go for a drink." I offered. "Shall I invite the gang?"

"Oh, why not?" Her voice brightened suddenly, sounding like the old Emma. "I'm flying up to Aberdeen to see Stewart next week so . . . after that."

"That will be good, seeing Stewart."

"We'll see."

Late August was unusually warm that year, especially for England. As I had promised Emma, six of us, all from the flying fraternity, had gathered at The Lamb, opting to sit outside at one of the picnic tables where we could all fit. Stewart, I noticed, was just coming along the path chatting with Samantha. He cast a concerned glance in our direction, his body language oozing awkwardness when he saw Emma. Philip offered to go inside and get the drinks, so I plonked myself down on the wooden bench next to her.

"How are you?" I asked.

"It's over!" she blurted, her head down.

"What do you mean?"

"With Stewart. When I flew up to Aberdeen last week, I had it out with him. I told him to piss or get off the pot."

"And?"

She sighed, her head sinking even lower, her fine auburn hair hiding her face. "It's no use. He said he *loved* me, but he wasn't *in love* with me." Her shoulders sagged. A long, slow breath came out of her as if someone had stabbed her with a pin and she was deflating.

I didn't know what to say. We had all known this, but Emma, God bless her, had continued to hold out hope.

She looked up at me, her very blue eyes shiny and desperate. "And I think the airline is going to lay me off, too, Natasha."

"Do you really think so? . . . Well, there'll be another–"

"Oh, I can't *stand* it," she snapped, tears gathering at the corners of her eyes. After a pause and softening she added, "I just can't bear to go through another training with yet another airline."

"I know," was all I could muster in commiseration. The process *was* exhausting. Though airlines came and went, and the jobs with them, the nature of the business demanded that we, like pretzels, adapt to ever-more demanding and varying expectations. But

Emma's own rebellion at authority had been the cause of at least two of her lost job opportunities.

"There you go, ladies." Philip put glasses of white wine down in front of us. He began to put a leg over the bench on the other side of the table, but I silently signalled to him with a please-give-us-a-private-moment glare. Tactfully he got up and joined the others behind us.

"What are you going to do?" I asked, peering behind to see where Stewart was standing. Although he was at a safe distance at the far end of the table, clutching a pint and chatting with Samantha through his pipe, he was throwing surreptitious and concerned glances at Emma.

"Oh, I dunno." She followed my stare. Seeing Stewart made her shoulders sag even more. She turned back to the table. "I'm going to get away. There's a place down in Dorset where I've booked myself in for a while."

"Good idea," I said, feeling helpless to console her. "If I can get time off, do you want me to come with you?"

"Nah." Emma shrugged. "Thanks, but I want to be alone. And anyway, I don't know how long I'm going to be away."

The sun-golden leaves of the trees around us rustled in a gentle breeze. Despite the warmth, I shivered. All my dear friends were gathered here. I should have been happy, but I wasn't. Somehow Emma was slipping away, and there was nothing I could do to reach her.

"Well," I persisted. "I was thinking of visiting Carol in Somerset. I can follow you part of the way, and then I'll go my way and you can go yours."

"Okay," Emma answered dully. "If that makes you feel better."

Not really, I thought, but it was better than feeling powerless.

The following Sunday, September 9, 1979, was one of those gorgeous sunny fall days where the sky is blue, the temperature warm enough and the leaves a rich mixture of copper, burgundy and green. Emma had agreed to drive to my place in Horsham and then we would leave in convoy on a pre-agreed route. Driving the narrow country lanes down to the west country would be a lovely road trip.

I was just putting my overnight bag in the boot of my car when Emma's MGBT swerved into my driveway and stopped precariously close to my kneecaps. The roof of her car was down and something in her expression told me that she didn't really want me to follow. But dammit, I wasn't going to give up that easily.

"Hey, Emma," I said, "do you think you could drive like a normal person today so I can keep you in sight?"

"Oh, *you* won't be able to keep up with *me*. Why don't we agree to meet somewhere for lunch instead?"

"Okay," I said but decided I would do my damnedest—without killing myself—to stay on Emma's tail. "There's a pub called The Bell Inn on the A303 just past Stonehenge. They do a great ham and cheese toasted sarnie. Want to meet there?"

She shrugged. "Okay." And before I could even wave, she had reversed and roared out of my driveway. I jumped into my car and attempted to follow, but she was already far ahead. Occasionally, at traffic lights and roundabouts or when Emma got stuck behind farm tractors, I would catch up with her. The back of her auburn head looked somehow vulnerable in the driver's seat. And when she accelerated again—as if trying to get away from me—her fine hair would lift in the wind in singular strands as if invisible hands were playing with it. As usual, she was taking risks, overtaking on double yellow lines and over hills where she couldn't have possibly seen the oncoming traffic. One of these days . . . I didn't finish the thought.

"What took you so long?" Emma was half-sitting, half leaning on the side of her car when I pulled up alongside her in front of the pub.

"Before I overtake, I prefer to see if something's coming the other way," I replied. "Call me weird, but I like to stay alive."

"Why?" she asked.

I laughed, thinking she was joking, but she was staring straight at me, her eyes boring into my soul.

"Shall we go in?" I gestured toward the black and white pub.

"Nah." She shook her head and her tousled hair half-covered her face. "I'm not hungry, and I want to keep going. You go in if you like, though."

"I'm not eating in a pub by myself, Emma!" I said, despite the pangs of hunger gnawing at my stomach. "I'll get something later."

"Your turnoff is about fourteen miles down the road," she said, pointing. "I remember there's a little café on that corner."

"This is where we part company then." I smiled at my friend. "Make sure you get some rest while you're away."

"Oh, I plan to." She climbed back into her car and revved up. "Thanks for everything, Natasha," she called over her shoulder as she reversed out of the car park.

"Try to have fun where you're going!" I shouted out of my car's open window, but the words were swallowed up in the roar of her black MGBT as she disappeared down the narrow country lane.

I so loved this part of the countryside especially where the roads became even narrower, more winding and prettier. In some spots the lanes barely had room for two vehicles to pass each other, so whenever I had to squidge over to the left to let an oncoming car pass, the hedgerow greenery tapped on my windows as if wanting to get inside.

Even the roundabouts were smaller here. At the second one I saw Emma just three cars in front. Strange how she's always racing, I thought, but her speed never really gets her that much farther ahead.

Well, I'm going to drive at my own pace and enjoy the scenery, I decided. I turned up my radio and listened to Michael Aspel's smooth voice on Radio 1.

On the next stretch of road, triangular orange signs posted on each bend warned MEN WORKING and SLOW DOWN, so I decelerated to 50 mph then 40. Emma was ahead and I noticed that, although she had slowed down, she was still driving above the speed limit. The roads were very curvy now and ever narrower. Suddenly a warning sign for a temporary traffic light appeared, around the next corner. I tapped on my brakes.

Around the next bend, and in front of a short line of cars, I saw a red and green temporary traffic light standing on a tripod blocking my side of the road. Beyond that, construction paraphernalia littered the left lane. Three cars in front, Emma was at the head of the line, still moving too fast. A worker in a bright yellow jacket and clutching a black walkie talkie was waving, signalling for her to slow down. As she reached the tripod, the green light switched to red. Instead of screeching to a halt, she quickly swerved onto the right side of the road and accelerated up the hill.

"Oy! You!" The construction worker yelled after her. "*Sto-o-op!*"

He was too late. Emma was halfway up the hill and a moment later, she disappeared around the next bend.

Oh no! What if another vehicle was on its way down?

Emma couldn't know how far the one-lane restriction was in effect. What was she thinking?

I got out of my car, and stood watching, waiting, holding my breath.

Then I heard it. The worst sound. Later it would be the volume and the violence of the noise that played over and over in my head. Metal on metal, screeching, groaning, tangling metal. It seemed to go on forever, So loud for so long, an eternity.

"Oh, *fu-u-u-ck*!" The construction worker exclaimed, then flattening his walkie talkie to his ear, he began to run up the right side of the road. The people in the two cars ahead of me stepped out of their vehicles but didn't move. They just stood looking up the road, knowing something awful was lying beyond the brow of the hill, something they could imagine but couldn't and didn't want to see.

I sagged down into my driver's seat, clutching my steering wheel for support. A trembling had begun somewhere in my body, and I realized I was now shaking all over.

Emma! Emma! Emma!

Then somewhere in the distance I heard sirens. Other construction workers appeared out of nowhere and were also running up the hill.

Another worker, his face ashen, approached the couple who had stepped out of the car in front of me. I heard him address the man, "It's bad. You better turn around and find another way. It's going to take a while."

"I saw her skip the light but . . . what happened?" The young man wanted to know. "Is she . . . ?"

The construction worker rubbed the front of his neck. He looked as if he was going to throw up. "There . . . was a milk truck coming down the other way," he said, shaken. "The sports car . . . went right underneath it. She's definitely . . . They say it's going to take a while to get her out. Best if you all turn around and go back another way."

I put my face in my hands and sobbed. Emma had warned me so many times she would do this. Her words echoed in my head, "Oh, I'll just drive into a tree and make it look like an accident." My God, she'd done it! But it had been a milk truck. The poor truck driver!

Pieces of the dream she had told me about—*narrowing roads, everything going black*—came to my mind. The dream had been a warning, of course. The 11-11 numbers.

Oh Emma!

My whole body was vibrating now. I couldn't think. What should I do?

The construction worker approached my window. My feet felt cemented to the floor of my car.

I put out a hand to stop his words. "Please . . . don't tell me!" I muttered. "I heard," not wanting to hear any more gruesome details. "She's . . . she was my friend. I was . . . following her . . ."

"Gawd love a duck!" He leaned on my car for support, lost for words. His already stricken face sagged in sympathy. "Then you don't want to see this, love. Better turn around."

"Was it . . . instant?"

The man still looked as if he was about to throw up. "Oh, yes."

"I-I don't know what to do. I-I can't drive." My hands were still glued to my steering wheel, and my body was vibrating in shock. Panic was threatening to take over. "What should I do?" I pleaded with the man. "Who should I tell? How can I get home?"

"Tell you what . . ." He put a beefy, tanned hand on my door frame. "When I've told these good people behind yer, and blocked off the road, I'll drive you back up to Woodmanscote, to the pub. Is there someone you can call from there? You're right. You shouldn't be driving, love. Helluva shock! Helluva shock!"

I nodded, grateful for his kindness.

Three hours later, after two stiff drinks in the Six Bells, sitting all by myself, I looked up to see Samantha and Philip who had come to take me and my car home. Samantha and I were back in Horsham before we spoke.

"At least she died instantly," she mumbled, her voice breaking.

"It was suicide," I whispered. "Emma wanted to die. Her death was not an "if" but a "when."

And as Samantha waited for a traffic light to turn from red to green, she said, "And today was the day."

10

BARBADOS, MON

September 1980

My Barbados flight was departing at 11:00 the following morning, just a week after Emmas "accident."

That Sunday, even as I threw various bikinis into a suitcase for my long trip, I was still torn about whether I should stay in ye rainy olde Englande and attend the funeral of my friend or go on what was essentially a week's paid holiday. No doubt there were plenty of Laker girls who would have leapt at the chance to take my place, but to go or to stay wasn't my only conflict. While part of me was angry with Emma's decision to risk—or end—her life, a big part of me was happy for her and for the peace I hoped she'd found. Mostly, I felt sad and bereft. Over the years, I had rescued her many times, but I couldn't help her anymore. Maybe I should just take care of myself now.

Still unsure, I silently asked Emma if she minded if I didn't go to her service. Words in her inimitable cheeky tone popped into my head and I heard, "Oh, hell, Natasha. Just go! Where I am, it doesn't matter."

As I finally snapped my bulging Samsonite shut, I thought, I will probably be miserable wherever I am.

In 1978 after Laker Airways had bought 51% of Caribbean Airways, our schedules to Barbados provided either a whole week to enjoy the idyllic island paradise or a laborious three-day duty with a "min-rest" return. Feeling a tad embarrassed about being rostered for yet another of these prized seven-day trips, Jonathan in Crewing had explained, "With all your languages, Natasha, you are the most qualified to do that route." I also rationalized that the luxurious on-duty week-long sun-tanning was my reward for the more frequent exhausting three-day Barbados there-and-backs. By the time we arrived at the hotel on those min-rest flights, showered and changed, there were only a few hours to enjoy a cocktail, eat dinner and then fall into bed. In the morning we would rush to don a bikini and get a few rays before getting back on the aircraft to do the same 16-hour long, long haul all over again.

While Jonathan's comment—though tinged with respect—made me feel a little less guilty about the plum trips bestowed on me, it did little to assuage the jealousy of the other girls who often saw me sporting the tell-tale dark Caribbean tan. "You're going to Barbados *again*?" they would complain, giving me suspicious looks as if to ask, "And who are *you* sleeping with in crewing?"

At first, I shrugged off the implications, but then I would simply state, "If you learned to speak four languages, you too could be rostered for these trips."

For a mid-September day in England, the next morning was surprisingly sunny. The trees lining the country lanes on my back route to the airport and the M3 motorway were still adorned in varying shades of golds, rusts and greens. While the bends on the Pease Pottage Road en route were now so familiar to me that I almost drove on autopilot, I tried not to think about the country roads where Emma had met her final destiny. I pushed the trauma out of my mind and instead, focussed on my imminent trip. Would there be any major incidents on this flight or would it, please God, be routine? On this route to Barbados—stopping in Luxembourg to collect

European passengers and then sometimes dropping into the Azores for refuelling—anything could happen.

Now as I neared the M3 motorway, I thought about how hosties were often accused of being biased or even racist if we complained about doing a flight with people of a particular culture. But the fact is when 365 people all of one nationality are confined in a slim metal container, each one stuck in a narrow seat for hours, some of them white-knucklers and all of them with their brain cells deprived of a full quota of oxygen, then yes, certain traits common to that nationality—good and bad—did emerge. Even though sometimes English passengers could be very rude, some of the girls would complain about certain nationalities and allow the obnoxious passengers among them to ruin their day. Often, because I understood the passengers' language—and had a deeper insight into their culture—I would explain that they were not being rude. Their language, when translated into English but spoken in the intonation they used to speak to each other, just *sounded* rude to us ever-so-polite British.

Working as part of a team, I had long ago decided—no matter what was going on in my life at the time—that I would not allow a grumpy, fearful or miserable passenger or crew member to contaminate my mood. On this day I also made a promise to myself not to inflict *my* misery on the crew or the passengers by mentioning Emma's death. Fake it till you make it was my motto. Or smile until you have cause to smile. "I will have fun on this flight, I will have fun on this flight," I intoned as I saw the M3 ramp ahead of me.

"Aw, naw-w-w," Anna-Jo, a tall, solid Bajan girl, moaned as she saw the captain and first officer getting on the plane. "Captain Wilson and Jo Smith are on de flight deck. Dat's gawin' to be terrible."

"Und vhy is zat?" Ingrid, one of the German girls on our crew, enquired as we sat in the middle cabin waiting for the IFD to check us on our emergency drills.

"Cos dey hate each other, dat's why!" Anna-Jo drawled in her lilting Bajan as she lolled in a window seat.

The conflict between the grumpy old captain and the only Bajan first officer employed by the company was famous. Crews often reported the chilly atmosphere in the flight deck and how the two men only exchanged words when necessary to fly the plane. Or so we hoped.

Looking around at the other girls, I was dismayed to see that I was the only English girl among the ten members of the cabin crew. Not that I didn't enjoy working with other nationalities, but on these flights, sandwiched between Bajans and Germans, I was often caught in the role of peacemaker. While the Germans were super-efficient and leapt into action immediately after take-off, the Bajan girls preferred to take their time. Perhaps this week away was not going to be the cheery diversion I had hoped for.

The popular and infamous IFD, Mary-Beth Clarke, suddenly appeared from behind the bulkhead. Although she was Bajan, she had unusually high cheek bones and an enviably lithe dancer's figure. She probably stemmed from a mixed gene pool, I thought, as she didn't share the stockier Caribbean physicality of Anna-Jo, Wendy-May and the other islanders.

Ingrid, sitting by my side, peered down her Teutonic nose at me, her shrewd eyes assessing me not too kindly. "Iss zis your first flight to Barbados?"

Looking up at Ingrid, it was difficult not to feel intimidated. "Well, actually. . ." I was just about to inform her that Barbados was one of my regular routes, then decided against it. "*Nein, nicht meine erste Besuch.*" No, not my first visit, I told her.

"Ach, you speak German, yes?"

"*Ja.*" With my jacket covering my dress, she couldn't see my German, Italian, French and Norwegian language badges.

"*Ach, dass ist gut!*"

I hoped so. My ability to speak German seemed to endear me to her. She softened and her eyes twinkled.

One hour later, with the aircraft checked, catered and finishing touches completed, a mixture of English and German passengers, and a few Bajans who were "gawin hawm," filed on board. Cabin crew assisted families and older people to squeeze their baggage into any available nook or cranny. I watched fascinated as Mary Beth took a heavy bag from one tall man struggling to lift it over his head and—as if it was just a bag of fluffy cotton wool—she picked it up and tossed it into the overhead bin. With everyone now on board, she went to Two Door Left, the main passenger door and swung the handle around, closing it.

As the majority of passengers were German, Mary-Beth instructed Ingrid to give the PA announcements in her language first before she followed up in English—or at least, that's what she called her strong Bajan dialect.

Let the games begin, I thought.

"*Guten Tag, meiner Damen und Herren,*" Ingrid began in her monotone, rapid-fire Frankfurter accent. German passengers sat up in their seats listening diligently. "*Im Namen von Kapitain Vilson und seine Besatzung, hoffen wir Sie wilkommen . . .* "

When Ingrid was finished, she moved away from the console and hung up the microphone. Mary-Beth, who had been halfway down the middle cabin, suddenly stopped and, realizing it was her turn to do the English PA, spun around and sauntered lazily in her loose-limbed Bajan way back up to the console. She picked up the microphone.

"Ladies and Gentlemen," she began, her sing-songy Caribbean accent filling all three cabins, "on behalf of Captain . . ." She frowned, turned towards the forward galley where three of the crew were gathered. Without taking the microphone away from her mouth, she called to them, "Aw, fock, what's his naime agin?"

A collective gasp spread throughout the cabin. All passengers and crew, German and English, suddenly sat up and paid attention.

"Vilson!" Ingrid hissed back at Mary-Beth from the forward galley. "Captain Vilson!"

"Ah yes!" Mary-Beth laughed at herself and slapped her thigh. "Dat's right. So, ladies and gentlemen, on behalf of Captain Wilson and Caribbean Airways, we welcome you on board dis DC-10 on your flight to Barbados."

At least she remembered our destination, I thought!

After take-off, with thoughts of being en route to paradise dancing in their heads, our passengers soon forgot Mary-Beth's transgression. The atmosphere in the forward cabin lightened and the lively murmur of voices rose as the holiday mood took over.

In my position as Number Seven, I worked at the rear of the plane with more of the Bajan girls. At the front of the aircraft, immediately after take-off, the German contingent had begun serving glasses of complimentary rum punch to passengers in Cabin A, while my colleague, Anna-Jo, was still lounging on the rear jump seat.

"Uh . . . maybe we should get going," I tentatively proposed to Anna-Jo. "The girls are nearly done in Cabin A."

"Oh, dawn't bother yer head, darlin'." She waved a floppy arm at me. "We gat lats and lats o' taime."

This isn't going to go down well with the Germans, I thought, when they end up serving two out of the three cabins while we are lollygagging down at the back.

"I don't mind getting started," I chirped, grabbing the massive container of sticky brown liquid and beginning to pour rum punch into plastic cups. Anything to prevent World War Three.

Finally, the reluctant Anna-Jo pulled herself up off the jump seat and helped place a maraschino cherry and orange slice garnish onto each plastic cup.

In the rear cabin passengers' faces lit up at the sight of a rum punch, a precursor to their Caribbean holiday. "*Vielen Dank,*" and "Oh, how lovely!" people cooed, carefully taking the plastic glasses from the tray.

On my return to the rear galley to collect yet another tray of drinks, I saw that Ingrid had come down from the front. I suspected she was excited about something, but it was hard to tell as her eyes were sparkling but her face remained impassive.

"Ja, I ssink it iss him!" she announced.

"Who's dat, darlin'?" Anna-Jo asked.

"Mel Smith! He iss on TV. *Not the Nine O'Clock News.*"

This comedy, spoofing British newscasters and current affairs, was the most popular comedy on English television at the time.

"Where is he?" I asked, familiar with the sullen-looking but oh-so-dry-witted Mel Smith.

"Last row in A. Center," Ingrid informed me.

"You better give him good service, or we'll be the joke of his next program," I warned.

After I had finished serving the rum punches and while we were waiting for the meal carts to arrive, I thought I would take a little stroll up to Cabin A. Pretending to be gathering up refuse, I glanced from side to side. But when I arrived in A and surreptitiously glanced over at our celebrity, I didn't see Mel Smith.

"Bill?" I asked, stunned. "Is that you?" Even though I hadn't seen him in ten years, the tall man sitting in one of the centre aisle seats was unmistakable. At six foot, five inches tall, with fine blond hair hanging down in strands, laughing blue eyes and a large nose, Bill was unforgettable.

"Natasha!" he beamed. "What's a nice girl like you doing in a place like this?"

"Oh, you have no-o-o idea!" I joked, hand-on-hip and rolling my eyes.

We both laughed.

"What a coincidence!" I exclaimed. "I'm sure I saw you in a Cadbury's commercial on TV recently. Was that you?"

"Oh, yes." He waved a dismissive hand, his eyes twinkling.

Just then I noticed that Mel Smith was sitting on the other side of Bill and staring at me with bored eyes communicating his displeasure. His fine blond hair hung down even longer than Bill's. His sullen face and stocky physique always reminded me of an unhappy bulldog, and right now the bulldog's body language oozed discomfort as if he was hating every minute of his current situation.

"What are you going to do in Barbados?" I asked Bill, pretending not to notice Mel, and immediately berating myself for asking a stupid question. What did anyone do in Barbados except suntan, swim and drink cocktails!

"Mel and I," Bill indicated the sour-looking man next to him, "are going down there for a week to write."

"Nice work if you can get it," I said, mimicking Bruce Forsyth, another English comedian, and smiling at Mel who merely responded with a tired flicker of his eyelids.

The banging of meal carts coming up from below reminded me that I should get back to work. "I have to go. I'm working at the rear."

"Let's get together," Bill said enthusiastically. "Where are you staying?"

"Paradise Beach Hotel," I told him.

He was writing something quickly on a cocktail napkin and handed it to me. "That's our number. Around midweek." He grinned. "We'll talk about old times."

"Great. I'll ring you, or you ring me," I said, tucking the napkin into my pinny pocket.

Throughout this whole interchange, Mel Smith's facial muscles had not even twitched. Maybe he was trying to stay in his drole TV character, or maybe, I thought, he was just plain miserable.

"Do you have everything you need?" I asked, addressing both men.

Mel finally came to life and raised his empty glass. "I could use another scotch."

"Of course," I responded, and then I asked the girls working in the front to make sure they kept our celebrity plied with drinks. He obviously needed cheering up. On my way back to the rear of the aircraft, I thought, this is going to be a fun week after all.

In between the dinner service and serving two teas and coffees and liqueurs, we were kept so busy with letting-loose-holiday-makers and their demands for an almost intravenous supply of alcohol that I didn't have a moment to break away to speak with Bill again. And then there was the Anna-Jo incident.

We had taken yet another drinks cart into the aisle when I saw that we were getting low on some of our minerals. "Anna-Jo," I asked, "could you please get some tonic waters and a few cokes?"

"Not a problem, darlin'," she replied and turned to go up to the forward galley.

I pushed the cart forward to be able to cater to the next few rows. As our cart was located at the rear end of the mid-cabin, we would just be serving about ten more rows before, ideally, the girls from the front would meet us in the middle and our service would be done.

Usually, it would take five to ten minutes to fetch additional minerals from the lower galley where all the boxes were kept, but after fifteen minutes Anna-Jo still hadn't reappeared. Maybe there had been an emergency up front?

"Have you seen Anna-Jo?" I called across to the girls on the other aisle.

Wendy-May shrugged, but Helga said, "I saw her go down to ze galley about ten minutes ago."

Then where is she?

As I was now completely out of the minerals we needed, I reassured the woman by the window, "I'll come right back with your coke." I couldn't leave the cart unattended in the middle of the aisle, so I finished serving the next three rows—minus minerals. Even after dragging the cart back to the rear galley and stowing it again, there was still no sign of Anna-Jo. Where the hell *is* she? I wondered, mystified. I'll have to get the minerals myself.

I took a tray, marched forward and hit the button to go down in the lift. Once down below, I stepped into the galley expecting to see Anna-Jo having a smoke, eating or chatting to a colleague, but the only person there was Valerie, the galley "slave," also Bajan, who was sitting on the jump seat at the far end, tucking into her dinner.

"Valerie, have you seen Anna-Jo?" I called. "She was supposed to come down here and get some minerals. We were right in the middle of a drinks service."

Valerie shrugged and carried on eating. The galley was always vibrating with a droning engine noise so maybe she hadn't heard me.

The mineral cupboard was the long, low one closest to the lift door. As I bent down to open it, I was faced with a sea of cardboard boxes. An assortment of minerals—cokes, tonics, ginger ales, soda waters and lemonades—were stored there, two boxes high and four deep. Of course, I thought, there are no cokes or tonic waters right at the front and within reach. Instead, I would have to scramble right into the cupboard and move about five boxes to get to the tonics. So much for my freshly manicured nails.

For a good five minutes, I fought to push the forward rows of boxes out of the way.

Finally, I saw the tonics almost at the back as I struggled to pull the heavy container toward me. Then something in the shadows at the back of the cupboard moved, something black and fuzzy.

I screamed, quickly let go of the box of tonics, and scurried backwards out of the cupboard. What the hell was it?

I got to my feet, watching, horrified and fascinated as the thing moved again. And it was much bigger than I'd first thought. Then a muffled grunt came from the rear shadows of the cupboard.

"Valerie!" I shouted hysterically, pointing at the mineral stowage. The boxes seemed to be moving by themselves. I stepped back even farther. Oh my God. What is it? Had an animal somehow got on board? A dog? No, it was much bigger than that. Maybe I should just close the door and imprison it in the cupboard?

"Th-there's something in there!" I exclaimed, addressing Valerie again.

The galley slave set aside her meal tray in a leisurely manner and began taking out a cigarette. Slowly she lit it, calm as could be. "Oh, don't worry, darlin'," she said, taking a long drag. "Dat's jost Anna-Jo."

"Wh-a-a-t? What do you mean? Anna-Jo?" How could she get in there? was what I wanted to ask but was too dumbfounded to speak.

"She's jost takin' a nap," Valerie added.

"A n-n-nap?" Before I could muster any more words, the boxes slowly shifted apart and a head of black hair emerged., the rest of Anna-Jo's tall body pushed her way out from behind the cases of minerals.

I stepped back to give her space as, on hands and knees, she crawled languidly out onto the not-so sanitary galley floor and into the light. She pulled herself up, unfolding to her full height, blinking in the stark, yellow brightness. "O-o-oh," she said, stretching like a cat, "why did you have to wake me opp?" Then she brushed the dust off her red dress and straightened her pinny. "I's havin' soch a lovely dream."

Speechless, I watched as she reached back into the cupboard and easily pulled out the box of tonics I had been struggling with, perched it effortlessly on her hip as if it were her toddler and stepped into the lift.

Gobsmacked, I loaded my tray with cokes and finally followed her.

Once the service was done and all the carts were stowed, headsets and extraneous refuse collected on trays, I sat down at the back and listened to the girls' chatter in their local Bajan dialect, not understanding a word. No doubt, once we landed in Barbados, these girls would all disperse to their family homes. My week would probably be spent with the German girls, that is, unless they all left to be with their big Bajan boyfriends for whom it seemed there was a natural and mutual attraction. The captain would, no doubt, prefer his own company while the first officer had a wife and family somewhere on the island. Presumably the engineer would hang out with the remaining girls or girl, which could be me. But maybe I just "vonted to be alone," which might be exactly what I needed—time to grieve quietly for my lost friend. And for a bit of comic relief, I could see Bill later in the week.

No one on the crew knew about Emma, and I wouldn't tell them. What was the point? They didn't know her, and I didn't want to spread any more misery. Mel Smith seemed to be doing a good job as it was. And anyway, I wondered, what *is* a lovely, funny man like Bill doing with a misery like Mel?

"Cabin crew, disarm your doors," Mary-Beth instructed us over the PA on landing in Barbados. Once the aircraft was stationery and "on chocks," we opened the passenger doors, and that familiar blast of Caribbean heat instantly filled the cabin.

Whenever the white chocks were placed under the massive DC-10 tires, I smiled, reminded of the scene from the recent movie *Airplane* when the aircraft did *not* stop but rolled forward through the airport's plate glass windows. That flight did not arrive *at* Gate 30 but *in* Gate 30.

Barbados, however, was no Heathrow. There were no plate glass windows or multiple gates here. Bridgetown Airport was a collection of single-storey yellow buildings slung together in an L-shape, with just one gate. After the rear door was opened, I could see the palm trees, beyond the terminal, their fronds waving in the slight breeze and the thrill of being back in Barbados surged through me again. Something about the island always made me feel like I was coming home. I remembered with a pang that this is where I had met Jose, who in so many ways had transformed my life from black and white to full technicolour.

After the passengers were deplaned, the crew stepped out of the aircraft to wallow in the hot air. At first, I felt as if someone had wrapped a warm blanket around me, but I knew that within minutes, as we took the short walk into the terminal, our polyester trousers would be clinging to our now-sweaty limbs.

"*Was willst du diese Woche machen?*" What do you want to do this week? Ingrid asked as she sat next to me on the seen-better-days mini-bus. Through the dusty windows of the transport, I surveyed the fields and fields of sugar cane as our driver took us via the back roads to our usual accommodation, the Paradise Beach Hotel on the west side of the island. I wasn't sure yet what I wanted to do. Perhaps just be alone? *"Ja, wahrscheinliches die normale Activitaten."* The usual, I told her.

The first order of business would be to get my hair braided on the beach so I wouldn't have to contend with my thick, fly-away mane going wild and frizzy in this humidity. Then perhaps a few of us would spend a day on the *Jolly Roger*, an infamous faux pirate ship that sailed around the island playing loud reggae music while the ship's crew plied everyone on board with rum punch and other deadly cocktails. The miracle was that, when the ship moored not too far from the beach and the drunken tourists leapt in paralytic ignorance from about fifteen feet into the shallow waters below, no one had died. Not yet anyway. But it wasn't unusual for people to be taken off the *Jolly Roger* on stretchers, not because of any injuries to their bodies, just to their brain cells. Afterwards many of them couldn't remember their uninhibited behaviour or proposing to a stranger, or even their own names.

Perhaps I might try improving my water-skiing, I thought, or just lie under a wafting palm tree and acquire a serious tan between dunks in the warm Caribbean waters. Stepping on sea urchins was to be avoided at all costs, of course.

Through the dusty windows of the mini-bus, I could see walls and walls of sugar cane rushing by, periodically relieved by clusters of pink, blue and yellow-shuttered shacks. We passed an older Bajan man riding his dilapidated bike. His white shirt was open at the neck, his brown trousers were held up by brown braces melded to his thin shoulders and his hat was tipped back on his head as he chewed a piece of sugar cane. He didn't have a care in the world—or so it appeared. All that sugar, I thought. No wonder the locals have no teeth. And even if they did have the odd, good canine, their remaining molars were often blackened with decay.

As we drove around the island, one by one the Bajan girls, and then the first officer were deposited at their homes. By the time we arrived at our hotel, our crew of thirteen had diminished to six girls, one grumpy captain and a very subdued engineer. Ingrid had attached herself to me, and it now seemed we were going to be each other's companions for the week. Her initial sternness had melted, and I realized that beyond her stoic manner, there was something very likeable about Ingrid.

On the first morning in my Caribbean home-away-from-home, I invested four hours sitting on a rickety chair on the beach while Embers, my Bajan hairdresser, transformed my long, thick hair into braids with multi-coloured beads and small pieces of aluminum foil on the ends to hold each one in place. One of the Bajan girls had told me that if I had the same braids done at Vidal Sassoon in London, the process would have taken eight hours and cost four times as much, so I was grateful and patient. The grandmotherly Embers, with her lavish Caribbean figure, thick Bajan dialect and an edginess to her friendliness, also had the aura of a witchdoctor. Tipping her generously, I thought, was a wise action just to prevent myself from any potentially bad juju. I certainly didn't need any more of that this week.

On the Wednesday, when I knew that Emma's funeral—with time change—would be taking place, Ingrid and I were lazing under the palm trees. As their fronds overhead fanned us with a gentle breeze, and we sipped on freshly made pina coladas, we read our books, though mine, *Sacajewa*, was proving laborious. And maybe I just wasn't in the mood to read.

I looked up at the view. The sea was a gentle blue while rainy-season grey clouds hovered on the horizon. Another pang of guilt surfaced but I reminded myself that Emma would have wanted me to live my life, and here I was on a beach in my favorite destination in the world.

Just as I was thinking how much I appreciated Ingrid's long periods of silence, she suddenly asked, "Do you haff a boyfriend?"

"No . . . no one special," I replied, though Jose was a constant in my thoughts. "Why? Do you, Ingrid?"

She shook her head. "*Nein, im moment, nicht aber. . .*" No, not at the moment, but. . . .

"What?" I could feel she was plotting something.

"I am ssinking about haffing a dinner party to vhich I vould like to invite you. Two friends of mine, Paul and Jack vill be zere. Do you ssink you would like to come?"

Another Jack! My flat mate, Ellen, would often tease me about the number of Jacks in my life and how she thought two of them were in love with me. I had explained that all five relationships were strictly platonic, one of the Jacks being my brother. The potential of a new relationship, though, whether it be with another Jack, or a Paul, might distract me from the void that Jose had left.

"Yes, I would love to" I told Ingrid. "I need something to cheer me up." And then without warning the words tumbled out of my mouth. "My girlfriend just died last week and it's her funeral today."

"Oh," Ingrid gasped. "I am sso sorry."

Grateful for her simple response, and that she had returned to reading her book, I lay back and stared at the ocean, imagining Emma's service, feeling the guilt of not being there.

Later, at the end of our beach time, and after I had navigated through the ferns and palms on the curvy paved path back to my room, a large Caribbean man suddenly emerged from the bushes. I stepped back alarmed. He beamed at me, flashing huge white teeth. Once I saw the hotel security insignia on his blue shirt, I exhaled and carried on. I stepped into the shaded #6 and was grateful for the blast of cool air from the noisy air-conditioner.

The red light on the phone was flashing.

"Are you free tonight?" Bill asked when I returned his call.

"Actually, yes I am." When Ingrid and I had discussed dinner plans for that evening, I had told her I wasn't sure whether I would be good company and had left her with Helga, another German girl. The funeral would now be done, but my sadness and guilt remained. Perhaps reminiscing with Bill about good times in Brighton ten years earlier would be good soul medicine.

"I'll come to your hotel," Bill said cheerily. "We're not far away."

"See you in the outside bar at, say, 7:30?" I offered, knowing that Bill would never be able to find my room in the evening blackness.

Two hours later I was sitting in the dark at a table on the hotel terrace. Though small lights were wrapped around the trunks of the surrounding palm trees, they barely gave off any illumination. If the Bajan waiter hadn't been wearing a white jacket and flashing a radiant grin, I would probably not have been able to see him either.

"Mai tai, please," I told him.

He nodded and placed a coaster in front of me. I sat back and basked in the warmth and the sounds around me: the now-black ocean lapping gently on the beach not far away, the whistling frogs and the rustling of the palm trees surrounding the terrace. How I loved the warmth—not just of the balmy weather—but also of the local people who embraced us on this island. I soaked it up like someone who'd been out in a snowstorm and needed warming right down to the bones. But some of the girls couldn't handle either the heat or the humidity, making some of them irritable. Those were the girls who became a little testy at the slowness of the Bajans in preparing drinks or serving meals. Once I came to understand the Bajan mentality myself, I explained to the newbies on the island,

"Don't take it personally." I urged them. "Their relaxed attitude is part of their charm. They're not in a rush. It's us who need to chill."

Just as my pineapple-garnished drink appeared, I heard voices behind me, turned and saw the light from the palm trees glinting on Bill's glasses and highlighting his smile.

"Natasha! I hope you don't mind," he said, grabbing a chair and positioning it across the table from me, "but I brought Mel."

"No," I said, with a mixture of excitement at getting to know the enigmatic Mel Smith and disappointment that Mel's presence might interfere with my reunion with Bill.

"Not at all," I told Mel who grabbed a chair and then placed it—not at the table—but off to the side as if he wanted to sit and observe. Or maybe, I thought, he just doesn't want to sit close to me. I smiled at him, but he just stared back at me, a strangely vacant, hooded look.

Maybe he's been drinking, I thought, but he didn't appear to be drunk, just very quiet. He had the same deadpan expression that he exhibited on TV and on the plane. Does this comedian *ever* smile? I shifted in my chair to be more inclusive of him while trying to be attentive to Bill. This was going to be an interesting evening.

Miraculously the waiter appeared quickly and took their drink orders.

"So, Bill." I smiled. "Where to begin? Are you still in touch with Frank and Janice?"

Bill and I gave each other a synopsis of our last ten years. After working for BMW in Brighton where I had met our mutual friends, I told him, I had gone travelling for a year, lived in Zurich to learn German, done some secretarial work in London and then begun flying with Dan Air. Now I was with Laker. Bill told me he had finished university in Brighton and immediately got into television in London, fulfilling various roles in front of and behind the camera.

"Good for you!" I said, wondering if I should have also pursued a career in television instead of travel. I was often told I was "entertaining"—whatever that meant. "Are you working on *Not the Nine O 'Clock News?*" I enquired of Bill while surreptitiously looking over at Mel and wondering, is he expecting me to give him special attention?

Despite my excitement at seeing Bill again and catching up on news of old friends, Mel's continued dour mood was unnerving. Does he disapprove of me? Why has he come then? Perhaps I was supposed to be fawning over him. He was the famous one, after all.

"I co-write with Mel sometimes" Bill continued. "That's what we're doing this week."

"It's my favorite program," I told Mel sincerely. He groaned as if that was the most inane comment he had ever heard.

"So, do you know where we can go and have some fun?" Bill asked, apparently sensing Mel's restlessness.

"There's this disco called The Garage. It's literally a structure made of pieces of corrugated iron, strung loosely together with rope. David, the owner, has cut vintage cars in half, and they are used as seats scattered around the edge of the dance floor. It's right on the ocean, and when the rains come, everyone just carries on dancing and gets soaked. When the rain stops and we dry off in the heat, we are literally steaming twits. It's a riot." I was grinning, but both Bill and Mel looked at me as if I was quite mad.

"Well, then, of course, there's also the Ship," I continued more demurely. "It's a great pub close to lots of other restaurants and fun places."

Bill glanced over at Mel again. This time he nodded.

"The Ship then?" I confirmed, trying to get a reaction out of Mel, but he continued to stare. He *hates* me, I thought. Why had he come tonight other than maybe not to be alone? I wished he had stayed at his hotel to write. "I've never driven there myself, but I know it's close to St. James."

"We've got the Moke so we can drive." Bill pointed behind me to where a small blue Mini-Moke, the Caribbean answer to the soft-topped jeep, sat under a palm tree.

"I'll just ask for directions," I said signalling to the waiter that we were ready to leave.

"Excuse me," I said. "Do you know a pub on St. James called The Ship."

"De Ship?"

"Yes, the pub?"

"De pub?" he asked, sounding surprised.

"Yes. It's just out of Bridgetown. It's a very popular pub. Lots of tourists and locals go there."

"Aw," he said, taking some money from Bill for the tab. "You mean De Ship Pub?"

"Yes." Isn't that what I had just said?

"Yes, Mon." He put the money on his tray and then pointed. "What you do is you find de driveway that gaws out of de hotel, den you gaw out of de driveway. Den you turn right. And you gaw for a lo-o-ong taime. Den de road fokks. But you don't take de right fokk, you take de other fokk."

"The left fork," I confirmed, trying not to laugh while mentally trying to sort out his directions.

"Yes, dat's right. Take de left fokk. But den you come to de traffic lights. Now if dey red, you can't gaw. When dey green, den you can gaw."

I smiled at the waiter's logic, but behind him I could hear Mel huffing. He was right. This might take all night.

"That's okay. We'll find it," I told the waiter. "Thank you."

As the three of us walked toward the Moke, I told Bill— full of a confidence that I didn't feel— "I'll probably recognize the road when I see it."

Mel pulled his bulk into the driver's seat, and Bill folded his long lean frame into the passenger side while I sat in the back.

"So let's gaw out de driveway and turn right," I said, mimicking our lovely waiter and trying to introduce some humor.

Bill laughed but Mel remained stonily silent.

As we drove the almost-black country roads with the only light coming from the porches of the multi-coloured houses, I tried to strike up a conversation with Mel about being on television. But he wasn't forthcoming. After fifteen minutes of driving, Mel asked impatiently "Where the hell is this place?"

We were nearing Bridgetown, but in the blackness, I couldn't see anything that I recognized. I had been to Barbados about fifteen times before this trip and had been driven around both during the day and in the night, but on this evening nothing looked familiar.

"Well . . . I'm sure if we keep driving down here, we will—"

"Oh, for Chrissake!" Mel snapped.

"I'm sorry, Mel, but I have never driven myself here before."

"I thought you said you knew the island really well." Though he was now finally communicating, I didn't like his tone.

"I *do* know a lot of places. I'm just not exactly sure how to get there in the dark."

"Fucking stupid blonde stewardesses," he muttered but loud enough for me to hear it just fine.

Bill turned to Mel and made a barely audible admonishment.

That was the moment I began to officially hate Mel Smith. I wanted to scream at him: My friend just died last week and was buried today, and I have something to be miserable about, you grumpy old sod! But for Bill's sake, and wanting to keep the peace, I addressed him instead. "Bill, maybe we should ask someone."

"Oh, good idea!" Mel drawled sarcastically.

We had arrived on the outskirts of Bridgetown, and a young local carrying a bulging sack over his shoulder was sauntering along the pavement on the brightly lit street. Suddenly Mel pulled over beside him and braked. "Ask him!" he ordered as if he was incapable of speaking English to the man himself.

"Excuse me," I called to the young man who had his head down as he walked. "Do you happen to know where a pub called The Ship is?"

"De Ship?" He looked up and frowned at us.

Oh, here we go again, I thought.

"Yes, the Ship Pub," I enunciated ever-so-slowly.

"Oh, no problem, mon. I know De Ship. It's clawse to my house," he said, and before I knew what was happening, he had climbed into the back seat of the Mini Moke, forcing me to move over to the other side.

"You gaw up dis street," he said, sitting forward and indicating with his long arm, "and den when de light's green, you can gaw ahead. . ."

I sat back in the corner of the seat, grateful to the young man that I was now off the hook and didn't have to deal with Miserable Mel. We drove for another fifteen minutes.

Then the young man pointed to a house on the side of a country road. "Mon! Here tis!" Mel pulled over.

"Where's the pub?" I asked him as he extended his long limbs over the side of the Moke and climbed out, dragging his sack full of God-knows-what behind him.

"Aw, I dawn't knaw. Thanks for the ride, mon," he called to Mel. "My feet's killin' me."

He turned and disappeared down a dark path into his home.

Uh-oh. Mel's response was not going to be pretty.

"Shit!" he exclaimed, banging the steering wheel. "What does it take just to get a fucking drink on this island?" This time he turned to look at me.

"Steady on," Bill told his friend. "It's not Natasha's fault."

"I'm really sorry, Mel," I told him, feeling bad. "There is another pub and I do know *exactly* where it is." Even though it is up the other end of the island, I thought. But I wasn't going to tell this misogynist that. "If we can just get back on the main road towards our hotel, I know where it is from there," I added.

He paused, scrutinizing me. "Are you sure?"

"Yes, I'm sure." This time, I *was* sure. "I know the people there. They're friends of mine."

For the twenty-minute drive back past our hotel on the west side and on to The Coral Inn, we drove in silence. Was this fiasco all my fault? If just Bill and I had got lost, we would have found it funny. Instead, I wanted to cry, but I wouldn't give this miserable brute the satisfaction.

As the Moke crunched into the driveway of The Coral Inn, I almost ran into the bar and into the welcome embrace of my German friend Kathy. She used to be a Laker girl but had met and married Robin, a local white Bajan man. The two of them were now owners of this quaint colonial style inn and pub. "Thank God you're here," I told Kathy. "We got lost looking for the Ship and one of my companions isn't very happy with me."

Armed with drinks, I joined Bill outside on a patio where the members of a band were setting up to play. To my relief Mel chose to stay inside at the bar to guzzle copious drinks.

"I'm sorry about that, Natasha," Bill murmured, shaking his head and chugging down a cold beer. "Mel's under a lot of pressure."

"That doesn't give him license to be so rude!" I told him, the remark about blonde stewardesses still ringing in my head.

"Well, every week he's got to come up with stuff, and it's got to be *really* funny," Bill said, still hoping for some compassion from me.

Maybe a sense of humor would help, I thought, marvelling that he was one of the funniest men on TV. Some comedians suffered from manic depression, I knew, and I wondered if that was Mel's problem.

"He's not normally this bad." Bill took another swig of his beer, a frown creasing his forehead.

"He hates me," I told Bill. While I might be a *femme fatale* for some men, others judged me on sight.

"No," Bill shook his head. "It's not you. He was toking earlier today, and he wasn't going to come with me, but at the last minute he decided to get out. He's having a bad trip."

"He's not the only one," I retorted. Then for the second time that day, I blurted, "My girlfriend died last week, and it was her funeral today."

"Oh. I'm so sorry," Bill muttered.

It was only then that I realized I wasn't looking for sympathy, just someone to assuage my guilt for missing Emma's funeral. "Well," I said softening, "I'm sorry that I got us lost, too. I was looking forward to a nice evening catching up with you."

I heard laughter behind me and turned to see Kathy and Robin emerging from the pub. Mel was walking between them and they were all laughing.

"Natasha," Kathy began in her mild German accent, "this man isss so funny. You must bring him here again."

Mel and I stared at each other and exclaimed simultaneously, "Not bloody likely!" He smiled then. Surprisingly, his ugly demeanor melted, and he looked almost handsome.

"A man could die of thirst with her," he said, pointing his glass at me, still smiling. With a couple of scotches under his belt, Miserable Mel had suddenly morphed into Mellow Mel—which was a great improvement.

"And you're supposed to have a sense of humor," I shot back. "And some manners."

"You could be right." He shrugged. "Forgiven?" He proffered his glass to clink with mine.

On another day, I might have acquiesced and accepted his apology, but today I was also having a sense of humour failure.

Briefly I thought about pouring my drink over his head. Instead, ignoring his outstretched glass, I turned to Kathy, who was also blonde. "*Weisst du,*" I said, indicating with my eyes that I was speaking about Mel, "*er glaubt dass alle blonde stewardessen dumm sind?*" Do you know that he thinks all blonde stewardesses are stupid?

"*Nein! Wirklich?*" No, really? She turned to Mellow Mel and gave him her evil eye. Robin took a step back, giving Mel a disappointed glance, the fan-shine in his eyes now not quite so lustrous.

"*Ja, dass hat er mir heute abend gesagt.*" Yes, that's what he told me this evening. "*Nur weil konnte ich nicht den richtigen Weg in Dunkelheit zum Pub finden.*" Just because I couldn't find the right road to the pub in the dark.

Mel's eyes narrowed. For all he knew, I could have been telling Kathy that he only had one testicle.

"*Ach,*" Kathy exclaimed, playing along with me. "*Dass ist nicht nett.*" That's not nice.

Mel, uncomfortable that he was being discussed, apparently in a derogatory way, had now clued into my intent. "Okay. Okay. I get it. You obviously speak good German and you're not dumb."

"No. Nor am I blonde." Then I added, smiling. "For the sake of your fans, I hope you develop a sense of humor this week." I turned away and walked over to Bill who was chatting with a band member.

"Bill, it's been lovely seeing you again."

"Are you leaving?"

"Yes, I think I will," I responded as we both glanced over at the now abandoned Mellow Mel. "And don't worry about taking me back to the hotel. Robin will give me a ride."

"I'm sorry, Natasha," Bill said, obviously feeling bad.

"I would love to see *you* again, but back in the UK. And just you!"

"Point taken."

For four weeks after that Barbados trip, I watched every episode of *Not the Nine O 'Clock News*. Not because I wanted to see Mel Smith's face again or that I would enjoy the program now. I did, however, want to make sure there were no references to "f... ing stupid, blonde stewardesses."

There weren't.

True to her word, and a week later, Ingrid invited me to her rambling house in Copthorne for dinner where I met Paul and Jack, both handsome, intelligent, successful and interesting men. Although it was Paul who kept me laughing all night, it was tall and lean Jack who, from the start, gave me butterflies. And so began my new romance.

11

POSITIVE THINKING?

January 1981
Aberdeen

"Do you want to go skiing?" Stewart's voice on the end of the line sounded like his old self. It was the winter of 1981 and Emma had been gone just four months. "I thought I'd get a crowd of us together," he added, chortling, "and go up to Aviemore."

"Aviemore?"

"Aviemore, the ski resort," Stewart explained, mistaking my surprise for lack of knowledge. "Two hours outside of Aberdeen."

While I *did* know of the Scottish ski hill, I was hoping he would have suggested somewhere more glamorous like St. Moritz or Arosa in Switzerland. But my skiing ability was minimal so maybe it would be good not to risk fatal injury on *real* mountains.

Back in 1976, as part of a year-long sojourn around Europe, my then-boyfriend Julian and I had lived and worked in southern Germany. While renting the upper story of the Muller house—and occasionally sampling the homemade Schnapps Herr Muller brewed in his cellar—Julian and I had borrowed the family's wooden skis. In the hilly cherry orchard behind his house, with the enthusiastic Herr Muller constantly yelling, "*Die Knie beugen!*" Bend the knees! We had slithered down the little hills—sometime colliding with cherry trees

—and instantly called ourselves skiers. So, Stewart was right. The gentle slopes of Aviemore would suffice for now.

"When are you thinking of doing this exactly, Stewart?"

"Mid-January."

Unlike Dan Dare, Laker was quieter in the winter months so I should be able to request four days off. And I remembered that Jack, my newish boyfriend, was going to be in Taiwan on business at that time.

"Why not?" I said. "Sounds like fun. Who else is going? Samantha? Philip?"

"Well . . . uh . . . they haven't committed yet," Stewart responded in his usual faltering voice. "But there'll probably be about twenty of us. If you can get yourself up to Aberdeen airport, I can pick you up. You can stay with me, and I think I have some skis here that might do for you."

"Is there lots of snow predicted?" Although I knew Scotland to be cold in January, could Aviemore guarantee enough of the white stuff?

"Oh, yes," he responded with a chuckle, the familiar sound of his unlit pipe-sucking in the background. "No worries there."

On January 15, 1981, Stewart was waiting for me in Arrivals at the small but clean and shiny Aberdeen airport. "My MGBT is parked right outside," he said, his customary pipe hanging from the corner of his mouth, "but would you like to go for a drink first at the end of the runway?"

"Isn't it a bit cold for that?"

"Ah yes." He grinned. "Perhaps I should explain. The End of The Runway is the name of the pub."

"Well, in that case . . ." I grinned.

"Jolly good, then."

While I tucked myself into the front seat of his drafty old convertible, my breath visible in the cold, dark air, I saw that there was a twinkle in Stewart's eyes. Phew. As it was the first time since Emma's death that we had seen each other, our meeting could have been awkward, but he seemed excited about our upcoming weekend adventure. Even though the night was still young, Stewart raced to the pub as if we might miss last call.

"So, who else is coming tomorrow?" I asked, my hand clinging to the door handle.

"Well . . . not too sure exactly." He grinned. "But we'll have fun, no doubt."

Uh-oh. Was it just going to be the two of us? Not that I didn't enjoy Stewart's company. I did. But I was just nervous about being alone with him after Emma's death. A crowd would be a distraction.

"Don't worry, Natasha." He patted my knee with a gloved hand and chuckled. "We'll pick up some airport strays along the way. I'm sure there's lots of willing victims out there."

The long, low Tudor-style pub was, indeed, not only located at the end of the runway, but ran right alongside the narrow, paved strip for quite a way. Stewart had to duck his tall frame as he entered the single doorway, but as I followed him through the crowd, I found the warmth and the hum of chatter comforting. Stewart was aiming for the far end of the bar, but everyone kept stopping him. They all seemed to know that he was going skiing the next day and kept pointing out the window. "Schtoowart, laddie, there's naw snaw!" And "Ach, Schtoowart," others exclaimed and launched into a Scottish brogue I could nae understand.

Schtoowart simply nodded. "Ah, not to worry," he said, taking his pipe out of his mouth and smiling like a benign professor. Finally, we arrived at the far end of the bar where we found a vacant spot with standing room only. Just as Stewart passed me my drink, a loud voice boomed over the long line of heads, most of them belonging to men, some of whom were still wearing their flight deck uniforms, not having even bothered to remove their captain or first officer stripes. "Schtoowart," the voice boomed, "you're not still thinkin' of gi-in' skiin,' are yer, laddie? Ah just flooo over tonight and there's naw snaw!"

Stewart acknowledged the man benevolently by raising his glass and waving his pipe. "Yes, yes. Thank you, Ian."

"Does *everyone* in this pub know you're going skiing tomorrow?" I asked, impressed.

"Er . . . probably, yes. These are mainly airport people, and it's not a big crowd, not like Gatwick," he pointed out.

"Do you think they're right, Stewart? Will there be enough snow to ski?"

"Oh, absolutely," he said, determined to hang onto his belief. "Even if we have to drive halfway around Scotland, we'll find snow."

Was it positive thinking, denial or just plain stubbornness that made him believe? Whatever it was, I was on his side.

Later when we drove to his rented house on the west side of Aberdeen, I could just make out—with the aid of the streetlights—the rows and rows of sterile grey granite houses, punctuated only by bright blue, red and green front doors. Once we were inside Stewart's austerely furnished house and sitting in the living room with hot brandy toddies to warm us, I wondered if I should mention the elephant in the room, Emma. Not feeling brave, I asked him instead, "Do you like it up here?"

"Oh, you know, it's not so bad." He sat back to begin the process of lighting his pipe. "It's like any airport really. We have our fair share of . . . uh . . . mishaps."

"Really?" I couldn't imagine this place on the east coast of Scotland being that exciting. "Like what?"

"Well, there was an incident about a month ago . . ."

"Do tell." I curled my feet up under me in the chair and settled in for his story.

"Well, you know a lot of our passengers are men who work on the North Sea oil rigs?"

I nodded, already aware that the oil industry was the main purpose for Aberdeen Airport and for the prop jobs he flew, 50-seater HS 748s that could land in smaller places.

"Of course," he said, "those men are on the rigs for months at a time."

"Yes." I nodded again. "Jenny's husband, Rufus, did it for a few years. It pays well."

"But they have to abstain from drink while they're there," Stewart continued, "so as soon as they get off the helicopter and onto our flights, they go at the booze with a vengeance. Coming and going from the rig, they drink themselves into oblivion. Well, one day this chap came into Aberdeen Airport to board his plane. The ground stewardess saw that he was really drunk and told him she was sorry, but he would not be allowed to board the flight in that state."

"Good for her!" I said. We had all long complained about the danger of allowing drunken passengers on board.

"Apparently, he yelled at her, 'Ah've gotta get awn on this flight,' and when she still refused to give him a boarding pass, he punched the poor girl firmly on the jaw and knocked her out."

"Oh, no!"

"Yes," Stewart nodded, puffing on his now lit pipe. "The ramp agent who was standing close by tried to stop him, but the man ran down the concourse toward the gate. The ramp agent got on his walkie-talkie and warned the security agents at the end of the concourse that this very inebriated man was coming. The guards were ready for him, or so they thought, and posted themselves on either side of the corridor in front of those huge windows."

I remembered seeing those windows on arrival a few hours earlier.

Stewart continued, "They told him, 'Sorry, sir, but you can't board that plane,' Instead of turning around, the man took on both security guards, sending one flying up against the window and knocking the other one out. Then this charmingly drunk fellow ran down the stairs and out onto the tarmac where the 748 was sitting. The stewardess had been warned not to let him on the plane, so she was just closing the rear door as the man ran up and banged on the outside. Of course, she didn't open up. He must have thought that he could get in another door and ran forward. But the flight deck had just started the engines . . ." Stewart paused, moving his pipe to the other side of his mouth, and studying me to see if I had comprehended what had happened next.

I envisioned the propellors whirring in the dark night air. "Oh, no!"

"Precisely!" Stewart said, making a furious sucking noise. "The poor bugger ran right into the port propeller. He was mincemeat from the waist up."

"Ugh!" I exclaimed, imagining the passengers already on board witnessing the grizzly scene. The carnage must have sprayed everywhere.

"The pilot told me he was just relieved that his DV window was shut," Stewart said, chuckling. He was referring to the sliding Direct Vision windows on either side of the flight deck, which the crew usually closed just before taxiing.

"Oh, that's awful!" And not funny at all, I wanted to say but for some reason we flyers had a macabre sense of humor.

"Yes. It was pretty bad," Stewart agreed more somberly. "The firemen had to come out and hose down the plane."

"How gruesome for them!"

"Of course, with the propellers already rotating at around 7,000 rpms, the blades would have been invisible to anyone, drunk or sober. All the man would have seen in the dark was the wing and the engine housing. A lesson, of course, not to be drunk outside an aircraft at night."

"Is that why a new directive came around the airlines a couple of months ago not to let anyone on the aircraft who was inebriated?"

"Probably." Stewart had settled back into his chair.

"That rule should have been implemented a long time ago," I huffed, remembering my hellish four-hour night Tenerife with a drunken woman when I was still with Dan Air. Although I had been the one to sell her copious miniature whiskies, I had not foreseen that she would instantly chug-a-lug them all.

After a while Stewart said, "Emma would probably have scared him into submission, though, don't you think?"

When he finally brought up her name, my shoulders slumped in a sudden release of tension I didn't know I was holding. "Yes." I smiled, thinking about the profanities that had sometimes come out of Emma's innocent-looking little face. "She could stare anybody down. . . or tell them where to get off." I paused, then asked, "How are you doing with. . .what happened, by the way?" I tried to make the question sound casual.

Stewart shifted in his seat, uncrossed his long legs, and then crossed them the other way. "Well, one just has to accept these things, don't you think?"

I sipped on my brandy, appreciating the warmth as it trickled down my throat and spread through my upper body. I wanted to ask; do you think she committed suicide? But then Stewart might think I was laying the blame firmly at his feet. And it hadn't been Stewart's fault. Instead, I said very quietly, "Emma wasn't strong enough for this life, you know."

He shifted his weight again, as if uncomfortable in his chair, and muttered helplessly, "I just couldn't give her what she wanted." His voice wavered as if his words were a plea for forgiveness, but his eyes were fixed on the gold fringe of the standard lamp just to the left of his head.

"I know, Stewart. You can't *make* yourself fall in love with someone. It doesn't work that way." I wondered if Jose had also "just loved me' but wasn't in love with me.

"No. I suppose not." He let out a large breath as if this was the first time that he had acknowledged this concept.

"Emma's need for love was bottomless," I added softly, "and in the end I do believe she did get what she wanted."

"How do you mean?" He stared at me; his eyes darkened suddenly with naked torment.

"Death," I told him. "She wanted death, Stewart. Why else would she have gone back to Iran in the middle of the revolution where she had already nearly died. Then the belly landing? And finally driving the car into . . .oblivion." I shuddered at the memory. "She taunted death until it came and took her."

"Oh." He studied his drink. Then as if choking on the words, and not looking up, he asked, "But do you think she's at peace?" The pain in his voice was evidence, I suspected, of many a tortured sleepless night.

"Yes. Absolutely."

"How can you be so sure?" This time he was searching my features, needing nothing but the truth.

"I can feel it. And perhaps you don't know this, Stewart, but for a long time she had talked about killing herself and . . . making it look like an accident."

"Good Lord!" He set his drink down on the arm of his chair. "She did?"

"Yes. So I don't think it was all about you. In fact. . .," I hesitated, wondering at the wisdom of speaking my next words as I didn't want to add to his devastation, ". . . on some level she knew it wouldn't work so she might have set herself up for failure with you."

I watched his reaction as he absorbed this concept. He blew out an exhalation, and the muscles of his face relaxed as if I had just given him a long, cold drink on a very hot day.

"I know she loved you," I added, "but you weren't the root cause of her misery. That dynamic had been set in motion a *long* time before you came on the scene."

"I do hope you're right." He exhaled another long sigh. "I do hope you're right."

For a while we both sat with our own thoughts, missing our friend, the funny, sometimes happy and often sardonic Emma we had known.

Suddenly Stewart snapped out of his reverie and stood up. "Well, we better get some shut eye. We've got to leave early if we're going to do some serious skiing tomorrow."

"Och, but Schtoowart," I mimicked, "there's naw snaw."

Laughing, we both retired to our rooms.

The next morning, as I dressed in the cold bedroom, my breath resembled a fire-breathing dragon without the fire. Despite the central heating and my coat tucked around my feet on the narrow bed the previous night, I had been cold. I squinted out of the window into grey bleakness. Aberdeen, or this part of it anyway, appeared even bleaker in the daytime. Through the misty drizzle, the rows upon rows of uniform grey granite houses could barely be distinguished in the greyness. No wonder they've painted their front doors such bright colours, I thought. How else would they know which was their home, especially if they came home from the pub two sheets to the wind?

The smell of coffee wafting up the stairs was welcoming.

"Ah! How's the skier this morning?" Stewart asked brightly as I entered his yellow-walled kitchen, bare of knickknacks. Were all Scottish houses so utilitarian or was it just his bachelor lifestyle? Too bad Emma wasn't here to add her feminine touch. She would have had a challenge making *this* place look cozy.

"I slept well," I lied. "But maybe tonight, if you have another blanket..."

"Yes, of course." Stewart stood up. "Would you like some toast?"

Just then the phone rang, the shrill sound echoing around the kitchen.

He picked up the receiver. "Yes? Ah, yes? Well, don't you listen to them, Cedric. We'll find snow..."

The group was diminishing by the minute.

"And if the worst comes to the worst," he told the caller, "We can all go to the End of the Runway."

This must have been the right thing to say because, before he hung up, he said, "Jolly good then. See you there."

Two hours later while Stewart negotiated the winding roads in his not-so-insulated MGB convertible, I sat beside him, bundled up in my brown ski outfit, jacket, scarf, hat and gloves. Behind us, a convoy of six cars containing twelve trusting souls were following us towards Aviemore. We had all met earlier in the car park of the End of the Runway and after poring over maps of eastern Scotland, the drivers had all agreed—in a conversation I could not understand—on a route.

Peering through the narrow windscreen at the grey drizzle and the rings of mist that—like halos around heads—hovered low over the surrounding green hills, I commented, "They were right, Stewart. I'm not seeing any snow."

"Well, apparently Aviemore is bare, so we've decided to try some other hills a little further on," Stewart informed me, clutching the steering wheel with his sheepskin gloved hands. We might end up in Inverness at this rate, I thought. Even though the collar of his sheepskin jacket was turned up to warm his neck and ears, I noted that his nose was almost blue. I was shivering myself. What madness had possessed me to agree to this, I wondered. And these hills looked intimidatingly high for my novice skiing ability.

"We're nearly there," Stewart said encouragingly. While I loved his optimism, I did wonder about his sanity.

Suddenly he pulled off into a small car park at the bottom of a hill. About six other cars were already parked haphazardly there between large puddles. Behind us, the rest of our convoy followed, splashing through the ruts filled with muddy water before coming to a halt.

"Just wait here, Natasha," Stewart said and climbed out to consort with the other drivers. Someone called Cedric who worked on the ground at Aberdeen airport and who knew the area well spoke to Stewart in his thick accent. After a few minutes of indecipherable conversation, Stewart climbed back into the car. "Well, there's no snow here either so we are going to look a bit further up the road. Cedric's leading the way. You better hold on for dear life."

There was a grinding noise as Cedric reversed his VW van in a spray of water and gravel and headed back onto the road. Stewart followed and the others drove behind us.

"That Cedric, he's quite a character, you know," Stewart said, chortling. "I'm not exactly sure, but I wouldn't be surprised if he had a bottle of Scotch for breakfast."

"Should he be driving?" I asked.

"Oh, probably not!" Stewart wiped the misting window with his gloved hand. "He probably shouldn't be allowed out of the house. But you know, these Scots have a different tolerance for alcohol."

Cedric seemed to be unaware that people were following him as he took off like an alcoholic who needed to get to the next pub before closing, the blue and white of his van disappearing around each corner and over each hill as we went. Having driven our own VW camper around Europe, I had never known those vans could go so fast. Fortunately, eastern Scotland appeared to have only one road so he couldn't lose us, try as he might.

"Ah, there it is," Stewart announced. In the distance, we could see Cedric's van turning to the right. As we caught up to him, I saw that the car park looked very similar to the last, with twenty cars parked in yet another be-puddled, graveled area.

"This looks good," Stewart said, peering through the windshield up at the mountain.

"It does?" I looked up at a very steep hill and saw only a thin layer of slushy brown and white stuff. Half of me was now hoping that we wouldn't find any snow, and like true Scots, we could return unscathed to the pub for a hot toddy. Seeing the size and steepness of the mountain, I was also having second thoughts. What had I been thinking? I hadn't skied anything close to this size even in Germany four years earlier.

"Alrightee, then," Stewart exclaimed gleefully, "let's go skiing!" We climbed out of the car, and I followed him over to Cedric's van to retrieve our skiing equipment.

"So, Cedric, I understand you're from this area," I said as we sorted out our gear. "Have you done a lot of skiing?"

"Ach, naw. Ah've never skied in ma life before, hinny. Mark an' I," he said, pointing to his friend who was donning a woolly hat, "jist thought we'd do it for a laff, if ya knaw what I mean. That crazy

Schtoowart fella thinks there's snaw up here. Is he a friend o' yours?" Cedric gave me a questionable look.

"Yes, he is." I smiled. "He means well."

"Ach, 'e's a bluddy nutter."

I stared at him, trying not to shake my head in disbelief. Who's to say *who* is crazy, I thought.

With trepidation, I pushed my feet into my ill-fitting boots and then hoisted too-long skis onto my shoulder—skis which I prayed would let loose if I fell. I *would* fall undoubtedly, but avoiding breaking a leg when I did so would be my focus for this day.

Once everyone in our troupe was kitted out, we trudged behind Stewart to the bottom of the hill. Cedric, I noticed, wasn't wearing any ski gear, just a big green parka covering his large not-so-athletic frame. No gloves, no hat and no scarf in sight. Even his jacket was flying open as if it was springtime and not the middle of winter in Scotland.

When we got closer to the hill, to my dismay I saw that the ski lift was not a T-bar but a button lift, which was comprised of a pulley with two ropes dangling down. At the end of each rope was a large disk or "button" about twenty-four inches in diameter. I watched as the skiers in front of us waited for a pair of ropes to swing around, saw them each grab one, place the button between their legs, sit back on the button and then hang onto the rope as it pulled them forward, two by two, up the hill.

"Stewart," I said, grabbing his arm in a sudden fit of nervousness, "I don't think I can do this."

"Oh, don't you worry, Natasha," he said, clicking on his right ski. "It's a piece of cake. You'll be *fine*."

Bloody hell! Why did Stewart have to be so infuriatingly positive about *everything?*

"Your faith in me is touching but completely delusional," I muttered as reluctantly I pushed my boots into the skis. There was no getting out of this now.

"Com'on," Stewart said cheerily as he grabbed my arm to pull me into the queue.

As the ropes swung around, Stewart seized a pair of "buttons" and handed one to me. He pulled his down, placed it between his legs, sat on it and leaned back. I did the same. All was well.

The rope pulled us forward.

"Keep your skis parallel on the ground, lean back on it and let the pulley do the work for you," Stewart instructed.

Okay. This is okay. I can do this, I told myself, as my skis seemed to glide over the wet and uneven snow beneath us. So far so good. I looked up ahead. The pulley was taking us up higher and higher. I hoped that the peak that was in view was indeed the top of the mountain. Behind me, Cedric and Mark chatted easily, but their conversation was unintelligible. I didn't dare look back, or to the side, to see the steepness of the incline we were climbing. Just keep your skis pointing forward, I told myself. This is not so difficult.

Then it happened.

Like a bad accident in slow motion, I could see it coming but was powerless to avoid the outcome. There was an icy bump in the snow ahead, right in our path. Relax, I told myself and leaned back even further. Apparently, this was the wrong thing to do as the next thing I knew, the button had escaped from between my legs and was flying into the mountain air. Suddenly I was lying face-down spread-eagled on that icy hump. I heard Stewart's voice carried away in the breeze saying, "Oh, no!"

I was lying right across the path of oncoming skiers, namely Cedric and Mark. If I don't move in time, they will be leaving tramlines across my buttocks. Get out of the way! I told myself furiously. Get out of the way! Like a duck-billed platypus on steroids, with all limbs flailing, I frantically inched my body and errant skis to the right, just before Cedric's ski tips zipped past my feet.

He shouted something I didn't understand, but I knew it wasn't complimentary. To my utter humiliation, I am sure that everyone on that button-lift was killing themselves laughing.

Fifteen minutes later, on those same buttocks that had narrowly escaped being marked for life, I had inched my way down the hill. Humiliating as it was to do that in front of uploading skiers, I felt that it was wiser than attempting something I could not do—ski.

Stewart, having swooshed down to the bottom of the button lift, met me there. "Are you okay, Natasha?"

God bless him, I thought. He was managing to keep a smile off his face and not make any bad jokes—to me anyway.

"I don't think I'm cut out for this, Stewart. Maybe you should just carry on. I'll wait in the car."

"Nonsense! You just need to get your ski legs. It doesn't take long. Come on." And with that, he grabbed another button, pushing it at me and I was yet again riding up the hill. "Just let the skis slide over each bump and keep your balance," he advised.

This time it worked. Phew.

When we arrived at the top of the button lift, which I now realized only took us a third of the way up the whole mountain, the entire group was waiting, discussing where to find the best sides of the hills to ski or more accurately, where there was snow.

Cedric, his parka flying in the breeze, followed by Mark, marched over to the top of a hill to our right that was half-covered with snow. At the bottom was a pond-sized muddy puddle.

"Now thain," he pronounced, planting his poles, and facing down the hill, his ski tips hanging over the edge. "How do yer doo this skiin' business?"

Before any of the others could respond with useful advice, he pushed off the top of the hill with his poles. We all watched in horrified amusement as, like a bat out of hell, his green parka forming a Batman cape and both skis parallel and pointing downhill, he went in a straight line to the bottom. When he reached the pond, his skis entered the puddle, bringing poor Cedric to a very abrupt halt. He fell forward, face planting into the pond. We all continued to stare fascinated as he emerged, like a dog, shaking the water off, and wiping the mud from his face and jacket., miraculously, uninjured. Undeterred, he marched back over to the button lift and reloaded. As he rejoined our group, he growled, "Ach, well, that's done. Is it time to gaw to the pub noo?"

But the group had decided to go higher where there was more snow, and somehow Stewart convinced me I would be "just fine." Like a lamb to the slaughter, I went, too. When I finally made it to the top on the accursed button lift, I stood with some of the others surveying the vista. Through the thin mist that hung over the surrounding landscape, I could see many more hills but, as the man in the pub had said, "Naw snaw." When I looked down and saw that just one side of our mountain was covered in a thick patch of slushy white and brown stuff before it disappeared into the mist, I gulped. With just these two wooden planks fastened to my feet, how the hell was I supposed to get down there without killing myself? Visions of breaking legs, twisting ankles, ending up in a tangled mess or spread-eagled again inelegantly across the mountainside came to mind. I contemplated my options but there were none. If I was going to avoid certain death, I decided I would just have to slide down on my bum—at least on the steepest part.

Stewart came over.

"I can't do this, Stewart," I whined, detesting my own weakness.

"It just looks steep, Natasha," he said. "Watch me and see how I do it."

I studied him as, effortlessly with feet together, he flipped his body from side to side and disappeared. Easy for him to say.

One by one the others followed. Then I was alone on top of what felt like a humpback whale of a mountain.

David, another Aberdeen-based Dan Air pilot, swished to a stop in front of me. "First time skiing?" he asked, looking maddeningly at ease on his skis.

"What was your first clue?" I smiled.

"I'll stay with you," he said.

Ah, chivalry wasn't dead then.

"If you feel you are going too fast, just do a snow plough," he told me, demonstrating how to place skis in a V-shape. "Shift your weight from side to side and push with one leg and then the other," he added.

"Okay," I said. "I think I can do that." Maybe I *could* get down the mountain and retain some vestige of dignity. Mr. Chivalrous then waved a ski pole in the air. "Follow me," he said, as he moved off down the mountain, also in a snow plough.

I trailed behind him, trying not to look out at the panorama. Heights have always made me nauseous. God knows why I was so drawn to flying and skiing—well, the idea of skiing anyway.

"Lean into the ski as you turn," David instructed.

I did and all was well . . . for a while.

Maybe there was a rock just below the surface of the snow, or maybe I lost concentration, or the thought of tumbling downhill like a snowball and breaking every bone in my body and never being able to fly again filled my mind, but suddenly the skis started sliding faster and faster, then going in different directions. I heard a scream. My scream. I felt myself falling.

David shouted, "Keep your feet together!"

Too late!

I was slithering down the mountain on my side, the long wooden skis sliding sideways with me. Miraculously I finally came to a stop, the skis further up the mountain than my head though both were still attached to my feet. David arrived by my side in a flurry of wet snow.

"You were leaning too far into the mountain," he admonished.

I didn't know what the hay he was talking about, but I felt frustrated and embarrassed.

"You know what, David?" I squinted up at him. "Thanks for your help but I think I'll just take my time. You go ahead."

"But you were doing so well," he said as he helped me up.

Sweet man. For the second time that day, I felt that someone else had more faith in me than I had in myself.

"You go and ski," I urged as I brushed myself off. Once he was out of sight, I could resort to my slide of shame on my derriere to where the slope was a manageable slant. David did not need to witness the Natasha Bottom Shuffle. "I'll just walk down," I told him.

"I can take your skis?" he suggested.

"Okay," I said, eager to be rid of the suicidal boards. David leaned over and disentangled the dangerous contraptions, effortlessly clicked them together and whipped them onto his shoulder.

"See you at the bottom!" he called behind him as he gracefully whooshed down the slope.

That night at The End of the Runway, as we all relished the warmth of the pub, I sat sandwiched between Stewart on one side and Cedric on the other as the Scot consumed inhuman amounts of "beer wi' whisky chasers." While Cedric talked excitedly about something to Stewart, who nodded and grinned, I was only able to catch every fifth word of their conversation. But I was content.

I silently thanked Stewart, David and my angels for the miracle of my having made it down the mountain in one piece without so much as a bruise—to my physical body anyway. My dignity was another matter. Still, both these men had inspired admiration in me. Against all odds and with positive thinking Stewart had found snow and he had fulfilled his vision of a ski-day with friends. And despite Cedric's lack of skiing prowess, unlike me, he had shown no fear. Was that bravery, copious amounts of whisky or sheer stupidity?

Maybe if I thought more positively and drank a bottle of Scotch for breakfast, I could become a fearless skier too?

Then again, maybe not.

12

FAMOUS PEOPLE DAY

LA LA Land
February 1981

"Praise be!" Franny, our Irish IFD, exclaimed, as she stood in front of us in the forward part of Cabin B reading the flight brief before our LAX-Bangor sector. "We've only got 112 pax, so we can take it easy today, girralls. However, we do have two celebrities, so we should try to give dem first class service. David McCallum and oh . . . let me see now," she said, flicking through her paperwork, "dat's roight, Henry Mancini."

"Oooh, David McCallum," I cooed to Maria, sitting next to me. "He was my teenage heartthrob."

Maria looked blank. "Who is he?"

"You know, Ilya Kuryakin in *The Man from U.N.C.L.E.*"

Maria shrugged. "I'm more interested in Henry Mancini," she whispered. "My Dad loves his music."

"Don't get too excited, Natasha," Franny said, having overheard my remark. "David McCallum's travelling wid his luverly wife and kids. And just a warning," she continued, "most of dese celebs are polite and gracious, but some of dem can be a handful." She grinned, her brown eyes twinkling. "Did yer hear dat we had John Cleese on our last LA? During de drinks service, he asked for one of de girrall's pinafores. As you know, dey barely cover our backsides, but on him—

he's about six foot five—it just about reached his navel. Well, he strutted up and down the aisle in the pinny doing his Ministry of Silly Walks and roaring at passengers, "What did you ask for? *A glass of water!* What do you think dis is? Bleedin' gift week?"

We all smiled, no doubt thinking how we would sometimes *love* to speak to passengers the way John Cleese did in his *Fawlty Towers* series. After dealing with the often-challenging public, watching his comedy program was pure therapy.

"How did the passengers react?" Maria asked.

"Are yer kiddin'? Dey loved it, but in de end, we had to ask him to sit down so we could do de service."

When the briefing was over, and we had all been tested on our emergency drills, we got on with our pre-flight duties. On these half-empty flights—as well as having an empty seat to nap in—we had more time to enjoy the sunrises and sunsets and converse with passengers, treating them like real people instead of like cattle who had to be merely fed and watered.

Once our "flying guests" were on board and we had all surreptitiously gawked at our celebs—David McCallum and family in the first row of Cabin A and Mr. Mancini on the other side—we looked forward to a relaxed flight. Even after the second meal service was cleared, we still had three and a half hours of flight time to fill, so I was happy when Franny suggested that—rather than make passengers come up to the carts in the forward and rear galleys to get a drink—that we could offer cocktails to them in their seats. But while I popped in and out of the galley fulfilling orders, some people were getting out of their cramped positions to stretch their legs or do yoga moves at the rear of the plane. Our two famous people remained in their seats, graciously accepting our attentive service, while others were striking up conversations with their fellow travellers.

Watching them, I wondered, how many romances began on flights? Despite the common belief that stewardesses were regularly propositioned by lusty male passengers, it rarely happened. With full loads we simply didn't have the time to chat, but during the snack service on this flight the tall, solidly built, blond-haired man seated beside Two Door Right had already attempted to engage me in conversation. Now as I stood in the forward galley making hot tea for a passenger, I saw out of the corner of my eye that he had stood up and was approaching me.

"Hi Natasha," he drawled. "I'm Roger."

Despite our first names being displayed on our name tags for all to see, it still unnerved me when passengers—without a formal introduction—casually addressed me by name. "Hello, Roger," I replied as I placed the cup of tea on a tray. "Just have to deliver this. I'll be right back."

"Sure," he said and stood back to let me pass.

"So," he asked me on my return, "what d'yer girls do when you're in LA?"

"Oh, you know, the usual," I told him. "Mainly Santa Monica and Venice Beach. There's not enough time to do too much else. On our direct London-LA flights, sometimes it's a min-rest of just twelve hours and then we're right back on the plane."

"Wow! That's fast. You must get tired."

"Comatose, actually."

He laughed, thinking I was joking. But after a sixteen-hour duty with just twelve hours in LA, which included the trip to and from the airport, and adjusting to an eight-hour time change, we barely had time to eat and sleep. And despite four days off after one of these marathons, I usually spent the first two days at home in a coma-like sleep.

"Do you ever go to concerts?" he asked.

"In LA? With our schedule? Not likely. Why?"

"Well," he said and puffed out his chest proudly, "I work security, and I know a lot of big names." As if he was slowly drawing a gun, he took his wallet from his back pocket and gave me a white card. *Roger Stewart, Security for the Stars* was written in plain black print with his phone number beneath. "Why don't you give me a call next time you're in LA, and I can take you to see some famous people?"

"Really?" I studied Roger's boyish face. Was he just full of it or . . .? "Okay, so who do you know?"

"Michael Jackson, Aretha Franklin, Pink Floyd, you know, those guys. But I also do private security, so I'm friends with quite a few celebs."

Was this All-American Boy bragging just to impress me, or did he really know all these people?

"Well, if I ever get more than twelve hours in LA, I will certainly give you a ring," I told him and put his card in my pinny pocket.

On each of my next three direct LGW-LAX trips, I did consider calling Roger, but as I had told him, our time there was too short. Then at the end of January an airline miracle happened. Thanks to the Flight Attendants Association protesting the brutality of our LA schedule, the company changed the length of our stay in LA from twelve hours to almost two days! Our return flight from LAX now departed in the evening of Day 2. Of course, our previous four-day-off recovery period post-LA was shortened to just two days off, but having more fun times in Santa Monica was preferable to being comatose in England.

When my first extended LA was rostered, I saw that the flight departed February 11 and returned on the morning of February 14. Darn! Since Jack and I were now on the outs after a big argument and not even a whiff of a fresh romance in sight, I knew that I would not be receiving any Valentine cards. Why was it that everyone else had a boyfriend except me? It wasn't true, of course, but I still felt justified in wallowing in self-pity. Well, at least I would be away from a rainy UK for two days and in sunny LA. Maybe, I thought, I *will* call Roger. But six weeks had elapsed since I had met him. Would he even remember me?

On February 13, the second day of my time in the City of Angels, with the Californian sunshine warming me through the glass of my Ramada Inn hotel room, I picked up the phone.

"Hello, Roger. It's Natasha Rosewood. Do you–"

"Hi, Natasha! Wow! It's so good to hear from you. Are you in LA?" Roger's boyish excitement took me by surprise.

"Y-yes, and I've got almost a whole day free. We fly out tonight but–"

"This is great timing! I have to go to Paramount today to see Henry Winkler. You could come with me, and if he's there, you could meet him."

Henry Winkler? Was he that older actor who played in war movies? No, that was Henry Fonda. Hmmm, Henry Winkler? I knew the name but when I searched my brain for a face to match the obviously famous person, I came up empty. Not willing to fess up to my ignorance, I simply replied, "I'd love to."

"Can you be ready in a half hour?" Roger asked.

"Sure," I drawled, unwittingly sounding like a true-blue American.

Now what should one wear in Hollywood? I had two choices: my Levis with a Marks & Sparks lacy top or a summer dress? I'm in America, I reminded myself. Jeans it is.

Thirty minutes later as I waited in the bright hotel lobby, Roger strode in, eyeing the hotel guests as if he was looking for a robbery in progress and ready to pull a weapon if needed. His face lit up when he saw me.

"Hi!" He took me by the arm and beamed at me as if we were old friends. "I'm parked out front." He pointed toward the street and ushered me through the glass hotel doors and into his humungous car as if he was *my* personal security guard. As we set off up Pico Boulevard, I took in once again the wide streets of Santa Monica with their tall palm trees, noting the famous peoples' street names.

"I didn't think I'd hear from you again," he said, sounding a little hurt.

"Well, this is the first long LA I've had so I couldn't call you before. Remember, min-rest?"

He nodded acceptance. "Oh, yeah. By the way, I'll have to sneak you into the studio, so let me do all the talking," he warned as the imposing archway of *Paramount Studios* came into view. "Security's tight here."

I couldn't hear the story Roger told the man on the gate to get me into the studios, but it worked. Once through, we immediately parked. "After Henry hired me for his security," Roger told me, taking a potted blue hydrangea plant from the back seat, "he referred me to another job, so I just want to give him this small gift as a thank you." As he talked, we walked past the massive sound stages. "You know, it's good business," he added conspiratorially as if I was also in "the biz."

We then turned down a street lined with small white cottages all joined to one another. "As well as acting, many of the stars have other companies" he told me, "and these are their offices." He reeled off names, some of whom I recognized and some I didn't. "They're always busy so I'm not sure if Henry will even be there, or that you'll be able to meet him, but hey, maybe you'll get lucky."

Suddenly Roger stopped in front of one of the cottages and knocked on the door. A tall, slim woman opened up. With her cropped black hair, cashmere sweater and pearls, she was all business though pleasant. "Can I help you?" she asked, eyeing Roger standing there clutching the small plant, while I, clad in my jeans and casual top, suddenly felt terribly underdressed.

"Hi, I'm Roger," he beamed, unabashed. "I did security for Henry a coupla weeks ago, and I've come to say a quick thank you for his referral and give him this plant. Is he in?"

Suddenly the woman lost her cool demeanor and appeared flustered. "Well, I . . .er . . . I don't know. I'm his new secretary and I don't know you." She was no doubt furiously struggling with the potential that we might be crazy fans or Henry's best friends. "What did you say your name was?"

"Roger. Roger Stewart."

"Well, er . . .yes. Why don't you come in and wait, and I'll ask Mr. Winkler if he can see you?"

She stepped back and let us enter the tiny living room area. Everything inside was just as white as the outside, even the furniture. The blue hydrangea would add needed color, I thought. I sank down onto a white two-seater couch. Roger sat beside me.

"He may not be able to see us," he said in hushed tones as if we were waiting in a doctor's office. "These people are always so–."

Suddenly there was a rush of energy and a handsome, dark-haired man burst into the room. "Hey!" He raised both arms and exclaimed as if he was greeting a long-lost friend, "Roger!"

Oh my god! Of course, I knew who this man was. Henry Winkler was *the Fonz!*

Roger stood up and shook hands with him, and then handed him the plant. As they exchanged pleasantries and thank yous, I also got up but stood rooted to the spot behind Roger, watching. Henry Winkler was much better looking than on TV, his eyes much bluer, his energy bigger. I inhaled. *The Fonz!*

Suddenly the star fixed his eyes upon me.

"Who's the pretty girl?" he asked Roger, sounding as if still in character. Then he reached for my right hand, picked it up and put it to his lips and kissed it.

I blushed, giggled . . . and couldn't think of a thing to say.

Roger came to my rescue. "Natasha's a flight attendant and is just in LA for a coupla days so I'm showing her around," he said. "I hope you don't mind. She wanted to meet you."

"Not a problem!" he said in his Fonz voice and beamed at me, flirting with me with those big blue eyes. Maybe the Fonz character *was* the real him?

I smiled inanely and just nodded.

"What do you think of LA?" he asked, trying to get some intelligent conversation out of me.

"Oh, I love it!" I said, cursing myself for my boring answer, but grateful that I was finally able to muster words.

"Yeah," he said, shifting his shoulders in his Fonz way. "It's co-ool."

The men chatted some more about another security gig for Roger, and then the Fonz said, "Hey, man. Great to see you, but I gotta . . ." He pointed both forefingers to the office from whence he had sprung, another Fonz gesture. "Hey, it was real nice meeting you," he said to me ever-so-graciously and disappeared into the room behind us.

Roger waved a hand at his back. "Thanks, Henry."

Outside in the sunlight again, I was a little stunned. Roger hadn't been bragging after all. He *really* did know people.

"Do you know the *Laverne & Shirley* show?" he asked as he steered me further along the pavement between more white offices.

"Oh, yes! We get that show in England." I stopped and gasped. "Are we going to meet them, too?"

He laughed. "No. Most of the shows are on hiatus now so they're not filming, but we can see their sets if you like?"

Five minutes later we were standing looking at the oh-so familiar *Laverne & Shirley* interior apartment layout. Without people, camera, lights and action, the set was eerily quiet, but I could still imagine Laverne's loud voice and the two actresses laughing and singing their song, *"We're going to make our dreams come true."*

"Com'on," Roger said and guided me to the next studio. "Do you recognize this?"

"Oh my God, it's the Mork and Mindy set!" For a moment I imagined Robin Williams leaping out from behind a door in his planet Ork suit, but again the stillness of the place without people spooked me—as if there had been a plague and everyone had died, leaving just a wisp of their energy and haunting laughter behind.

"Could you handle some lunch?" Roger, the oh-so-perfect tour guide asked as we retraced our steps to the road with all the white cottages. "The refectory is just up here."

We found a table in the sun on the restaurant patio, which was the studio canteen for executives, actors, producers, directors and crew. Roger sat facing me and from his strategic viewpoint, he could see who was coming and going. Between mouthfuls of his tuna sandwich, his eyes darted around the tables, and as surreptitiously as possible, he reeled off the names of the well-knowns who came in, very few of whom I recognized. Was Roger more starstruck than I was? And why, I found myself wondering, do we go gaga over famous people anyway? They were just humans with more . . . something. Maybe that something was the big mystery and the big attraction. We all wanted a little more of that . . . something.

"Who are your favorite stars?" Roger enquired as we lingered over coffee.

There were so many. "Well, I love Gregory Peck. He's not only gorgeous, but he seems like a good man."

Roger nodded. "He lives in Beverly Hills, and I have to go over there this afternoon."

Meeting him would be beyond exciting, but if I was speechless with the Fonz, I would be apoplectic in front of Gregory Peck. "Do you know him?" I breathed.

"I kinda know him, but actually I have to drop in at Zsa Zsa's place—"

I gasped. "You mean . . . Zsa Zsa . . . Gabor?"

"Yes," Roger said, holding up a hand and smiling. "But don't get too excited. She probably won't be home. These people are–"

"I know." I grinned. "Always busy."

"Right."

As Roger drove the wide, palm-tree-lined streets leading to Beverly Hills, I began to fear that he might be developing a romantic interest in me. Much as I enjoyed his well-mannered, all-American personality, I could not return his affections. I still felt that Jack and I would make amends so I hoped Roger would be okay with "just friends."

In Beverly Hills he sounded like a professional tour guide as he drove up and down the verdantly treed roads, pointing out who lived where and how many rooms, gold-plated taps, Porsches, swimming pools and marriages they had all acquired. Suddenly he pulled over to the side of the road. "Wait there," he commanded and leapt out of the car.

Ten minutes later he returned and handed me an envelope. Inside was a black and white photo. When I pulled it out, I saw Gregory Peck smiling at me. In the bottom right corner in a flowing hand was written *To Natasha, Gregory Peck.*

"Oh, be still my beating heart," I said, clutching the photo to my chest, and even though *I* was aware that his secretary—and not Mr. Peck—had more than likely autographed his photo, I chose to believe the latter. I beamed back at Gregory and then at Roger. "Thank you!"

"Your wish is my command, fair lady." These very English words sounded strange in his American drawl, but still touching.

"You are too kind, sir."

At the bottom of the hill Roger pulled into the driveway of a white mansion, its ornate cornices reminding me of the decorative frosting on a wedding cake. Running parallel to the straight driveway to the house was a massive flowerbed, abundant with tropical flowers. Once out of the car, I stood and surveyed the rich display of colors.

"Wow!" I said, again adopting Roger's vocabulary.

"Over here," he called.

I turned and saw that he was inserting a key into a garage door. I went over to join him.

"Is this . . .?" I asked.

"Yes. Zsa Zsa's house."

"You have a key to her house?"

"She's friends with my parents and I do some landscaping for her and her husband."

The garage door opened upwards, and we stepped into a short shadowy space where we faced another garage-type door. Roger unlocked this second one and we stepped into a walled courtyard. To our left was a three-car garage, the stable-like doors were open, displaying two shiny Bentleys, one blue, one white. As we stood in the centre of the enclosed area, we could see into the kitchen of the ivy-covered house. Visible through the window was a tall, slim woman, washing something at the sink. She waved at Roger and then poked her head out of the door.

"Hello, Roger! Do you want to see Mr. O'Hara?"

Roger nodded.

"Michael O'Hara is Zsa Zsa's sixth husband," he explained. "He's a lawyer, and he wants to discuss a landscaping job. We won't be long. I doubt that Zsa Zsa's here."

Roger didn't need to apologize. I was honored just to be there, agog with the beauty of the place.

"By the way," he added, "that lady in the kitchen used to be Joan Crawford's secretary."

Joan Crawford! *Mommie Dearest.* I shuddered at how her daughter's book had echoed my own alcoholic, abusive mother's behavior, except my mother wasn't famous—just infamous.

Just then I heard a grating noise and saw that in front of us, set into a tall brick wall topped with meandering clematis, there was an elaborately patterned wrought-iron gate. A small blonde woman had appeared on the other side of it, her outline barely visible through the intricate metal design.

Slowly she opened the gate and stepped into the courtyard. Oh my God. It was Zsa Zsa!

As she approached, I noted her legendary blonde hair piled high on her head and how the soft pink cardigan set and pearls she was wearing lit up her peaches and cream complexion. A radiant glow emanated from her petite frame so that she shone like the star she was.

Seeing Roger, she beamed and raised her arms in the air in greeting, her long pink nails pointing skyward. "Rrroger! Da-a-ahlink!"

He grinned and waited for her to come closer.

"You look like you've lost weight," he said, appraising her. No doubt, this was *the* thing to say to Hollywood stars.

"Oh, not really, dahlink," she said, brushing her skirt as if brushing her stomach away, "but ssank you. You are too-oo kind."

While they talked, I stared, fascinated. What struck me about both the Fonz and Zsa Zsa was how much more stunning they were in person. Both emanated some kind of light, an aura that wasn't apparent on screen. Perhaps their radiance was lost in translation, their powerful energy diluted between celluloid and real life.

Suddenly she turned to me. "Vot a pretty girl!"

I smiled, but I wanted the ground to open and swallow me up. In the presence of her exquisite elegance and with me dressed in jeans and a top, I felt like a crumb. Why hadn't I worn a summer dress? I mumbled a humble, "Thank you."

Roger explained my reason for being with him.

"Are you stayingk a long time in LA?" she asked me.

"No, sadly. We're flying home tonight," I told her, pulling a sad face.

"Yes, it's beeyootiful here, isn't it? I luff LA. Vell . . ." She raised her arms again and gave Roger a hug. "Enjoy, dahlinks!" She turned to go, then hesitated. "Oh, Michael is just finishink a phone call to London. He vill be out soon. I am so-o-o sorry," she added, addressing me and smiling, "but I must rrrush."

As soon as Zsa Zsa had sashayed into the house, a tall, slim, elegant man in a dark suit appeared and began speaking to Roger about plans for their property. He barely acknowledged me—for which I was grateful. I was still reeling from my meeting with the famous Zsa Zsa.

"Wow, you're so lucky that you got to meet them today!" Roger exclaimed as we drove back toward Santa Monica and the hotel. "It's so rare to actually see any celebs."

"My grandmother always accused me of having the luck of the Irish," I told him, "but it doesn't always work." I paused. "Thank you so much, Roger."

He beamed and puffed out his chest. "Too bad I can't take you to dinner. It *is* Valentine's Day tomorrow."

Oh no. Why did he have to go and spoil things? I hoped he wasn't thinking what I thought he might be thinking. "Yes, too bad, but I do have to get back to the hotel."

"I guess it'll just have to wait until next time, huh?" Roger added, glancing at me.

"'Fraid so," I said, grateful that I would be dodging a romantic bullet. For today anyway.

"When's your next LA?" he asked just as we pulled up to the hotel.

"Not sure. Our new rosters aren't out yet."

"If you are here mid-June, guess who's in town?"

I shook my head.

Roger beamed. "Elton John! And I'm doing his security. I could take you to the concert with me and then take you backstage to meet him."

"Wow!" I said out loud, horrified that I was now officially speaking American. "I'd love that."

After he gallantly helped me out of the car, Roger embraced me in a bear hug. To my relief, he did not attempt anything more.

"See you in June," I said as I waved and left him standing by his car, watching me.

Still on a high, I found it impossible to nap pre-flight, and without sleep I was not looking forward to the ten-hour night flight back to Gatwick. With luck, we would have a light load, and the passengers would all nod off. Should I tell the other girls about my "famous people" day, I wondered, or would it just sound like bragging?

By 1900 hours our DC-10 crew were all aboard, the aircraft isolated out on the tarmac, away from the terminal. As we carried out our pre-flight routines: emergency drill testing, flight briefing, emergency equipment checks and organizing the catering, Two-Door Left was open. Though it was dark outside, I inhaled the California air wistfully. Going back to a miserable wintry England and a loveless Valentine's Day was not a happy prospect.

As part of my preflight duties, I had to stock the toilets with dry goods, Kleenex, hand towels and toilet paper. I was just finishing dressing the port loo next to the flight deck when I suddenly heard excited voices in the forward galley. I peered down the aisle. Three of the girls were standing there gazing in my direction and giggling. Maria had something in her hand. What was all the fuss about?

"It's for you, Natasha!" Maria teased, waving a large white envelope. "From your l-e-r-r-vure," she announced in her comical Franglais accent.

As I didn't have a lover, and was curious, I abandoned what I was doing and walked down the aisle to meet them. I glanced at the envelope. She was right. *Natasha* was written on the outside.

"Your boyfriend delivered it," Janet cooed.

"What? I don't have a boyfriend, or a *le-r-vure*," I told them.

"Well, *he* thinks you do. Open it!" Maria urged.

I unsealed the envelope, puzzled. The three girls leaned in, peering over my shoulders, shamelessly nosy. Inside was a card featuring a massive picture of a cuddly bunny rabbit clutching a big heart, reminding me of Thumper from the *Bambi* movie. Sweet. The words, *Happy Valentine* were in a balloon coming out of the rabbit's mouth.

As I opened the 9" x18" card, the girls huddled even closer. Inside, the greeting read *You make my heart thump.* Then in large, slanted handwriting, he had written: *Missing you already. Until the next time. All my Love, Roger.*

Uh-oh. Houston, we have a problem.

"Aw-w-w!" "How sweet!" "Who's Roger?" "Oh, that's so romantic!" the girls chorused.

"But how did he get airside?" I asked Maria, puzzled and marveling at Roger's ingenuity. LAX airport was not noted for being lax on security. "And how did he know who to give it to?"

"You should marry that man!" the girls continued. "Oh, I wish someone would do that for me!" "I'm jealous!"

But in answer to my question Maria merely shrugged. "No idea, but the ground engineer told me the poor smitten man is still standing over there by the fence. You should wave to him."

"Wha-a-a-t?" I stepped up to the open door and peered across the tarmac. In the distance, just beyond the perimeter fence, some yellow lights shone on a vague black outline. I waved into the darkness, not knowing if he could see me or not. Maria stepped up behind me and waved, too. "Hi, Roger!" she called and giggled.

Roger could make anything happen, it seemed, and I admired that. Too bad I wasn't in love with him.

As I retreated into the aircraft to don hat and gloves ready for boarding, the girls still swarmed around me and plied me with more questions. "Who is he?" "Where did you meet?" "What did you do on your date?" "Does he have a brother?"

What the hell, I thought. They're already jealous. Maybe I'll just spill the beans and give them every little detail of my famous people day.

"Well, I met Roger–."

"Passengers!" Franny called over the PA.

Groaning, the girls immediately dispersed to stand at attention at their designated doors. My story of meeting famous people would have to wait.

"And by de way," Franny added while still on the PA. "We have a handsome TV celebrity coming on board. Cabin B. You single girls, behave yerselves. Try not to go gaga over him when you see who tis."

Hmmm? I thought. Maybe with a bit more luck of the Irish, my famous people day wasn't over yet?

13

AND THE INFAMOUS NIGHT

Feb 1981
Los Angeles – London Gatwick

"Can oy sit there?" the man with the Australian accent asked me just after take-off. Boyish-faced, blond-haired, short, stocky and a little scruffy, the man who had made the request appeared to have been travelling for not just days but weeks. He was pointing to the very last row of seats on our DC-10.

My colleague, Maria, and I were manhandling a fully laden drinks cart from the rear galley into the aisle. Our service strategy on these late day departures from LA to LGW was to offer drinks followed as quickly as possible by dinner so passengers could get to sleep. Hopefully, they would then stay asleep until our breakfast service, not long before our descent into Gatwick. As a result, we really didn't want anyone sitting in that last row because, when the plane was not fully loaded, we wanted that row for ourselves. On these long, long inbound return LAs—instead of being propped up on a metal bar box or on a jump seat nodding off in front of our passengers—we much preferred to rest in a comfortable passenger seat where we could grab a precious, and more dignified, 40 winks.

I waved my arm behind me at the rear cabin, which was only half full. "There are lots more seats to choose from. . .?" I suggested, hoping he would take my hint. For emphasis, I added, "And you know, our bar carts often bump into this seat and wake whoever's sleeping there." I shrugged the French way. "We just can't help it. These carts have minds of their own."

"Ah, don't frit, girls!" he responded cheerily, plonking himself in the back row. "I know you ladies loike the last row fer yer kip. When it's toyme, I'll move. Nah worries."

A well-travelled man with a sense of humor, I thought, liking him instantly.

With the plane sparsely populated, we were quickly able to provide drinks to the rear and most of the middle cabin. We soon reached row 18 and before looking down at the passenger in the center, I asked, "Would you like something to. . .?" And then I saw him. The strikingly handsome man in the aisle seat, 18D, was our celebrity, the dashing actor from one of my favourite TV shows.

"Oh . . .it's you!" I exclaimed. Then, blushing, I remembered to revert to my demure professional composure. "Sorry, sir. What can I get you?"

"Well, ladies first," he said in that oh-so-familiar suave voice as he pointed to the mature, female seated across the aisle. The blonde, voluptuous and overly made-up woman looked up at me, insolence in her body language. Was she model, actress or high-class hooker? I wondered. *Vixen* is the word that came to my mind. Was she going to cause trouble?

"What would you like to drink?" I asked her. "The gentleman is buying," I added facetiously. Drinks were complimentary.

"Give me a rum and coke, would ya, doll?" The chewing gum was missing for the full effect, but she was not high class anything. With her bright red lipstick and her V-necked, faux leopard, skin-tight sweater clinging to her very exposed breasts, she could have been going for a Marilyn Monroe imitation, but she didn't have any of

Monroe's class. My older, chauvinistic brother would have quipped, "If she had brains, she'd be dangerous." Unfortunately, there was something about this woman that suggested she *did* have brains, and she *was* dangerous.

"I'll have the same," Mr. Suave told me.

"Give us two more of those, would ya, hun?" Marilyn pointed to the rum bottles, her red fingernails fluttering over the miniatures' drawer. "We're thoysty!" she said and giggled.

After the two had their supply of drinks, and with that service completed, Maria and I returned to the rear.

"Did you talk to Mr. Dream Boat?" Sandra, who was manning the rear galley, asked us as we pushed the cleared-off cart back into its stowage.

"Who?" I responded. "Oh, you mean, Mr. Suave? Yes."

"What's he like?" Sandra's eyes were huge and dreamy.

"He seems very nice. A lot like the character he plays, a gentleman."

"O-o-oh." Sandra sighed, and just as I had done earlier about Gregory Peck, she clutched a hand to her heart, wistful.

"I hate to burst your bubble, Sandra," Maria told her, "but I think he has a girlfriend."

"That woman in 18C? That's not his girlfriend! She moved in on him even before we'd done the demo. Tart!"

Just then the smell of hot dinners permeated our nostrils as the meal cart was brought down from the front. Maria and I quickly loaded bottles of red and white wine, plastic wine glasses and a jug of water on top, then pulled the fully laden trolley out into the cabin. As we passed the first three rows of seats from the rear, Mr. Australia stirred. Sleepily, he sat up and put his lap tray down.

"Would you like red or white wine with your dinner, sir?"

"Nah, I'm alroyght. Just water, thanks."

I handed him the plastic glass. "Nah worries," I teased him.

As we worked our way up the aisle, we could see that our passengers were already getting sleepy, and the cabin was quiet. When we neared row 20, we heard loud voices and raucous laughter just ahead. I glanced up the aisle. The noise was coming from row 18. Peeking out above the seat next to Mr. Suave, I could see the top of "Marilyn's" blonde curls. Having moved over to the center, she was now leaning into him, talking loudly. Were they drunk already?

I sighed. Drunks were our worst nightmare, especially on nightflights. Give us a mechanical problem over a drunk passenger any day, I thought. At least, if it's technical, it's a problem to be solved. Drunks, on the other hand, were an unknown quantity.

As we arrived at their row, Mr. Suave was already slouched in his seat, his tie loosened, laughing and slurring his words. Marilyn was snuggling into him, giggling and nibbling his earlobe.

"Sir, would you prefer chicken or fish for dinner?" I asked.

She whispered something to him, and he looked up at me, his eyes now a little puffy and strangely dilated. "No dinner," he slurred. "Jush bring us more of those drinks, pleash."

We weren't allowed to serve more alcohol to someone who was already inebriated, but to avoid ugly confrontations, we employed a little trick. "Sir," I said, "if you can just wait until we've finished serving these dinners, I will bring you both drinks. Two rum and cokes?"

"Yesh, shank you," he said, barely able to focus. She, I noticed, was now not only nibbling on his ear, but also tracing those red fingernails along his inner thigh, going northward. He was grinning inanely.

"Well, it won't be long," I told Sandra when we returned our mostly empty meal cart to her galley, "before another couple join the

Mile-High Club. And you won't like it. It's your friend, Mr. Suave. Marilyn's getting her claws into him as we speak."

"Ugh. Disgusting!" Sandra shuddered, casting a glance at the loo, not three feet from where we were standing. "Well," she huffed, "if that's the kind of woman he likes, he's no hero of mine!"

As Maria and I stood waiting in the rear galley for Sandra to refill the coffee and tea pots, while keeping an eye on the cabin, we were not surprised to see Marilyn come sashaying down the aisle, closely followed by a staggering Mr. Suave, using the seat backs to steady himself. For a drunk, I thought, something about his body language was off.

Once they arrived at the rear, Marilyn saw us standing there watching. When we exchanged looks and she realized that we knew exactly what they were about to do, she changed tactics. She turned around, her back toward us, and put a hand on his chest. "Hon, wait there a sec. I won't be a minute," she whispered, grinning naughtily. Then before she opened the toilet door, she gave us a whadda-you-looking-at stare.

Confused, he leaned against the galley bulkhead for support and muttered to her back, "Ah, okay? So, I'll . . . I'll wait for you here then?"

"Yes, that's right, hon. You just wait there." She winked at him, disappeared into the loo and closed the door.

He glanced over at us, not sure what to do. Then he smiled sheepishly, staggered past the loo and over to the rear door and, with head drooping, slouched against the rear bulkhead. Feeling awkward, Maria and I each took a tray of creamers and sugars in one hand and a coffee pot in the other and left poor Sandra in the rear galley to either make idle conversation with Mr. Suave or ignore him.

Mr. Australia was, I noticed, gone from the back-row seat already. Had he also sensed what was about to happen in the toilet just behind him, or had he vacated on our behalf?

When I had finished serving second teas and coffees, instead of returning to the rear, I chose to head to the forward galley. Maria joined me there.

"Do you girls mind if we hang out here for a while," I asked the forward crew who were just setting up a bar cart for movie time. "Our famous actor is about to do coitus in the rear loo, and we really don't want to hear it."

"Been a while, has it?" Franny smiled at me as she hit the lift button to send garbage down to the lower galley.

"Yes, as it happens," I said, a little too defensively, reminded of my recent big fall-out with Jack and my hopeful-hopeless yo-yo emotions about Jose. "But that's not the reason. There's something about that woman I really don't like."

"Ach, he's a big boy," Franny scoffed. "I'm sure he can take care of himself, to be sure."

Maria giggled. "I hope he's using an Irish condom then."

"And what's dat?" Franny asked, trying not to roll her eyes at yet another Irish joke.

"They're double . . . to be sure, to be sure." Maria grinned.

Franny's face creased into a big smile. "Now dat's funny!"

Suddenly Mr. Australia arrived in the forward galley. "Any chance of a noyce cuppa? Outta the tap," he said, pointing to the hot water urn. This man was obviously familiar with the luke-warm tea that came from the pots.

"Of course," I said, grabbing two plastic cups and insulating them with a napkin. "So, are you on your way from Australia?" I enquired, always interested in passenger stories.

"Nah. I've been in Choyna fer the last six months."

"China! Hong Kong or mainland?"

"Mainland. Shanghai, Beijing. Oy travelled all over."

As I handed Mr. Australia his steaming cuppa, I saw over his shoulder that Marilyn was returning to her seat, groping her way up the aisle, using the headrests for support. Disheveled, she stopped halfway, pulled her sweater down and swiped her long, curly blonde hair over her shoulder. When she arrived at her original seat, she sank into it. Mr. Suave was nowhere to be seen.

I turned my attention back to my new Australian friend. "But wasn't it scary in China?" I asked, remembering the Pearl S. Buck books I had read about the revolution and the strict communism that followed.

"Ah, nah." He beamed, handsome when he smiled. "The people are beeeyootiful. Beeyootiful! I mean, they'll still shoot yer as soon as look at yer, but nah, the people are beeyootiful."

I wasn't sure I understood his logic, but I was grateful to be having this conversation to keep me from returning to the rear. "So, where did you stay? In a camp or . . ."

"Well, they called it a hotel, but I shot noyne rats in me room one noyght."

"Nine!" I shuddered. "And is it true about the Chinese airlines? I've heard some horror stories about them not being safe?"

"Oh, yayer." He pointed to our passenger seats. "You girls 'ave got it made in the shade. This plane is luxurious. In Choyna, we didn't 'ave seatbelts. Hell, we didn't even 'ave seats. On one airloyne, we was sitting on wooden boards and there was just a rope for a seatbelt and moyne was all frayed!"

"And I thought my previous airline was bad," I told him, handing him his tea.

"Thanks." He took a sip. "But you girls are fantastic!"

"Oh . . . Why do you say that?"

"I dunno 'ow yer do it, dealing with all these nutcases. Like those two who snuck into the back loo." He snickered. "Loyke we don't know what they're up to."

"Yup," I sighed. "You just never know what human beings will do."

"Look's loyke she's back in 'er seat already," he said, nodding in Marilyn's direction. "I guiss that means it's safe for me to go back." He grinned knowingly. "But I'll move from yer seat now if yer loyke. Must be toyme fer yer break soon. And I need a kip, too."

Who would have "guissed" that an Australian Bruce would be so considerate of the Sheilas?

"Thank you!" I said, impressed.

Franny then made her PA announcing that the upcoming entertainment was *Faulty Towers* and asked passengers to put their window shades down. As I headed to the rear and passed Marilyn, I saw that she was staring out of the window. Mr. Suave still hadn't returned to his seat.

"Can I get you a water?" I offered. She must be thirsty after all that activity.

"No, hun. Gimme another rum and coke, would ya?"

"And for your friend?"

"Oh," she waved a dismissive hand at his empty seat, flashing those nails. "Nah, I dunno. I think he's sitting somewhere else."

Coitus wasn't good then?

Except for the flickering light from the movie screens at the front of each cabin, the plane was now shrouded in darkness. When I served Marilyn her drink, using our trick—mostly iced coke with a little bit of rum laced around the rim of the plastic cup—I cast a glance around the rear cabin. In the dark shadows, with some passengers' heads already laid back, snoring or slumped to the side, I still could not see Mr. Suave. Maybe he had escaped up front, as far away from Marilyn as possible. Wham bam, thank you, ma'am and . . . next?

When I reached the rear of the aircraft, ready for my break, I saw that Mr. Australia had indeed moved his things from the last aisle seat. Maria was already on the far side snuggled under a blanket with eyes closed.

I sank down gratefully into my resting spot and replayed my exciting "famous people" day. Then I remembered Roger's unsettling declaration of love. What would I do about that? While I really wanted to meet Elton John, would it be fair to keep seeing Roger when I knew I wasn't interested? Heavy eyelids and sleep soon overtook my addled brain.

"Excuse me! Miss? Miss? Excuse me!" Someone was lightly shaking my shoulder.

I came to, trying to remember where I was. Oh yes. Back of a DC-10 with a middle-aged woman peering into my face.

"I'm sorry to disturb you, but I think there's a problem in this toilet?" She pointed to the starboard loo.

"What?" I sat up, slowly coming back to consciousness. "What's happening?" I asked, undoing my seatbelt.

"I keep hearing noises," she said, distraught, and put a hand on her cheek in horror as if it was a helpless child imprisoned in the toilet. "It doesn't sound good. Like a man is moaning. And it's been occupied for ever-so long now. More than an hour."

Oh no! Were Marilyn and Mr. Suave back at it? Or had he found someone else?

While I was tempted to say; Don't worry, Madam. It's just some people having sex, to placate her I got up out of my seat and stepped over to the toilet door. The slot was red, indicating that the loo was, indeed, occupied. Then I put my head against the flimsy fiberboard and listened. Sure enough, there was a low moaning sound. A male voice. He could be having sex . . . alone. I knocked gently on the door.

"Is everything all right?" I asked tentatively, desperately hoping I wasn't spoiling a moment.

The moaning got louder. Was it a pleasurable sound or someone in pain? I couldn't tell.

"Just a minute," I said, turning back to the woman who was hovering nervously behind me. "I need to check on something."

Leaving her standing, still with hand-on-cheek, I went up to see if Marilyn was in her seat. She was. Slumped over, mouth open, drooling and lightly snoring. Not a pretty sight.

I returned to the rear galley. Sandra was chatting to a little old lady on the port side.

"Sorry to interrupt, Sandra," I said, butting into their conversation, "but the starboard loo has been occupied for the last hour and I can hear moaning. I just wondered if you . . . you know . . . had seen anything?"

She turned away from the woman and in hushed tones said, "If you mean Mr. Suave, I haven't seen him since he slipped in there with that tramp. They made a helluva racket. Disgusting!"

"Something's wrong," I said. "She's back in her seat, but he's not. We *have* to open that door."

Sandra's face fell. "What do you mean—we?"

"Please let's do it together," I begged. There were so many possible ugly scenarios to discover. He could be masturbating, puking, dead, having a heart attack, foaming at the mouth with a seizure or—worse—he could be naked.

"Okay." Sandra sighed. She made her apologies to the little old lady and nudged me forward.

"You first, though." she said.

"Madam," I urged the nervous woman, "it would probably be best if you return to your seat now." No need for her to be traumatized by God-knows-what as well.

I reached for my ballpoint pen hooked onto the collar of my dress and lifted the metal flap with *Toilet* written on it, inserted the pen's nib into the small hole and slid it backwards. The red *Occupied* sign now read *Vacant*. Behind me I heard Sandra inhale as I put my hand on the door handle.

"Ready?" I asked.

She exhaled. "Go!"

I pulled the door open.

"Oh . . . my . . . god!" Sandra mumbled behind me, in horror and shock.

I could only stare and at the same time wished that I was not seeing what I was seeing.

Mr. Suave was Mr. Suave no more. He was sitting, slouched, almost lying on his back, his ever-so-expensive suit jacket hanging off his shoulders. His pristine white shirt was ripped open exposing a matt of black hair, while his pink tie hung loosely to the side. His lower extremities, however, were completely exposed as his suit pants and his white knickers were coiled around his ankles. With puffy red eyes half-open, he was waving his arms as if fending off an evil entity and moaning, "No, No! Keep them away. Help! Oh god. You monsters!"

I slammed the door shut. Sandra and I stared at each other.

"Well, I don't want to touch him," she said. "Do you?"

I could only shake my head, trying to get the vision out of my mind. If I got any sleep tonight, nightmares would be on the agenda.

Nervous Nellie had not budged from her spot. "Well?" she asked, "Is he okay?"

"Er . . . er . . . we're not sure yet, Madam." I responded, still in shock. "But thank you. You did the right thing. Now, please return to your seat and let us deal with it."

"Oh . . . Well . . . if you think. . ."

"Yes, I do," I said and nudged her forward.

Then I had an idea. "Wait here," I told Sandra. "I'm going to get help."

Sandra nodded mutely, grateful that I, at least, had a plan.

The movie was still playing, so if we could do this while the cabin was in darkness, I thought, we might save Mr. Not-So-Suave a few indignities and the passengers some trauma.

"Hello-o-o." Just as I had been woken up by Nervous Nellie, I was now doing the same thing to Mr. Australia in 14C. "So sorry to wake you," I whispered, as he finally stirred.

"Yayer." He sat up confused and rubbed his eyes.

"I'm so sorry . . . Mr. . . . er?"

"Ah . . . Bruce. Just call me Bruce," he mumbled, still sleepy.

You're kidding? What were the chances of an Australian man being called Bruce? High, apparently. "Well, Bruce, we have a big problem. You remember the couple that were . . . you know . . . down the back?"

"Oh, yayer." He grinned, coming awake. What's up?"

"Well, the . . . gentleman is . . . somewhat indisposed in the loo. We thought if you could help us put his pants back on, we could get him out of there and into a seat before all the lights and action start." Although Bruce was on the short side, he looked as if he could handle anything. "You see," I continued, "he's very famous, and it would be . . ."

"Embarrassin'?" He laughed, now wide awake. "Well, this is one for the books, eh?" he said, undoing his seatbelt. "Alroyght, let's do it!"

When we arrived at the back, some passengers were already grouped on the port side, whispering amongst themselves and tittering. Uh-oh. How did they know?

"Bruce here is going to help us with him," I told Sandra who was still standing guard.

She opened the door just wide enough so Bruce could slide inside, and we wouldn't have to be retraumatized. We heard the Australian whistle as he got the full picture of Mr. Not-So-Suave's situation.

"Well, you're a soyght for sore eyes, mate?" we heard him say to the still-moaning man. "Com'on, let's get yer dressed, shall we? Easy does it. There you go."

After a lot of banging, shuffling and more moaning noises, Bruce tapped on the door. "Okay, ladies. He's decent now. You can open up."

Sandra pulled the door open very slowly. The formerly classy actor was still disheveled and hanging off Bruce's shoulder. His bloodshot and dilated eyes darted from side to side, and he was pleading with Bruce, "Don't let them get me. Don't let those green monsters get me!"

"It's the men in white coats you should be afraid of," Sandra mumbled.

Was he drunk? Was he having a nervous breakdown? Or had he done some drugs with Marilyn?

"Where shall I put 'im, girls?" Bruce asked.

"Right here," I said, removing my blanket from my seat. I leaned forward to help, but Bruce said, "It's alroyght. I've got 'im."

Somehow, even in the tight space, our hero was able to maneuver the limp actor into the last center row, aisle seat. I noted that as well as pulling his trousers back on, Bruce had also straightened his tie, making him appear almost decent again. As soon as he was seated, Mr. Not-So-Suave's head fell to one side, and he fell asleep.

"Thank you so much, Bruce!" I exclaimed while fastening the actor into his seat and laying my blanket across his chest. "We'll be calling an ambulance for him at Gatwick."

"Poor bloke!" Bruce said, looking down at the now-peaceful man, "I reckon 'e's 'ad 'is drink doctored, and I bet it was that Sheila. If it was LSD, 'e'll be 'aving nightmares for a long toyme."

"He won't be the only one," Sandra and I said in unison.

Bruce studied the sleeping man. "So, 'e's famous, is he?"

"Well, he was," I commented. "But if anyone hears about this, he'll just be infamous."

Bruce nodded. "Mum's the word," he said and set off up the aisle to find his seat again.

14

SURPRISE!

LA or JFK?
July 1981

I should have known better. As a flight attendant I knew getting excited about an upcoming flight was as silly as planning a wedding in England in April and hoping it wouldn't rain. Roger, my new Californian friend had promised me that, as my next trip to LA coincided with an Elton John concert there, he would not only take me to the event but also escort me backstage to meet the British pop icon. After he had introduced me to two celebrities on my last LA flight, there was no reason to doubt his word. But it wasn't Roger who would disappoint me.

"Your LAX is changed," the young man in Crewing announced over the phone, "and we've put you on a two-day JFK departing 1300 hours tomorrow." Although the male staff in Crewing were in their early twenties, barely full-grown men, they had already acquired the "God Syndrome," knowing that they could wield the ultimate power over our lives and often our loves.

New York! I groaned inwardly. "But–" I started to whine about meeting Elton John in the hope he would feel my pain and still keep me on the LA.

"Sorry," he interrupted, "no changes."

Elton John's song came to mind: *Sorry seems to be the hardest word*. . . And now it was.

New York was one of our airline's destinations that I either dreaded or loved. With that city's crime rate at its height in 1981, even before leaving my peaceful home for Gatwick, I would psych myself up to deal with the constant threats we faced in the Big Apple. On other occasions, I looked forward to the noisy vibrancy of the city, the smells of so many ethnic foods emanating from the huge variety of restaurants as well as all the diverse and interesting people we encountered. Though I was still sad about missing my meeting with Elton, I took a leaf out of a Monty Python script and decided to "look on the broight soide of loife."

As we drove over New York's Brooklyn bridge with a soft pink sky casting a glassy, coppery light across the Manhattan skyline, I had a feeling that our two-day stay at the Doral Inn on Lexington was going to be. . . different. Juliana, a stewardess I had befriended on the flight, sat beside me on the transport bus from JFK Airport. She told me how, pre-Laker, she had been a dancer on cruise ships and had spent a lot of time in Brazil teaching passengers how to samba.

"I love South Americans," I said wistfully, thinking of Jose.

"Me, too," she agreed, her brown eyes twinkling. "They're so much more alive than stodgy old English people." She studied me. "Uh-oh. Are you in love with one?"

I smiled. "Is it that obvious?"

"Do tell!"

"Later," I whispered, not wanting some of the crew to hear.

When we arrived at the Doral Inn hotel, the vibrancy of the lobby once again reminded me of those 1930s' Hollywood movies where people bustled in and out, phones rang loudly, and everyone talked in urgent tones, all in a great hurry, the polar opposite of the dignified hush of high-end British hotels. Our crew of ten girls clustered in a mass of bright red together with our three flight deck crew—smart in their black uniforms—and waited patiently for the front desk clerks to issue us our room keys.

During the staying-alive-in-New-York pep talk we had been given during our training, we had been warned not to mention our room numbers while in public. Mine, I noted this time was 802. Many Laker girls refused to stay in certain rooms on the eighth floor because, according to rumors, three of them were haunted. But I couldn't remember which ones they were now, and I was too tired to care.

Once we all had our keys, Ritch Kievers, our popular, white-haired captain—ignoring all the security rules—announced to the crew while we were still in the lobby, "Okay, listen up! I want an early night so if you want to get paid, meet me in my room in 15 minutes. Room 915."

"Com'on, chuck," Julianna said, urging me toward the elevator that would take us up to our floor. Uncomfortable being anywhere alone in this hotel, especially in the clean but shabby lift, I was grateful for my new friend's company. When we arrived at our rooms, we followed the usual protocol before entering: *Unlock door, prop suitcase against door to keep it ajar as escape route. When entering room, be on alert for possible intruder. Look under bed, in closet, behind shower curtain and behind doors. When certain no one is in room, bring in suitcase and engage all three locks.* Living in a quiet Sussex town, these precautions had at first seemed a little over-dramatic, but after two years of flying to New York, I understood.

Twenty minutes later Julianna and I, having shed our uniforms, showered and changed into civvies, were now in the captain's room with the rest of the crew. After he had handed out our flight pay in US dollars, I folded the bills and put them in the small black crocheted purse I used for down-route as it was just big enough to hold a room key, two Kleenex and a lipstick. We had been asked not to linger, so unlike our usual post-flight routine where over a leisurely drink we swapped a litany of jokes and caught up on the latest airline gossip, we now downed a quick cocktail and left.

"I'm *hungry*," Julianna declared. "Shall we just go down to the bar?"

The other popular choice was to go to the deli on the corner, but the hookers who frequented the sidewalk outside the hotel often challenged us with "Get off our patch, bitches!" I wasn't in the mood for any confrontations that night.

"Good idea," I responded to Julianna's suggestion. "I could murder a bowl of their French onion soup."

The first officer and two more of the girls trailed behind us as we entered the elegant but shadowy restaurant. Although many of the tables were empty, we opted to sit on the high stools at the circular wrap-around bar. I placed my little black purse on my lap, but then decided that it would be too easy to steal, so I looped the strap around my ankle and placed the purse on the foot-rest underneath the bar. The purse was black so no one would see it, I reasoned. Soon all five of us were tucking into appetizers and engaged in each others' stories.

When it was time to pay my bill an hour later, I reached down and groped in the darkness for my purse. To my surprise, there was nothing wrapped around my ankle and nothing on the footrest. Had my bag fallen off? I slipped off my stool and, crouching down, inspected the dark shelf and the surrounding floor more closely. Nothing.

Had someone stolen it? Was it even possible *not* to notice someone lurking around us as we all sat so close together? But theft was the only explanation. Begrudgingly, I had to admire the thief's skill. Now what was I going to do? No money, no room key.

"You'll have to get a different room," the first officer pointed out. "They might be raiding yours as we speak."

"Ah, jeez. Not again!" the barman moaned wearily, his Bronx accent pronounced. He picked up the phone. "I'll let hotel security know and I'll have to bill your room."

Soon an overfed, middle-aged, bespectacled man appeared, introduced himself and drew me over to one of the empty restaurant tables. We sat facing each other as he took out a notepad and poised his pen ready to write. In the shadows it was challenging to make out his darker-skinned features.

"So, Ma'am, tell me exactly what happened." Why did he have to call me Ma'am? And his intense urgency seemed a little unwarranted for a missing room key and some money. This was hardly a murder investigation!

I tried not to smile. "Well, I looped my little black purse around my ankle, but when I went to pay, it wasn't there."

"What was in the purse, Ma'am?"

I told him.

"We'll have to change your room," he announced importantly as though at least a drug bust could be taking place in 802, but there would be no need to worry as he, no doubt, would be the hero of the piece. "Follow me." With that, he snapped his notepad shut and got up.

Like a duckling following its mother, I traipsed behind him into the lift. On the eighth floor as we neared my room, he put out an arm, stopping me in my tracks. Then in a Kojak move, he backed himself up against the wall and signalled for me to do the same thing. He patted something on his right hip. Did he have a gun? Then putting a finger to his lips, he warned me to be quiet. He cocked his head toward the door, listening. I wanted to laugh, but maybe Kojak was right about the danger. Maybe I was the naïve one.

Finally, reassured that no noises were coming from the room, he put his master key in the lock and threw the door open wide Rambo-style and shouted, "Security!"

I stood behind him, finding it hard not to laugh. He was enjoying this. He obviously didn't get to do Rambo-raids very often, or was he just trying to impress me?

"Stay there, Ma'am," he hissed over his shoulder.

Obediently I stood in the doorway while he checked under the bed, in the closet, in the bathroom. Oh no! I wondered. Had I left my knickers on the floor?

He reappeared. "All clear. Now pack up as quickly as possible, Ma'am, and I'll take you to your new room."

Enough of the Ma'am already!

As he stood, arms crossed, watching, self-consciously I scooped up my toiletries and delicates, then emptied the closet and threw my clothes back into my suitcase. Kojak grabbed the red Samsonite from me, and as we left, he locked the door behind him.

"You're in 819." He pointed as he marched ahead of me along the corridor and around the corner. Was it my imagination or did these rooms feel different from the others? Seedier? As we arrived at my new accommodation, he went through the same charade. Backs against the wall, listening, bursting open the door as if on a drug bust.

Wasn't this a bit over the top? I waited in the doorway. After he had checked the empty room, he called out another "All clear!" and I was allowed to enter. He had deposited my suitcase on one of the twin beds.

Keeping a straight face was not easy, but I tried to take the event as seriously as he thought it was.

Inside the room and suddenly feeling a little unnerved, I told Kojak, "I think I'll rejoin my friends in the bar now. I can unpack later."

"Okay, Ma'am," he responded, giving the room another once over and then handing me the key. "I'll take you down."

My crew were just finishing their drinks when I arrived back in the bar. "What am I going to do for cash?" I asked the first officer.

"You'll have to call Ritch. But not tonight. He likes his sleep."

"After all that excitement," I told the group, "I'm going to sleep like a baby, too."

"What's your new room number?" Juliana asked as we all ascended in the elevator.

"819." I showed her my key fob.

"O-o-oh. Isn't that one of the haunted rooms at the end of the corridor?" she teased.

"Ach, that's a load of old codswallop," the first officer scoffed.

"Well, I'm too tired to go through another dramatic room change with Kojak," I said, sounding braver than I felt. "So, if you hear someone banging on your door tonight, Julianna, you'll know it's me."

As I found my way down the shabby corridor, I thought that, if I had to choose, a physical invader might be preferable to a spectral one. But between jet lag, a few brown cow cocktails and the evening's excitement, maybe, just maybe, I wouldn't have difficulty sleeping.

When I entered 819, I surveyed the twin beds with their pink and blue flowered quilts, the faded pale blue of the walls, the chipped white paint around the open windows. Despite all the traffic noise from Lexington Avenue, the yellow taxis constantly honking their horns and the dense summer humidity, a stillness pervaded the room. How many hundreds of people had slept in 819? And what were their stories?

I reviewed my options. Keep the windows open and tolerate the humidity, noise and lights of a city that never sleeps, or close the windows and put on the air conditioner, which sounded as if a chopper was landing by my bed? I opted for the noisy air conditioner. At least I would be able to breathe.

Too tired to unpack, I left my suitcase on the far bed, retrieved my nightie, brushed my teeth and collapsed into the bed nearest to the door. Despite the closed windows, I could still hear—though muted—the honking of cabs and other traffic. I turned on my side to face the door so that the bright city lights shining through the curtains would not keep me awake.

I'm not sure how long I had been asleep when something behind woke me. A movement? Or was it a voice? I turned over and peered into the darkness. Yellow lights from the Waldorf Hotel across the street as well as pulsating orange neon signs cast shadows across the room. I squinted not sure of what I was seeing. I sat up. My suitcase was no longer on the other bed. Instead, in the shadows I could see the outline of a young woman lying there on her side facing me. She was half naked, clad in black lingerie, propped up on one elbow, her long black hair cascading over her shoulders. None of her facial features were distinguishable, but I felt that she was staring straight through me.

I gasped and froze.

The word *hooker* filled the air.

An ominous silence had descended over the room, which had somehow morphed into . . . the same room but different. No taxi horns now, no traffic, just a thick, heavy silence. And was it my imagination or was the décor also darker? I was in another time, in days gone by. And maybe I was dreaming?

She continued to lie there, staring. What did she want? I should be scared, I thought, but somehow, she was not threatening, just terribly sad. An overwhelming sense of remorse emanated from her. Then words came, not from her mouth but into my head–*Don't do anything you'll regret.*

Then I came out of my shock, grappled for the bedside lamp switch and, holding my breath, turned it on.

She was gone.

The bed was empty, my suitcase now back on top of the quilt. The décor had returned to the faded blue walls, chipped paint and flowered quilts of the present day. Outside the cacophony of traffic had returned. Compared to the former silence, the noisiness now sounded even more abrasive. But despite the humidity, the air in the room seemed to lighten.

Had I dreamt her?

Shaken, I lay back on my bed. Was the message for me, or had *she* regretted doing or not doing something? Being a hooker, maybe? And why was she haunting this room? Had she been murdered here? I shuddered. Was she the corpse we were told about during training who had been discovered after a week under the bed?

I needed to see life, other humans, even if they were just on a screen. With the light still on, I jumped out of bed and ran to switch on the TV. Rodney Dangerfield's routine was making Johnny Carson laugh on his *Tonight Show*. His familiar deep voice and laughter were a welcome relief. Soon I relaxed back onto my not-so-soft pillow, and by avoiding looking at the other bed and keeping the TV and the light on, I was able to drift in and out of sleep.

The next morning, I called Ritch Kievers and reported the theft of my purse. He reluctantly agreed to meet me in the hotel restaurant and replenish my flight pay.

"This is highly unusual," he commented, obviously not happy at doling out more dollars as if it was *his* money he was parting with. Or did he think *I* might be the thief?

"If you don't believe me, the first officer and Julianna are my witnesses," I huffed, not bothering to hide my insulted feelings. And do you really think I would have willingly gone through a room change with Kojak just for an extra $80? I thought but did not say.

"No-no, Natasha, I'm sorry. Of course, I believe you. It's just the airline will interrogate *me*, so I must make sure I have all the details in my flight report."

And maybe he had slept in a haunted room last night, too.

The front desk clerk was just as begrudging about doing yet another room change. When I told her that it was the noise from the street *and* the ghost of a depressed hooker that had kept me awake, she managed not to roll her eyes, though she was obviously thinking; Gee, another crazy Brit. She simply responded with a "Yes, Ma'am."

And don't call me Ma'am! is what I wanted to add but didn't want to push my luck.

"This one's at the back so you shouldn't be disturbed." She handed me the key fob.

"By ghosts or traffic?" I asked.

She just shrugged.

"Hey, Ratbag!" Julianna called over to me as she approached. "Do you wanna go for breakfast?"

After we had ordered bacon and eggs at our favourite Lexington Avenue restaurant, Julianna asked me, "So, how'd you sleep? See any ghosts?" Already on our second cup of coffee, she looked bright and refreshed, while I felt like a doped slug.

"Not sure." I shrugged. "But I never sleep well in New York anyway. Probably just had some strange dreams." By now I had convinced myself that the "visitation" had just been a nighttime fantasy.

"Was the dream about a hooker lying on the other bed?" She smiled, her freckles more evident in the morning light.

"How did you . . .?" I studied her, amazed.

"Well, you're not the only one. You know Brenda Jennings? She saw her, too, in that same room. She gives everyone a message. What was yours?"

I put my fork down, gobsmacked. We were talking about ghosts just as normally as if we were discussing live passengers. "Well," I told Juliana, "I thought I heard the words 'Don't do anything you'll regret . . .'"

"Hmm? I wonder what she meant?" she pondered as the waitress poured more coffee.

"That's the six-million-dollar question. I have no idea."

Julianna frowned. "It's probably to do with a man. It always is!"

"Com'on," I said as I laid my new dollar bills on the table. "Let's go shopping."

Back at the hotel and in my third room in two days, Julianna and I sat on the queen-sized bed and spread out the spoils of our shopping venture. Bloomingdales as well as a massive music store on Lexington and the warehouses down at the docks had, as usual, been our favourite spots for deals.

"So . . . tell me about your South American!" Julianna said as she tried on her new suede jacket and posed in front of the mirror.

Always happy to talk about Jose, I related the full story of how we met first in Barbados, then Bangor and finally England. "But he's married," I told her, remembering his painful revelation in Horsham. "So that's that." I shrugged. "But even though I know I should stay away from him—because he's off limits and he doesn't feel the same way about me—I can't let it go."

"When was the last time you saw him?" she asked as she removed her jacket.

"It's been two years since I actually saw him," I told her, realizing with shock that it had been that long since our wrenching farewell at

Gatwick. Our time apart felt so elongated in some ways, and in others, he was always present—at least in my thoughts.

She had flopped down in the armchair and was staring at me, entranced with the story. "Where is he now?"

"Well, the last time I was in LA, I was missing him so-o-o much, I just had to call him–even though I had promised myself it had to be over, and I would never speak to him again. He told me then that his company was sending him to Sao Paulo for two years, so I guess that's where he is now."

"Oh, I've been to Sao Paulo!"

"What's it like?"

"It's industrial and busy but there are some beautiful parts."

"It's crazy how much I miss him."

"You could call him . . ." She was grinning mischievously.

"I don't have his number."

"You could find it. You know the name of his company."

"Well . . . yes." Butterflies in my stomach were beginning to flutter.

I didn't need much encouragement to contact Jose, but still I hesitated. What was the point of staying in touch with someone unobtainable and so far away? But who was I kidding? Even though we had only spent a total of a week together, I had never felt so connected to, or so happy with anybody. Away from him, I felt as if a big chunk of me was missing. I now understood the lyrics in so many of the love songs, "You've stolen my heart."

Julianna suddenly sat up, her brown eyes wide. "Oh my god, that's the message from the ghost. Don't do anything you'll regret. Maybe she meant that you *should* call him!"

"Or shouldn't?"

She shrugged and tilted her head to one side. "Would you regret it if you *didn't* call him?"

"Always," I said, sighing. It was useless resisting. My heart had been hijacked and I was his prisoner.

Julianna giggled and came and sat on the end of the bed as I picked up the phone and called international information. She handed me pen and paper and I wrote down the number. "Here goes," I muttered, holding my breath.

Hoping I wouldn't need Portuguese, I asked in English, "Can I please speak to Jose Ramirez?"

"One moment," the operator responded.

I inhaled. Two clicks and then I heard the familiar husky voice. "Jose Ramirez."

Oh my God. I inhaled. "Hi."

There was a long silence. Was an introduction required?

"Hi," he finally responded, sounding breathless. Another pause. "I'm sorry, but . . . I am so shocked. How did jyou find me?"

"Information. I looked up your company in Sao Paolo," I said simply.

"I am so shocked," he repeated, breathless. When he had recovered, he said, "I haff to tell jyou . . ."

Oh, how his accent made me melt. Julianna was beaming at me.

". . .that I am so surprised because jost two weeks ago, I called jyou in England . . ."

Really? Or was he just saying that to make me feel good?

". . . but the guy I talked to told me that you weren't home."

Darn it! Why hadn't my new flat mate, Graham, told me that a man with a foreign accent had called?

"In fact, I tried calling jyou a few times, but jyou are *never* home."

That sounded familiar. My 9-to-5 friends often complained about the difficulty of connecting with me. Maybe he was telling the truth, after all.

"It's wonderful to hear jyour voice," he said, his soft tone making me tingle, warm waves flooding through me, my heart bursting with joy once again.

"How are you?" I asked, cursing the distance between us and wishing I could climb down the telephone line.

"Good . . . I called jyou because I haff good news. My company are moving me back to Boston earlier than planned! Next month."

"Oh, that's wonderful!" Boston's only an hour's flight from New York, I thought gleefully.

"Where are jyou now?" he asked.

"Oh . . . New York for a couple of days."

I felt his smile. "Jyou don't sound too excited."

"Well, I was supposed to be in LA and going to a concert to meet Elton John, but the airline had other plans."

"Too bad."

I hesitated. ". . . Maybe we can meet up in New York?"

"Jyou mean, jyou and Elton John?"

"No, you and me!" I said, laughing.

There was a sharp intake of breath on his end. "Maybe. When will jyou be there again?"

"At the end of next month, the 28th I think."

He was quiet again, and I basked in the sound of his breathing, knowing that he was just at the end of a phone line.

"Jyou know–," he began.

Then on his end men's voices began chattering in the office background.

"Oh, I'm so sorry," he said, sounding irritated. "I jhave to go into a meeting, but . . .thank jyou so moch for calling." Then he chuckled. "Jyou know, ... jyou're amazing," he added huskily. "Goodbye."

"Hasta la vista," I responded, refusing to say the "g" word.

There was a click and silence.

Elated, I laid down the receiver and beamed at Julianna. "He's coming back to the US!" Despite his marital status, I knew deep inside me I was still hoping that he would at some point choose me.

"Woo-hoo," Julianna cheered. "How was it?"

I laughed at her enthusiasm for my love life. "Lovely." I beamed. "He sounded *so happy* to hear from me."

"So? No regrets?"

I shook my head, still basking in the warmth of his voice and his breath.

"Maybe you should go back to 819 and thank the ghost?" Julianna moved over to my dresser and picked up my bottle of Chardonnay. "Or we could celebrate!"

"I wonder what the hooker regrets?" I pondered out loud. "Maybe she fell in love with a married man and regretted it, or maybe she pursued him and got her man and she's telling me to do the same?"

"She probably regrets being a hooker, not that some women have a choice about that!" Julianna posited as she emerged from my bathroom holding two glass tooth mugs filled with not-so-cold wine. She perched on the end of the bed and handed me my glass. "Oh my god," she exclaimed, eyes wide. "I hope it wasn't her lover who murdered her?"

"Well, we don't choose who we fall in love with," I said, "but we *can* choose what we do about it. I don't want to be a homewrecker, but if by some miracle he was to choose me . . ."

"No, no regrets," Julianna put down her glass and began dancing around the room holding up her arms and singing *Je ne regrette rien* in a dramatic imitation of Edith Piaf.

"You should have been a singer as well as a dancer." I said, leaning back on my pillow. "It's funny. If I'd gone to LA, I wouldn't have called him. So, I should thank you for sharing my love of South

Americans, then thank the thief for stealing my purse, so I had to change rooms, so I could see the ghost and get the message so I could call Jose?"

"Everything is as it's meant to be," she stated as she lay across the end of my bed. Propped up on one elbow, she looked like the hooker except for the short red curls framing her pretty freckled face and the fact that she was happy and alive. "Sometimes I think we have no control over our destiny," she added.

"Speaking of destiny, maybe I should thank Laker too, for changing my roster from an LA to a JFK. It would have been so-o-o sad if they hadn't because, right now, I would have been in LA meeting Elton John."

We laughed.

"So sa-a-ad. So sa-a-d!" And Julianna broke into song again, this time singing Elton John's *It's a sad, sad situation.*

"*So sa-ad, so gl-aad. It's a glad, glad situation,*" I rejoined.

As we clinked our tooth mugs, Julianna continued singing, "*And it's getting more and more absurd.*"

The next day, on arriving home, I encountered my recently moved-in flat mate, Graham, as he was about to leave for work.

"Graham, do you remember taking a message for me from a man with a foreign accent? He called here about two weeks ago?"

He peered at the ceiling. "Two weeks ago? Let me see . . ."

I waited.

"Well, there could have been. You know you have quite a few men calling with foreign accents."

Although he was making *me* sound like a lady of the night, he was correct. I did collect male friends, some of them foreign. Don called me from Texas, German Thomas from Barbados, my brothers from

Canada. But they were all platonic relationships . . . except for Jose.

"This one was South American," I added for clarification.

He shook his head, hand on the door handle, ready to go out the door. "Nope, sorry. Can't remember."

"Well, next time would you *please* mind writing down the names? It's important."

"Okay," he said blithely as he left, oblivious to the fragility of my love life.

Not even a month later, as I was climbing into my Morris Minor for my drive to Gatwick and was excited to think about arriving in New York and calling Jose again. He would be back in Boston by now and within reach from The Big Apple, unlike the agonizing gulf between us when he was in Sao Paolo. Perhaps we would even be able to see each other.

But as I put my seat belt on, a gentle voice popped into my head and it said, *You won't be together now, but later.*

Whose words were those? Not mine. And what did it mean? Later could mean next year or even next life. He was married after all, I reminded myself. Puzzled, I backed out of my parking spot and drove to the airport.

Once inside my Doral Inn bedroom for my two-night New York stay, I didn't wait to get changed into my civvies before I picked up the phone. I revelled in the delicious thought that Jose and I were in the same time zone, on the same continent and within an hour's flight of each other. Would he want me to fly to Boston or would he come up to New York?

"Surprise!" I began after he picked up the phone in his Boston office.

"Hi," he responded, but not with the usual breathless delight. Uh-oh.

"Where are jyou?" he asked, his voice sounding strained.

"New York!"

A silence fell between us, but it wasn't our usual you're-taking-my-breath-away silence.

"I could fly up to Boston to see you?" I blurted.

More awkward silence. I could hear his wheels turning. Finally, he said, "Well, I can't this weekend. . ."

I didn't even hear his words, just the dull tone of his voice and I knew.

The voice in the car had been right. I wouldn't be with him now, and maybe not later either.

15

DOUBLE WHAMMY IN MIAMI

November 1981

"What the hell is *that*?" I exclaimed as I studied my new roster and to no one in particular in the crowded crew room.

On that November day, rain was beating on the large, tinted windows of the crew room, and even though this was usually the quietest flying time of the year, long concertina buses, cars and crew transports were still busily coming and going on the Perimeter Road outside. The crew room was surprisingly full of "stewies" as well as the occasional steward, checking in and returning from flights.

Several of us were clustered around the wooden pigeon-holes on the left wall where we picked up notes to and from each other, as well as cheques, rosters and bulletins from the company.

My friend Francesca leaned over and peered at my white sheet of paper with its black scribblings and saw what I was pointing at: LGW-MIA-MAN-MIA-LGW.

"Oh, that's the double Miami," she explained. "They're new and they're bloody awful. Four trans-Atlantics in five days!"

"Wha-a-at?"

"Yes, you leave Gatwick, min-rest in Miami, min-rest in Manchester, and back to Miami again to do another min-rest and then back to Gatwick."

Whenever faced with something unpleasant, I usually reverted to humour. "Ee, ba gum," I quipped, doing my Monty Python imitation. "That's luxury! When I were wi' Dan Air, we did four sectors in a day, *and* we used to 'ave to load baggage onto t' aircraft."

"You won't be laughing by the end of that duty." Francesca then inspected her own roster and suddenly beamed. "Ooh, great! I've got one, too!"

"Why are you so happy about it?"

"Oh . . . I have my reasons."

"Don't tell me," I taunted. "It's a man and he's in Miami . . . or Manchester?"

"Now what makes you think that?"

"By the massive grin on your face."

"When's *your* double Miami, Natasha?"

I checked my roster. "The 15th."

"Same!" Francesca exclaimed. "Who knows? Maybe you'll get to meet him . . .in Miami."

"What does he do?"

"He's a pilot. But he's not flying at the moment."

"How come?"

"You know that Delta DC-9 that crashed a few years ago?" she said, folding her roster into her handbag. "Well, he was deadheading on that flight, and he was the only survivor. Can you imagine? He still has back issues, so he's on disability."

Two weeks later I was standing on the DC-10 in my position as Number Seven at Three-Door-Right and bracing myself for the next five days—the four Atlantic time changes and three minimum rests. On the other side of the aisle, Francesca was beaming at passengers, obviously looking forward to her reunion with her new man while I felt a stab of pain remembering Jose's recent rejection.

"Yer must like nights," a male passenger with a strong northern accent mumbled as he forcibly shoved his carry-on into the overhead bin.

At first, I didn't realize he was speaking to me. "I'm sorry. What did you say?"

He turned to address me directly. "Nights. Yer know. It must be nice for you girls to fly at night?"

Seeing my frown, he added. "Well, yer can sleep, can't yer, and yer don't 'ave to do all't work."

I shook my head. Unbelievable! I thought. The strange ideas that some passengers had about our job.

"Sir," I began, always happy to enlighten a member of the not-so-all-knowing public. "Whether it's day or night, we still provide the same service and have the same amount of work to do. Do you know that the primary reason we are here is to keep you safe in the unlikely event of an emergency?" And not to be slaves to your every whim, I wanted to add.

"Oh, aye," he said, no longer interested and sinking down into his seat.

Five hours and thirty-five minutes later, having negotiated yet another crossing of the dreaded Bermuda Triangle, the wheels of our DC-10 touched down on the runway at Miami's main airport. At our hotel and as per our usual routine, we all dispersed to our rooms to get showered and changed. Then we would meet in the captain's room to collect our flight pay and enjoy a cocktail together.

I was giving my reflection in the bathroom mirror one more cursory glance before leaving when there was a light knock on my door. Through the peephole, I saw that a female with long, dark hair was staring back at me.

Out of her bright red uniform, Francesca looked stunning. Her little black dress accentuated her dark tan and her long thick hair that hung luxuriously over her shoulders. "He's going to love you in that dress!" I remarked.

"Oh, do you think so?" She beamed, happy. "Listen, Dean is picking me up in a few minutes, so I wondered if you would get my flight pay for me. I called the captain and he's okay with giving it to you."

"Of course. But when can I get the money to you? I'm guessing you won't be here for breakfast . . ."

"I hope not!" She grinned. "No, I'll get it from you tomorrow. We might see you at the pool in the morning."

With a min-rest in Miami, we only had time for dinner, sleep, breakfast, a short tanning by the pool, a swim and a nap. By early the following evening we would be back on the plane.

"Have fun!" I told her as she headed down the balcony to meet her man and I went in the opposite direction toward the captain's room and our crew party.

"Sorry, ladies, I'm tired," the captain announced as we sat on his king-sized bed. "It's going to be a hard few days, especially for us on the flight deck, so I'm just going to pay you and then ask you to leave. Hope you understand. And I'm giving you your flight pay for the whole trip so be careful with it."

People mumbled their disappointment, but we understood. "Let's go up to the bar then," Julianna, who was sitting beside me, whispered. After our recent New York, she and I had become good friends, and she was one of the few crew who knew about Jose. "We can get something to eat there and then hit the sack early, too."

The bar of the Marriott resembled a large hotel room with lots of windows filled with thick mottled glass, but unlike many of the bars in our US destinations that were often shrouded in darkness, this place was light and bright. Small glass tables were surrounded by comfy white armchairs, and the white-padded bar swept in an arc halfway around the room. When we arrived, the place was abuzz with people and conversation and air conditioning blasting cold air that made me shiver. And aware that I was carrying both Francesca's and my own flight pay in US cash in my little purse, didn't make me feel any warmer.

Julianna and I found the last remaining chairs at a table where three men—likely there on business—were in deep conversation.

"Do you mind if . . .?" I asked the bespectacled man in the middle, indicating the vacant chairs.

He waved a hand. "Go ahead, little lady."

Texans, I guessed.

After we had ordered our pina coladas and were tucking into a shrimp salad, Mr. Spectacles asked, "So how do you like Miami?"

"We're air stewardesses . . . flight attendants," I told him using the more American title, which I disliked as it reminded me of the UK term, Lavatory Attendants. "Although we also fly to New York and LA which can be dangerous destinations," I added, "for some reason, I'm always more alert in Miami."

"Darn right," Mr. Spectacles said. "You girls better be careful. There are a lot of bad dudes here." He lowered his voice and leaned forward. "Probably every man in this bar is totin' a gun."

"Wha-a-at?" Julianna gasped and looked around. "Guns?"

I gulped and surveyed the room. But all the men and women in the bar were leaning into each other, laughing, talking. Everyone seemed like they were just enjoying a relaxing drink on a Friday night after work.

"And the crime rate's sky high," the third one added, jumping in, "on account of the Cubans coming over here en masse. It's caused a lot of racial tension, and now all the gangs are fightin' about who's top o' the pile."

Mr. Spectacles paid their waitress and they all stood up to leave. "We don't wanna scare you, but there's all kindsa bad stuff goin' down here that they don't talk about on the news on account of they don't wanna scare the tourists away."

You *are* scaring me, I thought. "Well, thanks for the warning," I said cheerily as they moved away, now even more nervous of all the cash in my handbag.

Almost immediately two very sharply dressed, Hispanic-looking men wearing dark glasses approached. Julianna and I exchanged looks. Drug dealers!

"Are theese seats frree?" the shorter, swarthier one asked, leering at both of us.

"It's okay," I said, standing up, but with head down trying to avoid eye contact. "We're just leaving."

"Natasha! Natasha! Where are you?"

The next morning most of our thirteen crew members were lying on chaises longues arranged in a chaotic cluster on the lawn close to the Marriott's rectangular swimming pool. Before departing for a not-so-sunny Manchester, we were soaking up the midday sun's rays. When I heard Francesca's voice, I sat up from my reclined position, opened my eyes and removed my sunglasses. The sun was already high in a cloudless blue sky and the brightness blinded me for a few minutes. The standing joke among crew members was that we were so used to seeing each other in bikinis or trunks that, when back in uniform, we would often exclaim, "Oh, it's you! I didn't recognize you with your clothes on."

In this case, it was clothes off.

"Yes, over here," I called and watched as Francesca picked her way through the array of steamy, prostate bodies. She was dressed in a pink moo-moo and now wore her hair piled on top of her head. A tall, slim, bronzed, blond-haired man followed close behind her. This must be the handsome captain Dean, I thought.

Suddenly self-conscious, I pulled my sarong around me.

"Take a pew," I offered, sitting sideways and making room for them both to perch on the end of my chair.

"Natasha, this is Dean."

We shook hands, his grip surprisingly weak. But he was indeed very gorgeous, late-thirties with sharp blue eyes that seemed to bore into my very soul. "Hello."

"Lovely to meet you, Natasha," he said in a deep, seductive drawl. His ingratiating manner was charming. No wonder Francesca was smitten. That voice would have melted me, too.

"Guess what?" Francesca was radiating excitement.

Things must be going well, I thought.

She beamed over at her companion. "Dean's coming back with me to Manchester! Just for a night! Isn't that a hoot? Just so he can be with me."

"Oh? Well, isn't *that* . . . romantic."

"Isn't it?" Francesca beamed at him yet again.

"So, Delta still gives you free flights then, even on disability?" I asked. Surely, he wouldn't pay full fare for a 24-hour return trip. Is any man *that* romantic?

"No, they don't!" He grinned sardonically. "Not after the first year." He took Francesca's hand, caressing it. "But this wonderful lady has signed me up as her boyfriend so I'm flying standby on Laker for ten pounds. Whatta deal!" He kissed the back of her hand as though she was the most precious thing in his world.

"I hope you get on board both ways," I commented, realizing that standby seats are never guaranteed.

"Of course, he will!" Francesca chided me. "Passenger loads are still light going in and out of Manchester. He'll be okay."

"Oh, Francesca, I nearly forgot." I reached behind me to retrieve my small handbag from underneath my towel. "Here's your flight pay." I said, handing her the folded wad of US bills. "I must say I didn't like carrying all that money around."

Dean suddenly stood up and started scrutinizing the area, first the crew, then the other people around the pool and finally the hotel balconies where more people were tanning, reading or hanging their towels. Who or what was he looking for?

"Honey," Francesca said, looking up at him and getting his attention. She handed him the cash. "Could you carry that for me? I don't have my handbag."

Dean peered at the money, frowned and quickly stuck it in his trouser pocket. "Sure," he said and smiled at Francesca. "No problem."

"Well, we're going to get some lunch now," Francesca stood up. "Dean, shall I introduce you to our flight deck so you can talk aeroplanes?" She turned to me and added, "He misses it so much, you know."

"I'm sure." A lot of pilots were like little boys, and airplanes were their toys.

Dean glanced over at the men. The captain was reading, and both the first officer and engineer had their eyes closed.

"Nah," Dean drawled in that deep voice. "It's okay. I'll catch up with them on the flight."

The crew were all surprised later that afternoon when Francesca appeared on the crew transport with Dean. They were even more delighted that he was in his captain's uniform and carrying the customary black flight crew bag with a few faded stickers still attached. In uniform, he was even more gorgeous, and some girls muttered, "ooh la la" as the couple made their way up the aisle.

Francesca blushed as she took her seat beside him at the back of the bus.

But why *was* he in uniform? Perhaps he thought that if he couldn't get a passenger seat, the flight deck crew would allow him to fly supernumerary in the flight deck jump seat. Although he was only checked out on a DC-9, it might be a good thing to have another professional on board in the unlikely event that our DC-10 captain should experience a heart attack, food poisoning or a mental breakdown.

"Listen up," our IFD, Mia Pascuole, announced from the front of the bus, already beginning her briefing as the bus driver negotiated Miami's rush hour traffic. "You might be aware that we are in hurricane season, and Hurricane Alan, the first one of the year, is building somewhere out there." She waved a hand obliquely behind her. "We'll be okay on this sector into Manchester . . . right, Captain? . . . but the Manchester-Miami might be delayed or diverted," she added. "We'll keep you posted."

"God, I'd rather get stuck in sunny Miami than not-so-sunny Manchester," I groaned to Julianna sitting next to me.

"Is it even possible to fly through a hurricane?" she asked.

"Better to fly into it," I commented, "like those little planes do all the time around here. What are they called? Storm busters? They go right into the eye to figure out how big the hurricane is. Kind of like *loife*," I added, mimicking Jesus's mother's high-pitched voice in *The Life of Brian*. "Better just to face it, dear, than try to go around it."

Once on board, Francesca was relieved when she heard that Dean was on the passenger manifest. As the plane was almost full, he had no doubt charmed his way onto the flight and got the last seat. Under the many curious and admiring stares of passengers, he took his place in the rear cabin so he and Francesca could chat during the service. She had never looked so content. I was happy for her.

Francesca had told the captain about Dean's story and how he was missing piloting the DC-9 so after a few hours into the flight, he was invited up to the flight deck for a visit.

The Elephant Man was now playing in all three darkened cabins and in between serving passengers drinks from the rear bar, Francesca and I were sitting on our jump seats.

"When do you think Dean will be operating again?" I asked her.

"Not sure," she frowned. "There's still some legal stuff to be sorted, and his spine isn't quite healed. You know he broke his back in the crash."

I vaguely remembered the story of a plane crashing with just one survivor, but there had been a few DC-9 crashes in the last few years and I didn't recall that the lone survivor on that flight was a pilot.

"Does he suffer from survivor guilt?" Julianna asked, always interested in people's psychology. Or she was just plain nosy.

Francesca shrugged. "He doesn't like to talk about it."

"Who could blame him?" I added.

During the movie, while some restless passengers came to the rear galley for a glass of water, a cocktail or just to escape the horror of the film, I heard the aircraft engine change pitch and felt the formerly smooth flight become a little jerky. Being at altitude and in mid-flight, the sound and the movement was highly unusual. For a moment, I wondered if indeed the hurricane was already chasing us, and the captain had been forced to change altitude.

Half an hour later Dean appeared in the rear galley, his face radiating excitement. "I flew my first DC-10!" he told Francesca.

"Oh, that's great," she cooed, happy for him.

"Is that allowed?" I muttered to Julianna, something about Dean's smugness suddenly bothering me and I didn't know why. "I mean, don't you have to be legally checked out on *this* aircraft," I persisted.

"Oh, Natasha." Francesca had overheard and immediately came to his defense. "It's fine. He's a pilot! Not just any old Jo-Schmo."

"Yeah. Don't worry, Natasha," Dean added ever-so-smoothly. "Your captain was sitting right behind me in the jump seat like a training flight. And," he added, pointing out of the rear windows to the blue sky, "we're still aloft, aren't we?"

I couldn't argue with that. Still, the niggle persisted.

Manchester Ringway Airport was, apart from our flight load of passengers, mostly deserted when we landed in the early morning. And when we walked into the hotel lobby of the Manchester Airport Hotel, I shuddered, remembering my last night there with Dan Air and the strange aftermath. Pushing it from my mind, I told some of the girls, "They do a great bacon and eggs in the restaurant here."

"I'm *so* hungry I could eat a cow," Margo, our galley slave, announced.

"Me, too," Julianna piped up.

"Can I join you?" the newest girl, Cynthia, asked.

The three of us stared at her and grimaced. From the beginning of our trip, Cynthia's nose had been stuck up in the air as if the rest of us had stinky feet. She had also constantly complained about the "slave conditions" of Laker schedules and had not smiled once. Like the majority of my colleagues, I was grateful for my job with the airline, so I had ignored her whining. Without answering, we moved into the restaurant. She trailed behind anyway.

During the week, this room would have been filled with businessmen reading newspapers or already in meetings, but at 6.00 on a Saturday morning, all the round tables covered in pristine white tablecloths were empty.

"Ee, our Margo, that's great, in't it?" I told her in my best Coronation Street accent. "There's no one 'ere so we don't 'ave to behave ourselves."

She giggled. "Eee, thank God!" she said as we all took our seats, removed hats, stripped off gloves, loosened our scarves and, underneath the table, kicked off our crippling high-heeled shoes.

Margo continued in the same accent, "Ee, it feels good to take a load off, doe'nt it?"

"Aye, it does that!" Julianna chimed in, just as good a mimic.

The three of us collapsed into uncontrolled giggles. Were we drunk with tiredness from the time changes, or was it hunger? Maybe it was hysteria.

Cynthia was not amused.

Soon the swing doors on the other side of the restaurant burst open, and a very buxom woman dressed in a starchy white apron and crisp white blouse bustled over to our table. "Eee, you poor loves," she said oh-so-soothingly as she turned our white cups the right way up on their saucers. "Yer must be just exhausted. I bet you'd all love a nice cuppa tea, wouldn't yer?"

The woman was so warm and loving--unlike my own mother who had gone emotionally AWOL a few years ago--- that I had an overwhelming urge to ask her if I could lay my head in her lap and rest for a while, or even take her home with me. Instead I said, "Yes, tea, please."

"Coffee! Give me coffee," Margo moaned as if she'd been stuck in a desert without water, and not just on a DC-10 with bad-tasting beverages.

"Right, then, chucks. I'll be right with yer."

Unbeknownst to the lovely waitress, she had innocently fallen right into our accents and our silliness. As soon as she disappeared back through the swing doors, the three of us looked at each other and burst into laughter again.

"Well," Cynthia huffed, "I don't know what you all find so funny, but I think it's disgusting that we have to fly four sectors in five days. It's not right, you know. We should complain to the union."

"Union?" I exclaimed, mimicking my favourite comedienne, Hilda Baker. Cynthia was bringing out the mischief in me, and I turned to Margo, grinning. "*We've* got a union? Eee, ba gum! I don't think so, chuck. Just an ass-oc-ia-shun," I enunciated slowly. Then switching to a Monty Python's Yorkshire skit, I said, "But, our Margo, wouldn't a union be a luxury! A real luxury!"

"Aye, 'appen," she replied, her face serious, but her eyes were twinkling with humour. "You could complain to the ass-oc-ia-shun."

Cynthia stared at both of us as if we had gone quite mad. She might have been right.

"And only four sectors in five days!" Margo continued in the Yorkshire skit. "Luxury! That's nought. When I worked fer British Midland, we used to 'ave to refuel aircraft, make sandwiches and then wash all't dishes! And afterwards fly 26 hours in just one day!"

"Twenty-six hours!" I exclaimed, "You were lucky.! When I worked for Dan Air, we 'ad to get up before we went to bed, refuel aircraft, lick tarmac clean and fly 16 days non-stop."

"You 'ad a bed?" Julianna jumped in. "Eee, you were lucky! We 'ad to sleep in puddle in middle o't runway and then move out o't way when aircraft landed."

Julianna, Margo and I were now giggling so hard that tears were streaming down our faces. I could not tell from Cynthia's tightly controlled facial expression if she was about to cry or laugh.

Just then our mothering angel appeared clutching a flowered tea pot and a metal coffee canister. Somehow, she seemed to understand

and forgive our silliness. "Ee, I can see you've all 'ad a long night," she commiserated as she poured our hot beverages. "Do you know what you want to order, luvvies?"

Her sage motherly tone brought us suddenly back to our senses. Mum placed the pots on the table and took out her notepad. With pencil patiently poised, she waited.

"I know what I want," I said. "Two poached, bacon, sausages, toast but no potatoes, please."

"You're 'avin' eggs *and* bacon *and* sausages?" Margo couldn't help it. "Luxury." Then straight-faced, she told Mum, "Me, too, please."

"Me, too," Julianna added.

"And for you, Miss?" When Mum addressed Cynthia, I heard a slight edge of dislike in her voice when she said "Miss." Cynthia was, predictably, still examining the menu, being picky.

"One poached egg, no butter please and could I get a fruit salad with no melon."

"Of course, dear," our new Mum said, again with a long-suffering note on the "dear." She put her notepad back in her pinny pocket and topped up the coffees.

As she leaned over, I told her, "You know, I used to stay here a lot when I was with Dan Air."

"Oh, is that right, chuck? Funny you should say that. I 'ad a feeling I'd seen yer before."

"The last time I was here, as well as dealing with our psycho first officer, there was a strange man in the bar who followed us upstairs."

"Oo-ooh, dear," she said, clutching her spare hand to her chest. "Do yer know, I remember that. That wasn't the first officer who ended up killing 'is wife in't Lake District, were it?"

"Yes, that's right! But the other man had been staring at us in the bar all night, and when we went upstairs to the third floor, he suddenly appeared out of nowhere, right behind me at my door, so I went to the first officer's room for protection. And then the first officer turned out to be the killer. You just never know with people, do you?"

She placed the coffee pot on the table and folded her hands under her ample bosom. "Eee, no, you dawn't, chuck." She was probably thinking we weren't too far from the edge either. "There's nowt so queer as folk."

I waited for her to return to the kitchen before I spoke again. "Speaking of queer folk," I addressed Julianna and Margo, "what do you think of Francesca's boyfriend?"

. "Oh, that man!" Cynthia patted her heart. "He's gorgeous. She's so-o-o lucky!"

"Lucky?" Margo grinned at me. Then more seriously she added, "I didn't really speak to him, but he looks like a dreamboat. Why do you ask?"

"Oh, I dunno." I played with my knife and fork. "There's something about him I don't–"

"Well, don't forget," Julianna interrupted, while holding up a mirror and wiping the smudged mascara from her cheeks with her serviette, "the poor man is still traumatized from that crash. He *was* the only one to survive, you know."

"Eee, lass!" Margo clutched her coffee cup to her chest as if she were frozen and it was warming her all the way down to her toes. "All I know is yer give a man four stripes and 'e' thinks he can 'ave whatever 'e fancies." Then she added a little more seriously. "To tell you't truth, I'm more worried about flyin' into t' bloody hurricane again."

"'Urricane?" Cynthia suddenly piped up. "Bloody luxury!" she said. "When I lived in Oklahoma, we 'ad typhoons with winds up to a thousand miles per 'our."

We all stared at Ms. Poker-Face gobsmacked. She had finally cracked a smile. Her face had transformed, and she actually looked pretty. There was hope.

Mum suddenly appeared and placed plates of piping hot food in front of us. A kind of silence fell over the table, the kind that happens when people are filling the gnawing emptiness in their bellies with sublimely delicious food and nothing else matters.

When the wake-up call came early afternoon, I emerged slowly from my deep cave of unconsciousness stared at the lemon walls in my hotel room and wondered, where am I? Once out of the single bed, I peered through the sound-proofed window and seeing the distant runway with planes in various stages of take-off, I finally remembered. Manchester!

I was not looking forward to this third sector back to Miami. Maybe the hurricane had kicked up a force and the winds would be too strong for us to fly, and we could all go back to bed. And pigs might fly, I thought. The weather had to be really, *really* bad before a flight was cancelled.

"The hurricane's touch and go," Mia advised us as we gathered in the hotel lobby in our uniforms to wait for transport. "But we're going anyway."

"I don't like the sound of that!" Margo, who was right behind me, muttered in my ear.

Dean and Francesca were standing close together in deep conversation, as if he was giving her instructions, and they were urgently exchanging contact information. Why did she look so worried?

"Transport!" Mia called, but as we all moved out of the lobby and into the bus, Dean and Francesca lingered behind. Then the whole crew watched as the couple kissed in what looked like a passionate goodbye.

"There's no room on this transport," Francesca explained as she sat down in front of me alone. "He's getting a taxi." She waved at him again and smiled sadly before our bus pulled away.

"Is everything okay?" I asked.

"We're not sure if he can get on the flight back. Sounds like it could be a full load."

"Won't the captain allow him to ride supernumerary?" I asked.

She grimaced. "He's not checked out on the 10."

"But the captain let him fly the plane before!" I pointed out.

Francesca just shrugged.

"That's too bad." I could relate to Francesca's pain. My romances had often been blighted by the vagaries of flying rules and regulations.

"If he can't get on the flight," Francesca added, "he's going to take the train down to my place in Brighton," she said, slumping down into her seat as if defeated.

"Well, that's great, isn't it?" I said. "That means he'll be there waiting for you with a big . . . hug when you get back on Monday."

"Yes, yes, he will," she agreed, a little cheered. "And he's given me the keys to his house in Miami so if he can't get on the flight, he wants me to go there and pick up some clothes for him."

"Well then, you've got a plan." I reassured her. "And he may still get on this flight."

"Yes," she replied, a little distracted. "He might."

Just an hour and forty minutes into the Manchester to Miami sector, the turbulence began, and the plane began to shudder.

"Captain said we've got to sit down!" Margo commanded as she stopped filling pots with boiling hot water in preparation for the beverage service in the rear galley. Her eyes were large with adrenalin. "We've hit the end of the hurricane, and it's going to get rough."

"Oh, bloody, bloody hell!" Francesca complained. The flight was completely full, so Dean had not got on. She was not a happy camper.

"Flush these coffee and teas down the toilets!" Margo snapped at the three of us as she struggled to push a heavy meal cart back into its stowage. "And be quick." We all knew how dangerous piping hot liquid could be on a turbulent aircraft.

"Alrioght. Alrioght," I told Margo, trying to make her smile with another John Cleese skit. "I didn't come 'ere for an argument!"

But she wasn't in the mood for humor.

Just as we shoved the empty pewter pots back into their cupboard, Mia's serene but authoritative IFD voice came over the PA. "Ladies and gentlemen, we will soon be experiencing some turbulence so we would ask you to please return to your seats immediately and fasten your seat belts. Keep them fastened until we advise you otherwise."

Her calm tone had the desired effect. As we checked that seatbelts were fastened throughout the cabin and that potential projectiles were secured, passengers were acquiescent. They did, however, begin to eat their dinners in haste, perhaps fearing that their potato salads or chocolate mousses might go flying in the turbulence, or worse, that this might be their last meal.

Over the PA Mia stated, "Cabin crew, take your seats . . . now."

As I hurried to Three-Door Right and fastened myself in, I looked up to see that all eyes in the rear cabin were focused on Francesca sitting on the portside door and me on the starboard side. Our job was, as always, to appear calm and in control, no matter how much we were praying or trembling inside. While I concentrated on remaining expressionless, I waited for the aircraft to start bumping, shaking, rattling and rolling through the air.

We waited. Nothing happened. Five, ten and then fifteen minutes went by. The plane continued to fly smoothly as per normal. I began to feel silly. These passengers, I could tell, were wondering;

why are the stewardesses sitting on their bums when there's no turbulence? And where's our coffee?

Frowning, I looked over at Francesca who had an intercom on her consul. Pick up the phone and ask, I mimed to her. As we communicated with signals from side to side, passengers' heads were swivelling back and forth as if they were watching tennis at Wimbledon.

She picked up the intercom. Now all eyes were on Francesca.

She spoke, she listened, she nodded and then she undid her seatbelt. It must be safe to get up, I thought, and so I undid mine. A collective sigh of relief wafted throughout the rear cabin.

Once at the back of the plane again, I retrieved the coffee and tea pots and placed them on the metal counter for Margo to fill. She was just topping off the first pot with boiling water when it happened.

The plane jolted up and down and then from side to side.

As I staggered backwards and forwards and backwards again, I watched Margo in horror, helplessly, afraid that she would get badly scalded.

"Shi-i-i-t!" she cried. But she managed to dance with the plane's movements, holding the pot so close to the urn's spout that no water spilled on her.

"What the hell . . .?" I cursed as I fell back against the starboard toilet door. The intercom above the jump seat buzzed. Still hanging onto the toilet door handle for dear life, I reached out and picked it up.

"Take your seats," Mia's more-ruffled voice ordered. "No time to check seatbelts. It's just about to hit."

While the plane rolled and bumped, I emptied the freshly filled pot of coffee into the toilet once again and helped Margo ensure that everything in the galley was stowed. Then, trying not to land in passengers laps, Francesca and I used the backs of passenger seats to steady ourselves as we worked our way back to our jump seats. Once buckled in at Three-Door Right, I stared out of the porthole window into the pale blue sky and the minus-56-degree temperatures and prayed. I could see that the three people sitting directly in front of me were white-knuckling their arm rests as, above them, the ceiling panels creaked and moaned under what sounded like a lot of stress.

An eerie stillness pervaded the rear cabin as everyone listened and waited. I heard the engines tones change and remembered not to frown. But something wasn't right. There was an odd whirring noise as if a mechanism was trying to get started but failing. The noise continued for an eternity and the plane was, even in the turbulence, behaving strangely. Still, I managed to maintain my all-is-well face.

And I held my breath.

So did the passengers.

The plane continued to jostle, roll, shudder and groan for a long time, time enough for me to think of the strangest things. I thought of Margo and Julianna down the back, knowing that in turbulence the tail of a DC-10 wags like a dog. It's the worst place to be. Could this plane handle this amount of buffeting? Where was Jose now? In a plane, too, or at home with his wife? I thought of Dean and what it had been like going down on a crashing plane. I thought of my time with Dan Air where potential emergencies and dramas were a regular occurrence, but nothing of any consequence had ever occurred in my almost three years of flying on Laker DC-10s . . . yet. Although we had experienced a decompression going into LA once, it hadn't been a dive-out-of-the-sky situation. And then I wondered was this going to be my first emergency with Laker . . . or worse, my first *and* last?

All we could do was wait.

The tone of the aircraft changed yet again.

The PA pinged and Mia's relieved voice filled the cabins. "Ladies and gentlemen, the worst of the turbulence is over. Hurricane Alan has now passed us."

There was a collective gasp from passengers. Some people muttered, "What hurricane?"

"But we ask that you please keep your seat belts fastened," she continued. "Unexpected turbulence can occur at any time. Flight Attendants, resume your service."

On landing on solid ground in Miami for the second time in three days, while I didn't get down and kiss the ground, I silently thanked God for terra firma. As the first through Customs, I was the first to join the flight deck crew on the transport bus. All three men sat huddled at the back. I took my place in front of the engineer who seemed agitated.

Were they arguing?

"That shouldn't happen," I heard him telling the captain. "I'll have to put that in my report."

The captain gave the engineer a we'll-talk-about-it-later wave of his hand, unwilling to discuss whatever it was in front of cabin crew.

"Was something going wrong during the turbulence?" I whispered to the engineer over the top of my seat. "I'm sure I–"

"It was close," he muttered so no one else could hear. "The de-icer on the starboard side failed for a while going through the hurricane. We could have gone into a stall."

Ohmigod! After my gliding course a few years earlier, I understood the danger. If the plane has enough height and speed, you can pull out of a stall and survive. But with ice on one wing, the plane's aerodynamics would not . . . I didn't want to think about it.

"Natasha . . ." The engineer tapped me gently on the shoulder, and when I turned, he put a finger to his lips signalling my silence.

I nodded, understanding. No need to spread fear.

Francesca was the next to appear and she plonked herself down beside me. "Can I ask you a favour, Natasha?"

Uh-oh! I knew what was coming. "Don't tell me. You want me to come to Dean's house with you to get his clothes?"

"Would you?" she pleaded. Her big brown eyes were as beguiling as Mr. Charming's blue ones. They made a good pair—the beautiful couple.

"Okay." I sighed. I didn't blame her for not wanting to go anywhere in Miami by herself. "But we'll have to do it tonight before dinner," I said. "I'm really tired."

Just over an hour later our crew was enjoying cocktails this time in the room of our first officer, Gary. The captain, he told us, had already gone to bed, officially tired, in a bad mood and like all of us, so glad that the next day was our last sector and that this marathon would soon be over. Hurricane Alan was picking up force but, rumour had it, the storm was hurtling in another direction, and we would not be affected by its path.

"Too bad your boyfriend didn't get on," Gary said to Francesca as we sat on his bed finishing our rum and cokes. "Seems like a good bloke . . . and a good pilot."

Francesca beamed at him. "Thank you."

"If we are going to do this thing," I told Francesca, empathizing with our tired captain, "we will have to do it soon, or I'll fall asleep."

But Gary had not finished his conversation with Francesca. "Now which DC-9 crash—" he began.

"Sorry, Gary," Francesca said, standing up. "Natasha and I have to go."

As we travelled down in the hotel lift to the ground floor, I asked Francesca, "How far is it to Dean's place?"

"I think it's close," she said, sounding uncertain. "Don't worry. We'll catch a cab. It won't take long. We'll be in and out."

She made it sound so simple.

Our Cuban cab driver seemed to know exactly where to go. As I watched his profile from the back seat, I felt a stab in my heart. He was a dead ringer for Jose. But then Miami was full of Jose dead ringers. Seeing so many lookalikes made my heart flutter every time I sat in the hotel restaurant or lobby and watched them walk by. I must forget Jose, I admonished myself. He's off limits.

Whether it was fatigue or whether I was lost in dreamy memories of my lost love, I did not pay attention on how we got to Dean's place, but suddenly, the driver pulled up on a residential side street.

"We'll be about an hour," Francesca told him, as she handed him dollar bills. "Would you be able to come back at, say . . . 8.15 and pick us up?"

"Si, Si." He nodded and smiled as we clambered out.

The house was, like many in Miami, small and white with yellow awnings decorating every window to keep the blazing sun out. As I followed Francesca up the short driveway, I wondered why a DC-9 captain, albeit someone who had been on disability but who must have received a large compensation from the airline for his injuries, would live in such a humble abode. Then I remembered how many of our captains had three ex-wives and monthly alimonies to pay. Maybe Dean had an ex and children somewhere, too? Some of the Laker flight deck not only lived in humble abodes but also drove old beaters for cars. Not quite the wealthy, sexy, cigarette smoking, glamorous image of pilots that were portrayed in the Rothman ads on the London Underground.

Although Francesca and I were both exhausted, I noticed that, as soon as we had arrived at his address, her energy had shifted. Was she afraid that she would come across something of Dean's that she shouldn't find? But he had entrusted her with the key to his home so he couldn't have anything to hide, could he?

Her jitters were catching. My spidey-senses were beginning to bristle, too as if behind us we were being watched. Just as she put the key into the lock, I turned around. In the garden on the other side of the road, a man watering his flowers was eyeing us. Just a nosy neighbour, I decided.

"Have you been here before?" I asked Francesca.

"No," she said. "We always stay in a hotel room close to the Marriott."

Hmmm? Why?

We were now standing in a short hallway with several arched doorways to choose from. The kitchen, we could see, was straight ahead, the door open. The wooden floors were clean, although the house felt a little stale. Did he really live here? Francesca seemed unwilling to move.

"I'm guessing the bedroom is that one." I pointed to a door on the left farther down the short hallway. "He just wants clothes, right?"

"Yes," she said, but still stood motionless.

"What's the matter, Francesca? You don't think he's got a dead body stashed under the bed, do you?"

She stared at me, horrified, as if I was serious—or as if she herself had contemplated that very scenario.

"Com'on." I laughed and nudged her. "We need to find some kind of a suitcase to put things in." I walked ahead and opened the door, and we entered the first bedroom. Although there were twin beds with yellow quilts on them, the room was dusty, filled with cardboard boxes, and it had that same stale smell. It occurred to me that this house was *not* lived in but was more like . . . a place to store things.

Suddenly a deafening cacophony of thunderous noise reverberated throughout the house. Francesca and I stared at each other and froze. She grabbed my arm. The loud banging, stomping, and crashing sounded as if it was coming through both the back and the front of the house as well as the walls. The noise was all around us. Then we heard men shouting "FBI!"

Francesca and I stepped back, cowering, clinging to each other, terrified. "What the . . .?" she hissed.

The banging got louder. More men's voices shouting, grunting.

"Oh my God . . .?" I put my hands over my ears to ward off the violent assault on my senses. I began to tremble, afraid of what would come through the door. Were we going to get shot? Should we hide? We just stayed frozen to the spot.

A black monster wearing a mask over his face with white FBI letters on its chest appeared in the doorway, almost filling it. He raised the gun he was holding and pointed it at us.

"FBI!" he growled through his mask, just in case we couldn't read.

Francesca and I instinctively put our hands up.

"Get on the ground, hands behind your back," he barked.

Whimpering, Francesca and I obediently lay down on the carpet and did what he said. A funky, mildewy smell instantly pervaded my nostrils. I looked at her with a "What the hell's going on?" question on my face.

"I . . . I don't . . .know," she whispered, but the monster was bent over us putting handcuffs on us. The metal hurt, digging into my wrists. Then in one swift movement, and with one beefy hand under my right arm, he lifted me up and sat me on the side of a bed before positioning Francesca next to me.

As I always did in adrenalin-fuelled situations, I had an overwhelming urge to laugh. Was this Dean's idea of a joke? Or had we stumbled into a movie set? But if the FBI were really after Dean, just what could he be guilty of? Airline spying?

I glanced at Francesca. Something in her eyes told me that this wasn't a complete surprise to her. Had she suspected something "off" with Dean and that's why she had been nervous about coming here by herself?

The monster was standing over us now, his hand still on his gun though now in a prone position as he talked into his pager to his superior, while in other parts of the house the crashing continued.

"All clear!" a man yelled from another room in the house, and the noise diminished. Now we could hear men and women talking in normal voices as drawers and cupboards were being open and closed.

Soon a tall, lean man in a tired tan suit and yellow checkered shirt appeared in the doorway. Was he really trying to emulate a taller version of the TV detective, Columbo?

"Who do we have here, Sergeant? Some B & Ers or druggies?" Tall-and-Lean now towered over us, no doubt trying to intimidate us. He needn't have bothered. We were both terrified. What the hell had we walked into?

"No, I . . . I . . ." Francesca's face crumpled, and she began sobbing.

"It's okay, Francesca," I told her. Showing more courage than I felt, I gave the detective my most evil eye. "*We* haven't done anything wrong."

"We'll see about that," Tall-and-Lean drawled. "We watched you from across the street. You let yourself in. Where'd yer get the key? Planning on a pick-up, were you?"

"Well, yes," I said. "That's exactly why we're here. To pick up some–"

"Sergeant, did you hear that? We even have a confession from these two . . ." He frowned. "You sound like you're fresh off the boat from England. Where do you live?"

"Listen, I don't know what's happening here," I told the tall man in my most dignified upper class British accent, "but we are two air stewardesses with Laker Airways, and my friend here has been dating

Dean, a pilot with Delta and the occupant of this house. He is stuck in the UK, so he asked Francesca to come and collect–."

Tall-and-Lean scoffed. So did the monster standing behind him. "Excuse me! You think he's a wha-a-t? A pilot, did you say? With Delta?"

Both Francesca and I looked up at him and nodded mutely.

The detective, or whatever he was, laughed and shook his head. "That's a new one. And you're flight attendants? Interesting."

"Yes," we both mumbled in unison.

"And how much exactly did he ask you to collect?" He looked around at the boxes and, just as I had done, frowned.

Francesca had calmed down now, but she was completely confused. "How much . . . what?"

"Com'on, ladies, I know how you flight attendants operate. How much snow were you planning on picking up? Save me some time. Just tell me where it is . . ."

"Snow?" I stared at Francesca. "Does he mean . . . cocaine?"

She began to cry again. "Oh no . . . no . . . How could I have been so-o-o stew-pid!"

"That's funny, detective," I told him, anger in my voice. "Or whatever you are. You see, we were just here to pick up some *extra clothes* for Dean as he got stranded in the UK for a few days. So, he gave Francesca his key and here we are. We don't know anything about any snow or cocaine. All we know is that Dean's a pilot who flies for Delta and that's all."

"Well, if you're telling the truth, girls," Tall-and-Lean said, softening, "and we *will* find out, I'm sorry to tell you that the man who lives in this house is not called Dean, and he sure ain't no pilot with Delta."

Behind hm the monster snickered again. "Then ... what ...?" Francesca's terror was dialling down now to confusion and simmering rage.

"If you *are* telling the truth, you been had." Tall-and-Lean sat down in a faded armchair across from us. "He has a lot of aliases, but your boyfriend's real name is Joe Reich and he's an international cocaine dealer and a real good con man. Re-e-al slippery. If I'm right about you two, he had you snowed, too." He grinned at his own joke.

"So ...you mean, he's definitely *not* a pilot?" I asked, remembering that Dean had flown the DC-10 with 365 innocent passengers and 13 trusting crew on board.

Francesca bowed her head, letting her thick hair fall over her face, and sobbed.

"Take the cuffs off," Mr. Tall-and-Lean instructed the monster who complied with surprising gentleness. "So, ladies, where is he now ... what d'yer call him ... Dean?"

Francesca rubbed her wrists then wiped her face. "He's at my house in England," she said, her breath catching. She stared at me; eyes wide. "He's got my credit card!"

"Oh, no, Francesca!" I put my arm around her. The shattering of her trust in him was going to be hard to live with for a long time, but a large credit bill might take even longer.

"You two will have come to the precinct with us," the detective said, all efficiency again. "The officer here will get your details and take you. We've gotta lotta questions to ask. In the meantime, if he does call you tonight or tomorrow, just act like everything's copasetic. Understood?"

"But ... we've got to fly out tomorrow. Will we ...?" I envisioned Francesca and I spending nights in an American jail with some really scary people. My hospital visit in Bangor on my first US trip had been terrifying enough.

"Don't worry, Ma'am," he answered, intuiting my question. "If you haven't been complicit in all this, you'll be able to fly back, and we'll probably be coming with you." He paused. "But if you *are* involved, we're gonna lock you up!"

That night from the precinct, as first Francesca and then I was grilled on our knowledge of Dean, aka Joe Reich, we were forced to call Mia Pascuole, our fearless leader, and get her out of bed. She in turn called a grumpy captain to let him know that two of his crew were being held by the FBI and Miami police under suspicion of drug trafficking. While the police finally accepted the fact that we were indeed just innocent victims in Dean's nefarious plots, the repetitive questions and the drinking of bad coffee was harrowing. It was midnight Miami time and 5.00 a.m. UK time before they delivered us back to the hotel. Desperate for sleep, I decided that the suntanning I had planned for the following day would have to wait.

On our final sector from Miami back to London Gatwick and home base, the whole crew was subdued. Three FBI men, including Mr. Tall-and-Lean sat in the forward cabin, a serious reminder of what had transpired. Our low energy was probably due to overwhelming fatigue, but I sensed that we were all feeling the loss of a potentially beautiful love-story, a loss of trust and a loss of hope as if another hurricane had blown through our lives, creating more turbulence and rattling our equilibrium.

Francesca wasn't the only one facing humiliation. On the return sector on the flight deck and later throughout the airline, the captain was the merciless butt of jokes for letting a con man fly his plane. But we had all fallen under Dean's spell, allowing him to make fools of the whole crew. Maybe we had just needed to believe in a happy ending?

When not serving passengers, a devastated Francesca sat on the rear jump seat and stared blankly out of the porthole into a cloudless blue sky.

"Eee, chuck, don't feel too bad," Margo said, trying to comfort her. "We've all given our hearts away for love, and sometimes we've given our credit cards too, or something even more precious."

But Francesca was inconsolable. She shook her head, tears sliding down her cheeks. "I'm such an idiot."

"Listen," Margo stood hand on hip in front of her, "if he can fool the FBI, the captain and everyone on this crew, you're not so daft, are you? We all believed him so that makes us idiots, too."

Francesca wiped her tears. "I suppose so," she said, lifting her head a little. "But when the credit card bill comes in, I will be the one left alone with a broken heart, a depleted bank account and total and complete humiliation."

"You could see it that way," I said, "or you could remember that he did love you in his way, he was gorgeous, and while you trusted and loved him, you *were* happy. That wasn't a lie. That's all still real."

"Ach, we all believe what we want to believe," Julianna added.

"I'll never believe in love again." Francesca sighed.

"Oh, yes you will," Margo said. "But it doesn't matter how gorgeous he is or how many stripes he has, next time you better check his credentials."

"Nudge, nudge, wink, wink," Julianna said and snickered.

Margo rolled her eyes. "I mean his *professional* credentials!"

"I think all our boyfriends need to be checked out," Julianna commented, "by the FBI, Interpol, the FAA, the CAA, *and* Scotland Yard."

"And don't feel too bad, Francesca," I told her. "A friend of mine married a real pilot, had a child *and then* found out he was already married. At least you didn't go that far. What can I say? Men lie."

Finally, Francesca lifted her head and smiled at all of us. "Thank God for girlfriends," she said, standing up. "Well, I better get back to the front. Would you believe the FBI guys are my new best friends? And they may want a drink."

With head held high, she picked up her tray and disappeared into the shadowy cabin.

16

RUDE AWAKENINGS

Barbados
November 1981

The bird-like trill of the phone brought me from a deep, dark and happy place to consciousness. I opened my eyes into pitch blackness. Where was I? Oh yes, Barbados. For a whole week! It must be the middle of the night. So, who was calling me at this godforsaken hour?

"Ms. Rosewood?" The masculine Bajan voice sounded sombre on the phone.

"Yes," I responded sleepily. Who was this? And why was he ruining my lovely deep sleep?

"You am got to be in de lobby in 30 minutes to report for duty," the voice commanded.

Oh, I know what this is, I thought. Though groggy, I smiled. The rest of the crew thought that I might be sleeping with my new local boyfriend, Lee, and had decided it would be a good gag to get someone to wake me up, get me out of my bed, make me get dressed and report for some bogus duty. But while my relationship with Lee was promising, it was still fresh, and I was sleeping alone.

"Very funny!" I told the male voice and put the phone back in the cradle. I turned over, snuggling into my comfy pillow and closed my eyes.

The phone rang again.

"Who is this?" I demanded, now annoyed.

"Madam," the same voice intoned, also irritated. "Dis am naw joke. You have to wok. De udder crew bin on de aircraft for 10 hours. Now you got to do de return flight."

"Wha-a-a-t?" I sat up in bed, trying to absorb what the man was saying.

"De captain say you got to be in de lobby in t'irty minutes!"

"I . . . I . . .yes," I mumbled, then clicking into professional mode said, "Yes. Okay. I'll be there."

After I hung up, I put my head in my hands and moaned out loud. "No-o-o-o." The prospect of getting up in the middle of the night after just two hours sleep, putting on a sticky uniform and doing a return sector of anywhere between 10 to 12 hours filled me with dread. Lee, when he found out, would not be happy either. Despite running a large local family business, a chicken factory, he had managed to get some precious time off so we could spend days enjoying the island and each other. But now I was being sent home.

"Fuddle! Fuddle! Fuddle!" I cursed, while clambering out of bed and fumbling for the lights. I hurriedly gathered up my scattered uniform, so happily discarded just hours earlier and remembering the moment when Lee had met me at Bridgetown airport at 4.00 that afternoon and suggested, "How about we gaw for a sunset cruise on the *Jolly Roger* tonight?" As well as being strong, dark and handsome, Lee also had an endearing Bajan accent, his island lilt always sounding strange coming out of a white person's mouth.

"That would be lovely," I had cooed. The *Jolly Roger* was the infamous faux pirate ship that cruised up and down the coast of Barbados and from which no one departed sad or sober. Instead of the usual daytime party on board with semi-naked, inebriated tourists, at night we could enjoy dancing and a romantic island sunset.

"You won't be too tired?" he had asked, concerned.

"Nah," I lied, thinking of the hectic flight we had just survived with over-excited holidaymakers. By the end of these Barbados epics, making stops in Luxembourg and/or the Azores–and constantly having to make PAs and answer incessant passenger questions in four languages, my voice was reduced to a squeak. Though German passengers found the sound of my strained vocal cords highly amusing, I was always mentally and physically drained.

"I'm fine," I reassured him, sitting back in his deluxe air-conditioned Cadillac as he drove me to the Paradise Beach Hotel where most of my crew were staying. "I've got all week to recover. But some of my colleagues might also like to join us if that's okay?"

Lee had shrugged. "Naw problem."

Now, at 2.20 a.m. as I climbed back into my uniform, I wondered what kind of tech problem could have caused a 10-hour delay. No doubt passengers had been stuck on the same aircraft we had flown on from Gatwick. I prayed that it was now fixed because the returning holidaymakers we would inherit from the out-of-hours crew would be very hot and bothered by now. There were no hotels on the island that could accommodate 365 passengers on short notice, nor was the airport lounge big enough to seat that many. In this humidity without air conditioning and with no smoking allowed on board, the delay that passengers had experienced would have been unbearable. But even without those conditions, a ten-hour delay and all its subsequent complications would not make for happy campers. Oh, joy!

And how was the other crew feeling? All their plans had gone to hell in a hand basket, too. Instead of doing just a min rest and then going home, they would now be enjoying seven unscheduled days in

Barbados, though only prepared for a quick turnaround with one bikini and one extra pair of knickers and a summer dress if they were lucky. While some of the crew might be ecstatic, others would be furious about this schedule change, all their plans with boyfriends, husbands and/or friends at home blown away in the wind. But none of us had signed up for this job because we loved a predictable routine. I, for one, thrived on last-minute changes, though not this kind of change, and not tonight.

As I wheeled my suitcase along the winding path through the dark shrubbery to the lobby, I felt a twinge in my lower back and remembered that while dancing with Lee on the *Jolly Roger* earlier, I had gone ass-over-teakettle on the slippery deck—probably due to the spilled cocktails—and landed unceremoniously on the base of my spine. Thanks to the anesthetic effects of two rum punches, I hadn't felt too much pain. After an amused Lee had pulled me back up—and once the initial winded feeling had passed—I had just carried on dancing. If I had caused any real damage, I still wasn't feeling any pain.

The expressions on the faces of my crew gathered in the lobby reflected my own dismay. Just five of the cabin staff had been staying at our hotel, the Paradise Beach. Our remaining colleagues were Bajan girls who had gone home to be with their families or boyfriends. One of the English girls was also missing, but we knew she was with her new husband at the Sands Resort just next door as this week in Barbados was supposed to have been their honeymoon. While they would be miserable at having missed out on a free week in paradise to celebrate their nuptials, I would eventually get over my cancelled plans with Lee. And hopefully, so would he. I knew that a lot of boyfriends got fed up with the disappointments of cancelled social events and soon ended relationships. There did seem to be a certain type of man, though, who didn't mind the last-minute changes. But would Lee be one of those?

Julianna was sitting in a lobby chair yawning. Mark, the fun-loving gay steward had his eyes closed as, like me, he was feeling the lack of sleep as both he and Juliana had partied on the cruise with Lee and me earlier. Then there was Ingrid, the tall Teutonic girl who had introduced me to my now ex-boyfriend, Jack. She was standing at the open entrance of the lobby, alert and the only one of us ready to leap into action. Our flight deck crew had already gone ahead to the airport but how long had it been since those pilots had imbibed alcohol? I wondered. Like us, definitely not the regulatory eight hours. Even now I could feel the wooliness of an oncoming hangover, fatigue and lack of sleep encroaching on my brain. This flight was going to be the longest flight of my life.

Franny, our Irish IFD, was on the phone at the front desk, tracking down the new bride and then giving the bad news to the Bajan girls, dragging them away from their homes and families and boyfriends. What a rude awakening!

Lee wouldn't appreciate a call at this time, so I scribbled a note for him and asked the man behind the front desk, the same man I had hung up on, to please call my boyfriend in the morning and give him the message. "Aw, naw problem," he said, recognizing Lee's name. Barbados is a small island.

As we climbed into the transport, I felt an emotional wrench at leaving my paradise. Barbados had this strange hold on me, as if it was really my home. Perhaps in a past life I had also been a Caribe, though maybe what I felt for Barbados was just simple gratitude for how my vacation here, and meeting Jose, had healed my wounded soul. The joy I always felt being on the island liberated me, and being sent back to a cold, rainy England in November now felt like punishment for some crime I had not committed.

As our crew was driven over the pitted roads in the pitch-black night, we were silent, either too tired or too upset at losing our week in paradise to speak. Over the noise of the old van barrelling along, we could still hear the whistling frogs and the gentle rustling of sugar cane in the breeze.

Inside the too-warm DC-10 sitting on the tarmac, the weary and exasperated inbound crew were beyond relieved to see us. Already wearing their hats and gloves and clutching their crew bags, they were clustered around the door like flies on treacle, eager to make their escape, get out of their polyester tunics and trousers sticking to their perspiring frames and collapse into their beds. Behind them, the passengers in the cabin were sprawled in their seats, hot and bothered, tired and restless, the whole plane stinking in the heat. Not a good combination. Tempers would be short and frayed, I thought. As they saw us arrive, some of the passengers sat up in their seats, hope in their eyes. Something was happening, they sensed, but what?

Mary-Beth Clarke, the popular Bajan IFD of the crew we were replacing, huddled in the galley with our IFD, Franny, briefing her on the information she would need for the flight. While more catering was loaded, we juniors stood around, awaiting instructions. Two of the Bajan girls hadn't appeared yet, but locals weren't known for their speed. Legally we could fly with just eight out of the usual compliment of ten crew members—one stewardess per door and per fifty passengers—but that would mean extra work for everyone, and no one was in the mood for that.

Before Mary-Beth left the aircraft, she turned to us all, standing there almost asleep on our feet with hangovers officially kicking in. Seeing our sad demeanours, she shrugged helplessly and said, "Saw sorry, but dawn't bother yer heads, darlin's. Once you take off, dese passengers will just gaw to sleep." When we didn't react, she grabbed her bag and with a "Have a good flight," tossed over her shoulder, and flounced happily off the aircraft and down the stairs.

The bride, Diane, appeared in the aircraft doorway looking stunned, accompanied by a despondent man, presumably her new husband. Mary-Jo was right behind them, wearing a red dress, but not the Laker uniform.

"I washed me dress as soon as I got hawme," Mary Jo explained to Franny, "but it was still wet when I got de call, saw I couldn't put it on."

"Ach, do yer tink I care?" Franny snorted. "As long as yer're here. But you're a Number T'ree, aren't you, so you can work downstairs." Then assuming her IFD mode, Franny waved us all into the galley where we were out of the passengers' earshot. "Gather round, girralls and Mark."

"So, dis is de deal," she started. "Dere was a fuel leak, which dey've fixed now, but de poor bastards have been stuck on dis plane for a helluva long time, so we'll need a little sympat'y for deir bad behaviour. After take-off we'll do de usual drinks service and dinner and den let's hope to God dey all go into a coma until we land, but we'll put de film on anyway. T'ank heavens, we're flying direct to Gatwick. We've got mainly Germans, some Scandinavians, and some French, so Ingrid, you can do most of de German PAs and, Natasha, you'll do de other languages. I know dis is tough for all of us, but let's do de best we can and smile. Okay?" She surveyed our glum faces. "Now we're still missing . . ." Franny checked her paperwork. ". . . Anne-Marie. If she doesn't show up before doors close, we'll go wit'out her. She's Number Seven, so Julianna, you take her place up front. Do I need to test yer on de emergency drills fer dat position?"

Julianna shook her head.

"What's the movie?" I asked, knowing that German passengers would give me the third degree. "Vhere is ze movie screen?" "Vat iss ze movie called?" "Vhat iss ze film about?" "Iss it a good film, *ja*?" "Who iss in ze film?" were just some of the questions they would fire at me in English or German as I handed out headsets.

Franny consulted her written brief. "*Where Eagles Dare.*"

"Isn't that about World War Two?" Mark enquired, concerned.

I smiled, remembering how at Gatwick, before all our German passengers had boarded for the outbound flight, Franny had goosestepped down the forward aisle, finger under the nose, doing her John Cleese imitation and announcing, "Don't talk about ze vor!"

"Ach," Franny said now, waving a dismissive hand. "Dey'll all be asleep by den, to be sure."

Now resigned to our fate, we moved toward our respective positions, removing hats and gloves and preparing for an epic flight. Even before Franny, Ingrid and I made our pre-take-off PAs, fatigued passengers were tidying up their belongings, putting games away and preparing for take-off.

Three hours later, at cruising altitude in a cooler, air-conditioned aircraft, and after having been fed and watered, both smoking and non-smoking passengers seemed content knowing that they were finally on their way.

"Ladies and Gentlemen," Franny began her PA, "we will now be showing the film *Where Eagles Dare* starring Clint Eastwood and Richard Burton. We would ask dat you please pull down your window shades so dat you can see de movie and so dat others can sleep." While Ingrid repeated the instructions in German, and I followed in French and Norwegian, passengers reclined their seats and got comfy.

We dimmed the lights and set up bar carts in the lighted forward and rear galleys. As the film credits began to roll, a quiet settled over all three cabins, and the crew breathed a collective sigh of relief. For at least one and a half hours passengers would watch the movie—or sleep. And we could rest.

"You two," Franny said, pointing at Julianna and me, "go on first break." Without any argument, we both descended, along with Mark who'd been working at the rear, into the lower galley.

"Good job you had a red dress," I commented to Mary-Jo, our Bajan galley-slave, as she handed me my hot meal. "At least you kind of look like a member of the crew."

She harrumphed. Like the rest of us, she was not in the mood for chit-chat. "I'm gawin' to miss me mudder's birthday party," she moaned. "She cried when I had to gaw."

"Oh, I'm so sorry," I commiserated. We all had our sad stories.

The intercom on the wall above the sink buzzed and Mary-Jo turned and grabbed the receiver. I watched as she frowned and then nodded. "De IFD wants you all upstairs right *now*," she told the three of us. "Dey is a problem."

We exchanged looks of alarm. *Oh no*, I thought immediately. *The fuel leak!* Did we have an emergency? Please God, not tonight, I prayed.

Julianna, Mark and I abandoned our half-eaten meals and squeezed into the lift. What was awaiting us up there? But even as we ascended, we heard loud noises coming from the cabin, like a raucous pub crowd out of control. What the hell was going on?

The lift clunked to a standstill, and we stepped out. Four crew, including Franny and the Number One from the rear were huddled, alarmed, around the drinks cart.

Shouting and yelling was coming from both sides of the forward and rear cabins. Sick bags, plastic coffee cups, paper, pens, miniature bottles, magazines and mineral cans were flying like missiles past the galley, some landing adjacent to us on the floor. The energy in the cabin was no longer docile, but more like the aftermath of a

Manchester United football match after they had lost to Man City. Why were passengers rioting?

"Sorry to interfere with your break, but we're going to need yer help," Franny shouted over the din.

"What's going on?" Julianna asked, shocked at the hullabaloo and frightened by the flying debris.

"All I know is," Franny explained, clearly shaken, "dat de film's been on for about forty minutes. At first all was fine, but den a low grumbling started down de back and spread t'roughout all t'ree cabins. Passengers were getting antsy in deir seats, and den dey got louder and angrier. And now you can see dey're fit to be tied."

Julianna peered cautiously from behind the galley starboard bulkhead into the middle cabin but quickly dodged back in again, narrowly avoiding contact with a low-flying coke can. "What are they saying?" she asked me.

From the shouting in the forward cabin, I could distinguish some German swearing. *"Scheiss Koepfe!" "Dass ist Quatsch!" "Nicht Wahr!" "Dumme Amerikaner!"*

"They're calling the film rubbish and saying it's not true. Is it?" I asked Mark.

"Well, the premise is," Mark supplied, "that at the end of World War Two, an American and a British soldier get into this supposedly impenetrable German castle and fool the Nazis into revealing their spy network which essentially ends the war—or something like that." He shrugged. "It's safe to assume that these pax don't like how the Germans are portrayed."

"But it's not a true story?" Julianna asked.

Mark shook his head. "No, but maybe they think it's *our* version of how the war was won."

Franny and I tentatively peered around the galley bulkhead. She looked forward, peering into the darkened Cabin A, while I looked down to the middle section. Some people were leaning out into the aisle to lambaste the movie and swear at Clint Eastwood and Richard Burton. Others were standing on their seats and shaking their fists at the movie screen, throwing whatever they could lay their hands on toward the front of their cabin and the flickering images. Others were tossing mineral cans, cups and any other kind of debris they could find and hissing, "*Dass ist Scheisse*!" and other even ruder German curses which I didn't care to interpret. The few French and Scandinavian passengers were cowering in their seats while a full-scale riot was taking place in all three cabins!

Franny and I both pulled quickly back into the lighted galley.

"Geez!" Franny exclaimed. "Dis is like bluddy Belfast on a Saturday night. I'll do a PA and try to calm dem down, but I'll be needin' yer all to go out dere and shut down de movie screens. Yer better go in pairs or de bastards might kill yer." She addressed her Number One. "Anna, you do de same ting down de back."

In my mind the biggest danger in-flight had always been an out-of-control passenger, but now we had over 300 of them, all going nuts. This could be very dangerous.

From the safety of the galley, we watched as Franny, with her shoulders hunched, moved toward Two Door Left, dodging missiles. Just as she picked up the intercom, a miniature bottle grazed her arm.

Her body language suddenly changed. Instead of cowering, she straightened up and I could see her fiery Irish temper coming to the fore. "Ladies and Gentlemen," she yelled into the PA. "If you are going to behave like children, den we must treat you like children! You must all return to your seats *now*. For the remainder of dis flight, dere will be *no* bar service, except if you are lucky, we might give you a glass of water. The cabin staff will be shutting down de screens immediately. You must stop t'rowing tings! If *any* of my crew or other passengers are hurt or de aircraft is damaged by your bad behaviour, you will be taken off at Gatwick and arrested."

Over the noise of their continued ranting, even Franny's authoritative words could barely be heard, but in the galley Julianna and I exchanged good-for-you-Franny looks! I had never witnessed a stewardess speak to even one passenger like that, let alone an IFD scold a planeload of troublemakers. But for everyone's safety she needed to reassert control.

The anger, yelling and cursing became a little quieter but still continued. Frustrated, she called me over. "Natasha," she said, handing me the phone, "tell dem what I just said in German . . . exactly."

"*Meine Damen und Herren*," I began, thinking about how to paraphrase Franny's stern warning and hoping they wouldn't take their wrath out on me. "*Sie mussen jetzt . . .*"

Suddenly a hush descended inside the whole aircraft. Perhaps it was hearing the message in their own language that caused them to pay attention, but magically the missiles stopped flying. Like shamed children having been reprimanded and told to go to their rooms for time out, everyone—even the biggest, angriest male passengers—quietly slunk back into their seats. With garbage everywhere, the cabins now resembled a football stadium where hoodlum supporters had done battle.

Silence reigned.

"Tank de Lord," Franny muttered, exhaling. "Okay, girralls. Shut down de screens and dismantle de bar cart. Den I need all of yer on deck to make sure the plonkers behave. Sorry girralls—and Mark—you'll have to take yer break up here."

Could this night get any worse?

The answer to that was, yes, it could.

Once the screens were up in their stowages and there was no alcohol in sight for enraged passengers to consume, each of us took up our positions on our jump seats. Maybe they had just needed to expend their rage at being stuck on this aircraft for so long, and a politically incorrect German war movie had given them a good excuse to go wild.

Soon, with no entertainment, and with all three cabins darkened, most passengers slept. How I envied them!

An hour later while sitting on my jump seat at Two Door Right, I was fighting to stay awake. Despite being on my third cup of disgustingly tar-like airline black coffee, my eyelids were getting heavier and heavier.

"Bul-o-o-o-dy hell!!" The sound of Franny's curse and the slamming of her clipboard on the metal galley surface made me jump. She had just come from the flight deck. *Uh-oh.*

"Now what?" I asked.

She waved me into the galley where we were out of earshot of passengers. "You'll never guess what?"

I shook my head, too tired to think. Anything was possible.

"We have to divert into Gander!" she moaned.

"Gander? In Newfoundland?" I frowned. "What for?"

"Dey're still worried about de fuel leak, and dey don't tink we'll make it across de Atlantic without refueling. Passengers will stay on de aircraft."

My brain was foggy and refused to figure out the implications. "So . . .?"

"It means," Franny snapped, "instead of another t'ree hours on this flight, dat now we'll be landin' in Gander in an hour, and den we have anodder five-to-six-hour sector from Gander to Gatwick."

I was right. This was going to be the longest flight of my life. "Won't the flight deck go out of hours?" I tried to do the math in my head, but my tired brains cells were clogged, and nothing came.

"Probably," Franny snorted. "But de Captain has decided in his wisdom dat dey can go as long as it takes so we don't have to stay in Gander. Legally, as yer know, dey can go up to 14 hours, but he just wants to get home. Now we won't have time before landing to serve dese poor buggers breakfast, so dey'll have to wait until we take off again, and it'll be another hour before dey get fed. Den we'll have 365 angry *and* hungry pax. Dey might do more dan just riot . . . dey might just bloody well kill us. Will dis nightmare never end?"

Apparently not.

We were afraid of disturbing sleeping passengers with a rude awakening, but Franny still felt obliged to keep them informed, and I followed her announcements with the other languages. Although a collective groan rippled throughout the cabins, people's reactions were surprisingly mild. Until, that is, we were on the descent into Gander.

That's when children began to cry, and some adults began complaining of feeling faint with hunger. We plied them with teas and coffees and tiny biscuits, hoping to stave off their pangs, but that wasn't enough for some. With no time to serve a hot breakfast before landing, the only food we could offer was our crew snacks, which Franny asked if we would be willing to surrender for the children. Despite our own gnawing empty stomachs, we, of course, said, "Yes."

At that moment Ingrid appeared in the front galley with a full tray of debris. She emptied her load into a garbage bag, and said, "You know, zese Americans are so bloody rude!"

I just nodded. The Americans weren't the only ones to have a franchise on rudeness. Every nationality had its bad 'uns.

"Zis man just asked me for a second cup of coffee. So, I told him, 'I am sorry, sir, but vee are just landing and I am unable to serve more coffee.' Do you know vot he said?"

I waited.

"Give me anosser fucking cup of coffee!"

"How rude!" I managed.

"So, *I* said . . ." Ingrid's face remained stoic, but I could see from the twinkle in her eye that she was pleased with herself. 'I am sorry, *sir*, but vee only serve normal coffee on zis flight. Zee fucking you vill haff to do for yourself!"

I smiled, imagining Ingrid looking down her Teutonic nose at the man and him shrinking under her disdain. "How'd he like them apples?" I asked.

"Ach, he just stared at me und said, 'Huh?'"

Our drole retorts were often lost on passengers due to diverse cultural backgrounds, language difficulties or fatigue, but a sense-of-humour failure, the most common of all, was what—on finally, finally arriving home—I would also experience.

Waiting for me on the living room coffee table was a note in Ellen's handwriting:

Lee called. He was sorry not to be able to say goodbye. He insisted that I give you this message. While he really likes you, he doesn't think this relationship will work long-distance. He wishes you well.

Well, I sure know how to pick 'em, don't I? I thought, doing an inventory of my most recent and failed romances; a gorgeous travelling South American businessman–who had turned out to be married—a single, wealthy aristocrat who was a non-committal workaholic, and now Lee, a handsome and successful entrepreneur who couldn't handle a long-distance relationship with an air stewardess.

Maybe this was another rude awakening? Was the universe trying to tell me that I needed to change my choices in men and pick someone local and more ordinary like . . . an accountant? But this was too much to think about. Right now, today, I needed to sleep for a very, very long time.

As Scarlett O'Hara intoned in *Gone with the Wind*, "After all, tomorrow is another day. . ."

17

HIJACKED!

Barbados
December 1981

"Did I hear you correctly?" I asked the young Crewing member on the phone. "You mean you're rostering me to fly to Barbados as a *passenger* for a whole week, do a three-hour duty to St. Lucia on the Tuesday and then deadhead back to Gatwick. . . after a week. . . as a passenger?"

"That's right," he affirmed.

This sounded too good to be true. "Why?"

"They need a language speaker."

I knew he wasn't just referring to my German-speaking ability. When we dropped into Luxembourg en route to Barbados, we picked up passengers from all over Europe and a speaker was required for French, Italian, Spanish, Scandinavian and others. Unlike Dan Air—who had exploited my linguistic ability and worked me to the bone, Laker had often bestowed prize trips on me, like weeks in Berlin, and now this one. So instead of the usual laborious fourteen-hour Barbados flight, I would be deadheading—travelling as a passenger—there *and* back. As Monty Python would say, "Luxury!" Paying me to go on what was essentially a week's holiday in Barbados seemed an expensive proposition for the airline, but who was I to argue?

"Departure Sunday at 1200 hours," Crewing man added. "You can travel in civvies."

Phew. If I didn't travel in uniform, that meant that they couldn't change their minds and make me work.

Excited, I hung up the phone, but who could I tell? Both my flatmates were away, and my flying colleagues often jealously commented, "What? You're going to Barbados *again?*" to which I now bluntly replied, "Well, if you learned four languages, you could, too." Bragging, though, didn't win me any popularity contests.

And then I remembered. Jack! Recently, my love life had taken another turn, for the better. Since my New York in June when Jose and I had had our last conversation leaving me numb, then last month, after my rudely interrupted Barbados trip caused Bajan Lee to bail on our budding romance, my intention had been to swear off exciting men and go for some local Mr. Boring. But as soon as Jack—dashing at 6' 4" tall and with strawberry blonde hair—had beamed at me from the other side of the host's kitchen at an airline party, that idea flew right out of the window. Like magnets, I knew Jack and I would get back together again soon. And so we did.

This time it would be different, I told myself, and it was. Thankfully, Jack, being a workaholic and world-traveller, wasn't fazed by the unpredictability of my occupation. "Have fun and see you when you get back," was his nonchalant response when I told him of my upcoming week away.

As I took my seat at the rear of the plane on the Sunday, I was apprehensive about the crews' reaction to me sitting on my bum deadheading while they worked. My friends Amy and Margo as well as Katie and the lone steward, Simon, were working down the back. To my relief, they all seemed pleased to see me, even if I was in civvies.

"Ee, yer jammy bugger," Margo commented good-naturedly. On the many min-rest Barbados trips we had done together, she knew how much harder I worked than the other girls, doing all the PAs in different languages as needed and running up and down the aircraft interpreting passenger's questions or requests.

"Who's the captain?" I asked Amy, as she handed me the customary after-takeoff rum punch.

"Oh, we've got a grand crew!" she said in her soft Dublin lilt. "Sexy Lexy and . . . Ben Atkins! And yer know, of course, Cathy's de IFD."

"That's great, but let's hope it's not pouring in Barbados." Amy and I both laughed, remembering our rain-filled Toronto trip the previous year with these same crew members. This is going to be the best trip, I thought as I relaxed into my seat with my drink. "Well, if you need any help, just let me know," I offered.

"Oh, don't worry, dear," Simon piped up from the other end of the cart. "We'll put you to work if we need you."

"I didn't really mean it!" I grinned. "I was just being polite."

Once on the tarmac at Grantley Adams International, or BGI as we knew it, and the crew had finally opened the front and rear doors, I relished that first blast of warm, humid air as it wafted into the aircraft. In my hotel room, and having liberated myself from restrictive English winter clothing, I donned flimsy summer wear, savouring the feeling of freedom. Unlike some of my colleagues, I found the humidity and the lackadaisical pace of the locals to be part of the island's charm. Compared to some of our other destinations–New York, LA and Miami–Barbados with its happy, friendly people was for us the safest in our otherwise unsafe list of destinations.

The next morning my first order of business was to go to the beach and find Embers, the generously figured older Bajan woman who braided hair. While I sat on her battered plastic chair under the shade of a densely-leaved manchineel tree, Embers once again tugged at and tightly interwove my long thick strands and then put a colourful bead on the end of each thin plait followed by a tiny piece of silver foil. Although the process took four hours, it freed me for a whole week from having to deal with my long humidity-damaged, fly-away hair.

While Embers created her work of art, I faced the ocean and enjoyed watching the comings and goings on the beach in front of me. Twenty yards down the sand to my right, some of my bikini-clad crew were lined up like soldiers on chaise-lounges close to the water's edge soaking up the hot sun while Margo and two other girls were splashing in the turquoise Caribbean Ocean.

Embers chatted to me in her strong Bajan dialect while she worked—most of which I couldn't understand. I only half-listened as the rhythmic lapping of small waves on the beach hypnotically soothed my soul. I closed my eyes.

Suddenly a piercing scream came from somewhere to the right, behind Embers. She turned around to look. I tried following her gaze, but her ample bosom blocked my view.

"What's going on?" I asked.

"Aw naw!" Embers exclaimed, still peering at the water. "De poor girl got needles. Dat naw good."

"What. . .? Who?" I asked, leaning forward, trying to see.

"Sea urchins, darlin'," Embers said, standing to the side to give me a wider view. "Dey hurt like hell!"

Now I could see that Margo was limping up the beach, supported on either side by Simon and Amy, her right foot held above the sand. They assisted her to her chaise where she sat, still holding her foot aloft. Then while Margo whimpered and grimaced in pain, the rest of the crew gathered around her, peering down at what was causing her distress.

"Dem bad," Embers muttered, returning to my braiding. "She gotta get a man to piss on her or dey stay in de skin."

"Piss on her?"

"Yes, mon. De man's urine makes de needles dead an' den dey coom out."

Ugh! I immediately had visions of poor Margo, standing on one leg, and holding the other out for the treatment. "Couldn't they just collect the urine from someone and pour it over her foot?" I asked.

"Aw, naw, mon. Got to be fresh piss, straight from de tap."

Suddenly the group parted, and I saw that they were helping Margo to stand up. Our first officer, Ben, in his bathing trunks, was approaching accompanied by one of the waiters, who was dressed in the full white uniform of the hotel. They seemed to be in a discussion. Were they talking about another antidote or, worse, discussing which man would do the deed?

The Bajan waiter pointed to a tree further down the beach, away from the tourists.

Uh oh.

I watched as Ben and the black waiter half-walked, half-carried Margo along the beach to the tree. Poor thing! I sat back in my chair, hiding behind Embers ample bosom, grateful now that I could *not* see what was taking place.

The next day with a developing tan and my newly braided hair pinned up in a bun, I boarded the transport bus from the Paradise Beach Hotel to the airport for our short St. Lucia flight.

"Margo!" I said, surprised to see her on the bus. She had been absent for dinner the night before. "Are you okay?" I asked as I sat beside her.

Surprisingly, she laughed. "Ee bah gum, lass, after 'e peed on me foot, it were a bluddy miracle. All the needles just died and worked their way out and then broke off."

"Who did the honors?"

"I don't rightly know. I told them I didn't want to know. I just covered me eyes and let whoever it was do their worst."

"Ooh, yuck! But no pain?"

"Not anymore."

"Ee bah gum. That's a good story for the Laker newsletter. . . and your grandchildren."

She grinned. "Oo-oh. I'll never tell."

The noisy transport bus started up and moved out of the hotel's circular driveway. "Isn't he forgetting people?" I asked. "There's only five of us?"

"We've only got nine passengers on the flight," Margo supplied. "And then we fly back empty."

"You mean Laker flew me out here for a week just for a twenty-minute flight for nine pax?"

"They'll all be wonderin' who you're sleepin' with in Crewin'?" Margo elbowed me teasingly. "Nudge, nudge. Wink, wink."

I scoffed. "You know, I've never even visited Crewing. They're just a voice on the phone."

"Funny you should say that, chuck," she responded. "Did you know that they call you The Voice?"

"Wha-a-at! No. Why?"

"It's that low, husky voice of yours. They think it's sexy."

I shook my head and laughed. "It's all those Dunhills I used to smoke. Who says smoking's bad for you?"

"I'll have to start smoking," Margo said and grinned. "Then maybe I'll have a sexy voice and get the best trips, too."

The bus was now bumping along the back-country road from the Paradise Beach Hotel toward the airport. I never got tired of seeing the expansive fields of sugar cane punctuated by the occasional brightly coloured homes.

"What's the flying time to St. Lucia?" I asked Margo.

"About twenty minutes," she replied absently, checking her reflection in her make-up mirror. "It's an up-and-downer."

"This just gets better and better," I said. Maybe having a "sexy" voice did curry favour with the crewing boys.

We seated all nine passengers in the forward cabin for take-off and landing so I didn't need the PA system to make the German announcements. But when we landed in St. Lucia, none of us were expecting the rough ride over what felt like bomb craters in the bumpy runway. Thankfully, the airstrip was short but then the plane came to a sudden and juddering halt. As our small load of passengers disappeared down the stairs and into the small airport. I wished them *Schone Ferien,* Great Holidays.

With no returning passengers, we expected a quick turnaround and to be back in Barbados in time for dinner but then Cathy, our leader, emerged from the flight deck to announce to the four of us sitting in A, "Our front wheel is stuck in the mud." She grimaced. "We might be staying overnight."

I had wondered why the aircraft had curled around on itself at the end of the runway and come to that convulsive stop. This landing strip wasn't built for a jet aircraft, let alone a big bird like a DC-10.

As always on unscheduled night-stops, the princess in me reacted with, Oh no! I don't have any spare knickers, toothbrush or civvies. Then my adventurous self kicked in, and I thought, Oh yay! I've never seen St Lucia. A new place! But just as my adventurous self won out, the plane shuddered and moved backwards.

"That means we're going!" Cathy sighed and returned to the flight deck for confirmation. Disappointed, we all took our seats for the take-off back to Barbados.

Lying on the beach the following day, I became restless. When I asked my crew whether any of them wanted to go into Bridgetown to explore the capital, they all declined, content to sunbathe.

"You could take one of the Mini Mokes," Ben suggested, peering up at me over his sunglasses from his chaise. He was referring to the two small open jeeps that were kept at our remote hotel on the west side of the island, ready and waiting and at the disposal of the Laker crews should we decide to go sightseeing or out for dinner. Although, like England, they also drove on the left in Barbados and I had driven one of the Mokes before, I felt that I would be safer on local transport for some reason. "No, that's all right," I demurred. "I'll just catch the bus, Ben." The Bajans were such a friendly lot, after all.

As soon as I boarded the old blue bus that pulled up on the roadside opposite our hotel, the dismay on the black driver's face told me he was *not* happy to see my white European face. *Uh-oh*. Maybe travelling alone had been a mistake. When I turned and saw the bus full of even more resentful black faces staring back at me in anger, I gulped. Definitely a mistake! This is what it must be like, I thought, to be the only black person in a white group. Scary.

Maybe the rumors were correct. Just weeks earlier Lee had warned me that the Rastafarian contingent from Jamaica were slowly bringing their communist and anti-tourist attitudes into Barbados. The atmosphere was changing, he had warned. Some tourists had been attacked.

"No-o-o," I had argued, fighting for the sanctity of my heavenly paradise. "The locals have always been so friendly." But maybe he was right. Maybe things *had* changed in Barbados. The white tourist was now the enemy.

Humbled and aware of all the unfriendly eyes on me, I sat in the one remaining seat in the middle of the bus. The local woman beside me leaned away from me as if I was infected. As we bumped along the road into town, I felt sad—sad for the Bajans and the loss of their natural joy, and sad for the loss of yet another freedom, the freedom to go it alone in Barbados. Maybe now it would be unwise to go anywhere unaccompanied on the island. Why, I wondered, when different races come together in one place, do the behaviours become worse? Rather than give rise to animosity and hate, why can't we enrich each others' lives and learn from and celebrate our diversity?

But the locals' resentment was justified. Even after independence from British rule, many of these people still lived in their colourful shacks close to the beach or in town, some in abject poverty. They had to watch as spoiled, rich, mainly white people came to their island home and took over the luxurious hotels, partying to their hearts content, lollygagging on the beaches, glugging down cocktails while the locals waited on them hand and foot. And all the while, the Bajans often labored for a pittance, fishing, cutting sugar cane or, worse, serving those tourists. The glaring imbalance was evident. If I had been born Bajan, I might have resented us, too.

The bus was now getting close to the south end of the island. Maybe, I thought, instead of going all the way into Bridgetown by myself, I would get off close to the Hilton Hotel where I had met Jose on my amazing vacation. I could take a stroll down memory lane or at least sit on the Hilton Beach with other tourists and remember.

I walked through the Hilton's open-air lobby with its water fountain gushing into the man-made pond while small chirping birds swooped in and out of the water and around the vines hanging down from the balconies. So many happy memories came flooding back. I glanced up to the third floor and noted room 310 where I had stayed and where Jose had left me flowers.

Outside, beyond the shadowy lobby, I was back out in the brilliant sunshine again. Tourists in different stages of a tan, were lying, swimming or conversing as they lounged around the very blue pool. At the beach bar, the Bajan waiters chatted in their strong dialect as they took their time making cocktails. On the sand a steel drum band was softly beating their magical island sound while prostrate bodies lay under sheltering palm trees, their fronds fanning them with the warm breeze that was coming off the ocean. Yes, it was just how I remembered it. Only it felt empty. Something was missing—my holiday companion, Maria, the friends I had made . . . and, of course, Jose.

I kicked off my sandals, relishing the finer texture of white sand at this hotel's location, walked down closer to the water's edge, plonked myself down on the beach and gazed at the water.

"Scuse me, lady, are you stayin' here?" A tall man with a wild Afro and dressed in the Hilton's red uniform shirt towered over me. "Do you be needin' a chair?"

This wasn't the same man who had brought my lounger every day of my holiday, the one I had laughed with. I could have fibbed and given him my old room number, but suddenly I didn't feel like staying. It was all wrong. I should have let the memories remain where they were. In the past.

"No, thank you." I stood up and brushed the sand off my skirt. "I was just . . . looking for someone, but I don't think they're here."

Tall and Slim gave me an odd look, shrugged and returned to his post at the top of the beach.

Clouds were moving in over the horizon, and suddenly I felt unnerved as if the line of dark grey cutting across the blue sky represented something ominous. I wanted to get back to the familiarity of my hotel and feel the warm friendship of my fun crew. Forget the bus, I thought. I'm getting a taxi no matter how much it costs.

Even as the driver dropped me in front of the Paradise Hotel lobby, I could hear the familiar sound of Margo's raucous laughter coming from the pool bar. I instantly felt relieved and exhaled.

"Ah, dhere you are!" Amy exclaimed as I joined the group, grateful for their smiling faces. "We're just talking about dinner plans. We t'ought we'd go to de Flying Fish near de Hilton on de beach dhere, and dhen go to de jazz club."

The term "club" was a little exaggerated as the location was an old two-storey house on the outskirts of Bridgetown. "That'll be fun," I said as my spirits began to lift again. "How many are going?"

"About nine of us. We'll take both Mokes."

"The petrol gauge doesn't work on one of them, you know," I pointed out, feeling some angst rising again, "so you have to look into the tank to make sure it's got petrol."

"Aw dawn't bother your head, darlin'," Margo joked, mimicking our Bajan colleagues. "We is good." She gyrated her hips in a Bajan dance movement. While attempting calypso, she sang, "He put de lime in de coconut, and Alex put de petrol in de Moke."

Amy and I giggled.

"We're meeting here at 7.30," Amy added.

"So, I've still got time for a cocktail?" I asked, suddenly wanting to get into party mode. It had been a strange afternoon.

"You've got time for a whole barrel of rum, darlin'," Amy answered, "and time to sleep it off!"

An hour later as I wended my way along the winding paths that led back to my room, I encountered a large security guard just standing in the lush undergrowth that lined the path. We nodded to each other as I felt another small stab of sadness. Until a year ago the hotel hadn't needed security guards.

After a rum-induced nap, a hot shower and a change into a sleeveless pink summer dress I was ready for a fun evening. Before leaving, I gave myself a final inspection in the mirror. As an afterthought, I slipped on a gold bracelet to match the gold chain around my neck. I liked the way the precious metal shone more brightly against my deepening tan.

Whether it was stumbling into a different security guard on my way to the lobby—who in the darkness I could barely see—or some leftover sadness from the afternoon that was still lurking in the recesses of my mind, I began to feel uneasy about the evening. Don't be silly, I told myself. We're in Barbados. We're going to have fun.

Most of the crew were already gathered in the hotel reception, but once the stragglers arrived, Alex announced, "Okay, people. There's nine of us, so four of you will have to squeeze into my Moke, and Ben will take three. Who's with me?"

As well as Cathy, who was standing next to Alex, Simon, Amy and I also raised our hands.

"Good. Everyone else goes with Ben. Let's go."

The Mokes were only meant to hold four people. As I was the first to get into the back seat, followed by Amy in the middle, Simon had to squeeze himself into the tight space on the other side. Cathy sat up front, next to our captain and chauffeur for the night.

Twenty minutes later we were in the open air at the shack-like restaurant. Being so close to the Hilton for the second time that day, I somehow felt as if I was receiving another psychic nudge. What *was* it? To be careful? But a warm breeze whipped around us from the sea just a few feet away, and with gusto we all tucked into our fresh-out-of-the-ocean fish and salted chips. Seeing the girls with their humidity-afflicted fly-away hair now made me grateful that Embers had braided mine. As usual, the crew shared a litany of jokes, and as I laughed with my newly tanned friends, the cloud that had threatened to dampen my spirits lifted.

A year earlier Sexy Lexy and Ben Atkins had been my "flight deck" on that rainy seven-day Toronto trip also with Cathy, Amy and Margo. Both men had taken such good care of us. Our captain's name was well deserved. He was tall and fit with movie-star good looks, and though his nickname might have inferred that he was a philanderer, he was actually a loyal husband and very respectful toward the female crew. Intelligent and extroverted, Ben was also cut from the same cloth. Not many of the crew would have guessed that he had suffered a tragic loss just four years earlier. But now, in our paradise, he and the rest of the crew were all relaxed and in good spirits.

The drive from the Flying Fish to the jazz club lasted a torturous twenty minutes over uneven, cratered roads in a jeep with barely any suspension, but our great mood, and no doubt the copious cocktails we had already imbibed, lessened our pain. As we drove into town, our liveliness attracted the attention of local men walking the streets who shouted, "Hey mon, are yer havin' a good taime?" We laughed and waved back, shouting, "Yeah, mon."

Alex pulled up in a side street close to the Belair Jazz Club. I looked around at the somewhat dilapidated single-storey houses in this area, which were all painted in yellow, green and apricot orange pastels, and wondered why our English houses were so drab. Probably to match the grey weather, I thought. I still did not understand why Bajans often left their sunny island paradise to come and live in miserable rainy England, while the English could not wait to escape to sunny Barbados. Maybe we always want what we don't have.

The other Moke, I noticed, was already pulled up ahead of us on the pavement and empty. Ben and the rest of the crew, including Margo, were apparently inside.

From the upper storey of the colonial house, music blasted into the humid air of the surrounding quarter. The tempos didn't sound like pure jazz, more like a mixture of calypso, jazz and other influences I couldn't pinpoint, but the sound was rich and happy. I glanced up and saw with horror that the balcony seemed to be hanging off the house at a precarious angle as if it might collapse at any moment and all those people who were standing there, casually enjoying a cocktail, would come crashing to the ground. No one up there seemed concerned.

We climbed the rickety stairs and entered what might have been a living room before the house had been converted to a club. The band sat in one corner playing a strange assortment of instruments producing an infectious harmony, while the Bajans and some tourists were clustered at small low tables. The locals danced in their inimitable way, standing in the same spot and moving their bodies subtly but rhythmically to the music, in contrast to some of our male flight deck who threw their arms and legs around in wild abandon as if something itchy had crawled down their backs and they were attempting to escape it.

Before we knew it, Alex appeared in front of us, grinning and clutching five rum punches in plastic glasses. "That's all they're serving." He shrugged as we relieved him of our drinks.

"De others are out dere," Amy said, pointing to the balcony. We followed her outside and stood on the wooden structure, which didn't feel as "tippy" as it had appeared from below. I still stayed close to the door, just in case. Maybe, I berated myself, you should stop imagining the worst?

Ben took my drink and placed it on a ledge. "Com'on, Natasha. Let's dance!"

Happy to be off the balcony, I let him pull me inside and we soon lost ourselves in the music. I tried to emulate the Bajans "cool" style of dancing, barely moving. Then I saw that Alex and Margo had come onto the dance floor, too. Suddenly a very tall Bajan--at least six foot four—approached us. I wasn't sure whether it was his scruffy beard, his long dreadlocks or the bright yellow and blue shirt he was wearing, but he gave off a strange vibe. I wondered if this was the infamous Bamboo, the Bajan who had used my colleague's cheek as an ashtray on a flight last year. What did he want? When he finally spoke, I thought he was addressing Ben, but his eyes were glazed and unfocused, so I wasn't sure if he was even speaking to us.

"Hey, Mon," he said, fidgeting with the buttons on his bright shirt. "You got any dope?"

Ben's eyes twinkled with amusement, and he shook his head. "Nope, sorry," he responded, protectively steering me away from the stranger. We resumed our dancing, but the man still stood there in the middle of the floor. He continued to stare at me with a strange piercing look. What did he want *now*?

"You am better be careful," he muttered. "Dey's bad juju here tonight."

I shivered, but before I could ask what he meant, he moved away and disappeared onto the balcony.

After several more dances, Margo approached us. "Hey, Ben. We don't want to spoil your fun, but we're just lettin' yer know that, when you're ready to leave, we're good to go."

He nodded. "After this dance. Okay?"

As Ben left with the girls trailing behind him in single file, I called after them, "See you all back at the ranch for a nightcap?" Ben just raised a hand and waved while Margo turned and grinned.

I joined Alex and my carload on the balcony. At the far end, leaning against the precarious railing, the tall stranger was talking to some locals. Thankfully, he ignored me.

"Well," Alex said, knocking back the last of his drink. "Ready to go, girls?"

"Oo-ooh yes," Simon responded, hand on hip, "I'm definitely ready for me bed." He cast wary glances at the threatening looks from the large Bajan men in the club. Being so blatantly gay was probably dangerous for him in this very macho environment. "But just look at Cathy!" he added. "Look at her go! She might be difficult to drag away."

We followed his gaze and saw that our IFD was dancing with not one but two locals. And grinning from ear to ear.

"Too bad," Alex retorted. "This bus is leaving."

A few minutes later we were all piling back into the Moke, taking up the same seats we had before.

As Alex carefully negotiated the streets back through the town and out into the countryside, pleasantly tired, we all rode in comfortable silence. Now, except for a few lights shining from the odd house, we were shrouded in the pitch-black night. On either side of the road the sugar cane rustled, and the whistling frogs were loud in the balmy night air. We had just turned a bend and were now on the last straight stretch of road leading back to the Paradise Hotel when suddenly the Moke shuddered and slowed.

Alex steered the vehicle onto the left verge, and it bumped along the rough grass until it spluttered and then died.

"Wha-at?" he exclaimed more to himself than us. "We can't be out of petrol! I filled . . ."

He turned and unscrewed the petrol cap in the panel on the left side of his seat. He peered in, but in the darkness, it would have been difficult to tell if there was petrol in there or not.

"Bloody hell!" he muttered. "Some of those bastards at the club must have siphoned it."

Just as Alex was replacing the cap, a noise erupted behind us that sounded like a big old car without an exhaust, coming closer. We could hear men's voices hootin' and a hollerin' as if they were drunk.

Uh-oh.

The noise got louder just as a vehicle appeared around the last bend, its driver nearly losing control as, with tires squealing, he barely negotiated the curve. That earlier sense of foreboding now landed in my stomach like a lead brick. We were in trouble.

We all turned and looked back into the dark night. Just one headlight was bearing down on us. Although the Moke was mostly off the road, we were holding our breath. Would the car crash into us, or go past us? The vehicle slowed, pulled over and just yards away from our rear bumper, screeched to a halt. As if they were arriving at a prearranged meeting. Could these be the culprits who took our gas and then followed us?

Four men got out of their old beater and muttering in their Bajan dialect, swaggered toward us.

"Maybe dhey can give us some petrol," Amy, ever the positive thinker, said.

"They're probably the ones who took it," Alex mumbled.

Cathy gasped. "Oh my God! Those two were dancing with me at the club!"

"Ooh," Simon muttered. "I don't think they're thinking about dancing now, duckie."

"Oh, shi-i-it!" Alex hissed and looked around as if he was frantically trying to form an escape plan.

I gulped. We were sitting ducks. What, I wondered, would they do to us?

The four men circled the Moke. One of them held a torch and shone it into our captain's face, standing over him smirking. In the light I noticed he had a bad scar by his left eye. Then I saw a flash of metal in his other hand. Oh my god. He had a knife!

"Dawn't even tink about tryin' to be a hero," Scarface threatened, putting the knife up to Alex's throat and spitting the words into his face.

A second man, younger, taller and leaner, had positioned himself next to Simon in the back seat, behind Alex. When the steward squealed with fright and put his hands to his throat, Tall and Lean, realizing that Simon was gay, spat at him in disgust and ran around to my side, but then hung back, not sure exactly what he should do next.

Then he moved closer in to join the other two who were standing leering down at Cathy in the front. In the blackness of the night, I could only see their shadowy movements, not sure what their intentions were. One of them, bigger and stockier, then turned his attention to me, ogling not my face, but my throat.

My heart was beating out of my chest as my assailant's eyes stared at me, his eyes bulging with fear and excitement, the whites of his eyes more prominent in the darkness. He was panting, breathing heavily. There was something in his hand. A dagger? Was he planning on slitting my throat? In my mind I shrieked, somebody do something! But I was too frozen to open my mouth.

Then looking me in the eyes, he raised his arm. I gasped and instinctively put my hand up to protect my throat. Beside me, I felt Amy being pulled away and hearing Simon yelling, "Run, Amy! Run!" Then a scuffling. I turned and watched helplessly as they escaped the Moke and ran forward, disappearing into the black night.

There was a sudden pain in my little finger. When I looked down, I could see blood and realized that, while I was looking away, Mr. Big had cut away the gold chain from my throat and in the process had sliced into one of my fingers. The sight of my own blood spilling onto my pink dress turned the mild trembling in my whole body to shaking.

"Shit, Mon! Gaw get 'em," the fourth man who was ogling Cathy shouted to Tall and Lean.

"Aw, let 'em gaw," Alex's attacker, Scarface, muttered. "Dey is nobody for miles. Jost get de jewellery!"

I exhaled slightly. Maybe this was just a robbery then and they didn't plan on killing us?

"Dat's a fancy watch, mon," Scarface said, eyeing Alex's wrist. "Gi me dat."

I felt Alex's bottled rage as very slowly he did as he was told and removed his Rolex. He handed it to his hijacker.

"Gi me all your money, too!"

Alex reached into his pocket and put some Bajan dollars in his assailant's outstretched palm.

"You got mo, mon?" Scarface pushed the knife tighter against Alex's throat.

Alex mumbled a strangled "No!"

"Gi me dat," my attacker, Mr. Big, still at my side, snarled. He was pointing at my wrist and the slim gold bracelet I wore. "Or I cot yo arm."

With trembling fingers and with blood still dripping onto my dress, I tried with my left hand to undo the fragile link on the narrow gold bracelet. In the front seat of the Moke, I was aware of an equally terrified Cathy giving over her handbag and her jewellery. Amy's small black bag was still lying on the seat beside me. Maybe they wouldn't notice it.

"I do it!" Mr. Big snarled impatiently. Closing my eyes, I held out my arm. He flicked the point of his knife under the chain and quickly broke it.

"Okay, Mon," Scarface shouted, "now we gonna have some fun wid de girls. I'll stay wid 'im," he said, still holding his knife against poor Alex's throat while inclining his head toward me, "and de one in de back." Addressing the other man who was busy pocketing Cathy's spoils, and nodding at her, he said, "You take her fost."

I froze as I understood what they were planning. Two of the men on my side closed in on Cathy while Mr. Big stood guard over me.

"No!" Cathy cried. "No!"

I gulped. After Cathy, I knew it would be my turn. Until now, she had sat there paralyzed with terror. But as they manhandled her out of the Moke and dragged her back towards their car, she began to whimper. "No, God! No! Please don't!"

In the light of Scarface's torch, I could read Alex's body language, his broad shoulders stiffened, his torso frozen, anger, rage and powerlessness seeping out of every pore. With the blade digging into his throat, one false move might have been fatal for him. He was helpless.

Do something, Natasha! I told myself. Do something! But what? "You bastards!" I screamed at Mr. Big. "Leave her alone!" I sobbed, "Leave her alo-o-one!"

He sneered at me with an almost toothless grin, and brandishing his knife close to my face, he taunted, "Dawn't you bother your head, darlin.' You'll get yo turn soon enough."

While trying not to listen to their snickering and Cathy's whimpering behind me, I closed my eyes and prayed hard. Please God, I begged. Please, God. Help us! Help us!

Suddenly, there was a light in the darkness. I opened my eyes, and through my tears I saw a set of headlights coming around the bend toward us. But would they stop, or just carry on afraid to "get involved?"

"Aw, shit!" Scarface, still holding Alex hostage, shouted to his friends. "Dey is someone comin'!" He pulled away from Alex, turned and ran back toward their vehicle.

Mr. Big stared at the lights, and suddenly scared, also ran to their car.

I heard a voice from behind. "Get rid o' her."

Car doors slammed.

Still too afraid to turn round, I thought, Please God, I hope they didn't have time to rape Cathy. Or were they taking her with them?

There was more scuffling, followed by a dull thud and a scream, but the noise seemed to come from the ditch behind me. I heard a low moaning. It was Cathy. What had they done to her? That's when I turned around.

The attackers were backing up their car, doing a U-turn in the narrow road, and with tires squealing, they disappeared back into the night.

Perhaps I wouldn't be raped or murdered tonight after all. I exhaled and began to cry.

Immediately Alex leapt out of the Moke. "Natasha, are you okay?"

Though my finger was bleeding badly, that was minor. "Find Cathy," I muttered. through my sobs.

The oncoming car now slowed and pulled over onto the grass verge, the headlights casting shadows onto the Moke. Could they be attackers, too?

The two back doors of the vehicle flew open and two people leapt out and ran toward us. Then a black middle-aged man and a woman climbed out of the front seats and stared at our vehicle, stunned.

"Jesus, Mary and Joseph!" It was Amy's voice. "Oh my God, Natasha!" she called as she ran toward me. "Are you okay?"

I couldn't move, and I couldn't speak.

"For the love of God, you're bleedin'! I'm so-o-o sorry. But where's Alex, for God's sake? And Cathy?"

Simon ran by on the other side of the Moke, searching in the darkness. "Alex? Cathy? Oh no!" Then, "Oh dear! Is she okay? Oh, my go-o-od!"

The two locals stood there not sure what to do. Little did they know then that they had probably saved us women from, at least, being raped—if not murdered. But I wasn't sure yet if they had saved Cathy from every woman's worst nightmare.

"Do you have any first aid?" Amy turned to ask the dazed couple. "My friend's bleedin' like a stuck pig here."

I looked down at my hand. In my shock and fear, and in the darkness, I hadn't seen that the top of my little finger was sliced almost half-way through. Still nothing compared to Cathy's trauma. And for some reason I wasn't feeling any pain.

While the local woman suddenly came to her senses and offered to take care of my wound with her first aid kit, Amy went to assist Alex and Simon, then soon reappeared at my side.

"Dear Lord, dey're helping poor Cathy out o' de ditch."

"Is she hurt?" I asked Amy. "I mean, did they. . .?"

"No, tank God, but de poor ting, it looks like she broke her wrist when dey t'rew her in the there. Dose *bastards!*"

I watched as Alex and Simon half-carried Cathy to the stranger's car where they gently placed her in the back seat. The woman tentatively laid a blanket around her shoulders, careful not to touch her wounded wrist as our IFD cried and moaned in great pain.

Amy pulled me very gently out of the Moke, but as I stood, I felt faint and leaned on her. "I tink we arrived just in time," she muttered, to herself.

"Poor Cathy," I whispered while also thinking that it could have been so much worse. "Amy. . . How did you find. . .?" I asked, inclining my head toward the couple.

"Simon dragged me down de road until we found dis house with lights on. We kept banging on deir door . . . until dese nice people. . . Oh, I'm so sorry for leaving you, Natasha, but . . ."

"Thank God you did!"

"Dis is Mr. and Mrs. Johnson," she said, pointing to the couple who still appeared scared, like awkward bystanders. "Dey called de police straight away so dey should be here soon."

"Thank you," I said to the Johnsons. "You saved our lives."

They just nodded, stunned and embarrassed. They were obviously not just sad for our plight but also ashamed that this had happened on their island. Barbados would never feel safe again for any of us. Looking at the devastated Johnsons, I suddenly wanted to cry. Instead, and despite the humidity, I began to tremble with cold.

Amy sat me in the back seat of the Johnsons' Ford Fairmont next to a moaning Cathy. "We need an ambulance. . ." I mumbled.

"It's comin'," Mrs. Johnson told me in a light Bajan accent.

As we, the physically injured, sat in the back seat, and Cathy continued to groan, I whispered, "I'm so sorry, Cathy . . . There was nothing . . ." What could I say that would make her feel any better?

She barely shook her head. We were all in shock and she was in excruciating pain. While we waited for the police and ambulance to arrive, I hoped for Cathy's sake that they were faster at delivering emergency services than making cocktails. Otherwise we were in for a long wait.

In the darkness, Alex, Simon and Amy stood on the verge talking to the couple in low voices. Alex, I could tell, was very shaken. I wondered how it had felt for a man whose whole career had been about being responsible for other people's safety suddenly finding himself so powerless to protect his own crew. None of this was his fault, nor could he have done anything different to save us. Ironically, the spat-upon Simon had been the quick-thinking hero of the night.

An hour later and while still at the hospital, once Cathy's broken wrist had been set and the tip of my finger had been stitched back in place, the local police had put us through a surprisingly brief interrogation. They knew the identity of our attackers, but we weren't sure how justice would unfold. In the early hours of the morning, the five of us were finally dropped off at our hotel. All we wanted was a hot shower and oblivion.

As I lay in my bed that night, doped up with painkillers, I thanked God for our rescuers— whether Amy had found them, or God had sent them—and that they had magically appeared before. . . .. It was too horrible to think about. I cried for a long time— for Cathy's trauma, for Alex, my crew, for the loss of trust, for the loss of innocence and for the loss of my Caribbean "home." Barbados would never hold the same charm again, for me anyway.

Once the news of our attack spread around the airline, we weren't the only ones who suffered shock. All crew members were officially warned about the new dangers in Barbados and so the island, formerly our friend, was now just another destination—like New York, LA and Miami—where we always had to be on alert.

Three months after our "incident," while on a New York trip, my crew and I were enjoying a bowl of hot French onion soup and drinks in the Doral Inn's restaurant when my colleague Pauline pointed over to the bar.

"Isn't that Sexy Lexy?"

I turned to see Alex sitting all alone, nursing a drink.

"Just a sec." I got up and went over to him. He was dressed in a pale blue sweater that accentuated his clear blue eyes. Despite his good looks, he still appeared shocked, frozen and sad, just as he had that night.

"Hi, Alex."

He appeared startled to see me, as if I had dragged him back from another reality.

"Oh . . . Hi, Natasha."

I hoped seeing me didn't bring back awful memories, but looking at him, I was shocked to realize that he had never left the scene. "How are you?" I asked, though it was obvious.

He shook his head and took a swig of his cocktail. "Not good," he answered, staring down into his empty glass and frowning, as if wondering who had imbibed his drink.

"Alex . . ." Should I say anything? I sat down on the stool next to him. "You know, it wasn't your fault. You know that, don't you?"

His shoulders slumped and he leaned on the bar. "I should have done something!"

"But you had a knife at your throat! It never occurred to any of us, including Cathy, that you could have done anything differently."

My soup was getting cold, but I hated to leave him alone in his torture. "It could have been so much worse."

"Could it?" he asked, desperately searching my eyes as if seeking redemption.

"Yes! At least we all survived, and with our virtue intact."

He twirled his empty glass, perhaps wishing it would refill itself and make this all go away. "But it's humiliating that it was the gay steward who saved our lives. Some flight crew have given me hell about that." He waved a hand at the bartender to get his attention.

"Ach, how do *they* know?" I snapped, angry at those who had judged him. "They weren't there!" Why couldn't Alex see that he was a cut above so many of the other captains. "I bet some of them would have screamed like big girls' blouses and run away or tried to be silly heroes and made the situation much worse."

He stared at me intently, some faint truth dawning on him. A small smile appeared on his lips. "Maybe you're right."

"And," I said, looking him straight in the eyes, "if I had to go through it again, the only captain I would want with me in that Moke would be you."

His eyes began to water. "Really?"

"Absoblootly!" I smiled.

"Thank you, Natasha," he said, sitting up straight and, as if for the first time in months, relaxing those broad shoulders. "That means a lot."

As the bartender served Alex his drink, I said, "Why don't you come over and join us?"

He glanced over at our table and saw the three women deep in conversation. "Nah. Thanks anyway. I think I'll hit the sack." He twirled the glass containing his scotch and water and then threw it back in one.

"Alex? . . . Are you going to be all right?"

"I think so." He stood up and threw some dollar bills on the bar. "Eventually."

I could see that my words were appreciated but had only grazed the tip of his iceberg of grief. Alex was still traumatized. We all were. And nothing I could say would change anything. While we appeared to be the same–on the outside–we would never be the same on the inside. Our trust had been broken into a thousand pieces. Something precious had been hijacked, and just like Humpty Dumpty, they would never be able to put it back together again.

Not for a long time, anyway.

18

DESPERATE MEASURES

London
February 1982

"Hey, guess what?" my colleague Barbara announced, beaming. "Rumor has it that Freddie's getting a Hong Kong contract and maybe Australia, too." She was sitting in the galley of the DC-10, enjoying a cigarette before going back up to the cabin to work the meal service on our outbound JFK.

I was checking the ovens, focused on the brand-new first-class service Freddie was offering. Would I be able to balance the cooking of Chateaubriand steaks and Salmon en Croute for Cabin A while heating shepherd's pies and lasagnas for the "punters" down the back, as well as serving the flight deck's meals on time? While I was keeping my beady eyes on the hot food, Mary-Jane, our Bajan Number One, was struggling to retrieve a box of ginger ales from the lower cupboard at the other end of the galley.

"Dawn't get too excited about Hong Kong, darlin'," Mary-Jane said as she finally pulled the box out. "*I heard dat we're gawin' bost.*"

"Bust? No-o-o-o!" Barbara exclaimed, dismayed. "What about all the new airbuses Freddie's bought?"

"Tink about it, mon," the Number One said as she dragged the ginger ales toward the lift. "He jost bought ten aircraft durin' a recession and den all de cartels in Europe want to sue him for planning 666 routes at a tenth of deir fares." She shook her head. "Mon, *dat* number got to be ba-a-ad juju. Naw, dey jost dawn't like 'im."

"But I've only been flying for a year," Barbara moaned, standing up. "I don't want it to end."

"Oh, dawn't bother your head, darlin'," Mary-Jane said over her shoulder as she pushed the button for the lift. "Dere's lots mo' airlines."

If Freddie did go "bost," would I want to train with yet another air carrier? And if he didn't, would I want to keep doing this galley malarkey? Hong Kong, though, would be exciting.

Was turning the forward cabin into a first-class service Freddie Laker's latest desperate measure to stay ahead of the competition? The Royal Doulton china, stainless steel cutlery and champagne glasses that had been added to the usual plastic supplies were creating a spatial and logistical nightmare in the galley. What *was* he thinking? He had, after all, branded himself as a cheap, low-fare carrier and that's what it was. People didn't expect first class. Providing a superior service on this configuration of a DC-10 was like trying to make me—at 5 feet 4 inches with a tendency toward a Rubenesque figure—look like a super model.

One of the ovens binged. The captain's meal was ready. As if on cue, the lift descended, and Janet, the training stewardess peered out. She was on board to check on the new service–and my performance–with first class. When she saw me bearing the captain's meal tray, she retreated into the shadowy lift. "I'll ride up with you."

Uh-oh. Here we go. I stepped inside the lift and faced her. Okay, let's have it, I thought.

"I must say, Natasha, I'm very impressed," she began. "You're *so* organized!"

"Oh." *What?* While I was taken aback by her praise, I didn't admit to lying awake all night thinking about how to juggle ovens, timing and space before deciding it would be a bloody miracle if I could pull it off without giving anyone food poisoning.

"And they said it couldn't be done," Janet added, beaming at me.

Oh no. Had I made it look *too* easy? "Well . . . it's a lot more work."

"Yes, but we'll all get used to it. Good job."

A few minutes later as I handed the meal tray to the grumpy captain, I suddenly heard a voice in my head saying; You don't want to do this anymore.

The day before my next rostered LA, I woke up with severe stomach pains. When the airline doctor examined me and asked, "Have you fallen on your lower back recently?" the pains made sense.

"About six weeks ago," I told him, remembering, "I slipped on the deck of the *Jolly Roger* in Barbados and landed right on . . . the base of my spine."

"You'll need a course of physiotherapy then." He began writing a prescription. "And you're not to fly for a month."

Oh, goodie! A month off! Maybe Jack and I could go away somewhere. Our deepening relationship was helping me to forget Jose who was gradually becoming a ghost of a memory—on some days at least.

Only thirty minutes after I informed Crewing of my prescribed leave, Deborah, the deputy chief stewardess, rang me. "Are you fit enough to work in the office?"

Ugh. I couldn't lie. Yes, I was, and they had my resume on file listing my secretarial skills. Curses! "Well . . . yes. I think so."

"Then report here at 09.00 hours tomorrow," she commanded and hung up.

The next morning Deborah ushered me to a desk facing a blank yellow wall on which sat an electronic typewriter and a stack of forms. Harried, and not her usual pleasant self, she quickly gave me instructions. I watched as she scurried away, and I resigned myself to four weeks of boring paperwork.

In the following days, as I drove along the Sussex country lanes toward Gatwick and my new temporary job in dismal January weather, I was shocked at how much relief I felt at not having to fly or deal with a DC-10 galley. While I had absolutely *loved* my eight years of flying adventures, the fun with my colleagues and some eccentric passengers and crew, I knew it was time for a change. But what?

During that first week, in between plonking away on the typewriter, I heard whispered snippets of tense conversations behind me in the large office. From the fragments I could glean, the airline was either in deep trouble or had great prospects. Then one day excited murmurings pervaded the whole floor. Apparently, Freddie was in a meeting with a banker who could grant him the massive loan he needed to keep his planes in the air. By the end of the day the office mood had gone from hopeful to jubilant. The request had been granted. I decided that if Laker was going to the Orient and Australia on new aircraft, maybe flying would be interesting again. Hong Kong and Sydney here we come!

That Saturday morning, Ellen and I were relaxing in the living room with our coffee and reading. Her head was buried in a *Time* magazine while I was fascinated by a *Reader's Digest* article on Libya and how Muammar Kaddafi (Qu'adafi) had turned that country's oil resources into a thriving economy that was ending poverty there.

Ellen suddenly checked her watch and stood up.

"What's up?" I asked.

"I'm driving down to Brighton to see a psychic called Maggie Cullen. Do you want to come with me?"

"Oh, is that the one I saw on TV reading the paws and bellies of lions and snakes?"

"Yes! She's supposed to be *really* accurate."

"Can she read humans, too?"

Ellen laughed. "Yes, of course. She's a palm reader."

"Hmm. She must be good then." I grinned. My own palm reading ability had been developing slowly over the years, and sometimes when passengers, crew and friends allowed me to read their palms, they scared *me* with their declarations of *my* accuracy. "How could you know that?" they wanted to know, and I would respond oh-so-intelligently with, "I dunno."

I had lost faith in my regular card-reading psychic, Mrs. Ainsley, who in every session over the last four years had insisted, "You're getting married this October." Despite changes of boyfriends during that time, her predictions, and my unwedded status had remained the same. Maybe Maggie Cullen could give me more accurate information. Perhaps she could tell me if Jack and I would be getting married? After all, recently the romance between us had warmed up significantly. "I'd love to," I told Ellen.

Two hours later we stepped inside Maggie Cullen's "office." Was it because the small, shadowy waiting room was empty of people or because the place was solemnly church-like with pews for seats and navy velvet curtains hanging over doorways that I wondered: Are we in the right place? The tall, slim figure of Maggie Cullen, with her long, wispy, grey-brown hair—making her look every inch the witch—soon appeared from behind a curtain at the back of the room. Without introduction, she asked, "Who's first?"

"You go," I told Ellen, a little nervous of what she might impart.

I plonked myself down on a wooden pew and took out my *Readers Digest* again to finish the article on Kaddafi. Twenty minutes later, Ellen emerged. "She sees a wedding!" she announced beaming before ushering me toward the back. "Your turn."

Maggie welcomed me into a tiny private cubicle encircled with more blue velvet curtains and pointed to an uncomfortable-looking wooden chair.

"Show me your left palm," she ordered without preamble.

Nervous, I laid my hand on the small, bare wooden desk, while she sat opposite and peered at my lines.

Occasionally she touched the tips of my fingers or moved my thumb. Expressionless and without pause, she rattled off initials, names and events. "There's a big change coming."

Perhaps a wedding? I thought.

"Something's ending," she stated. "You will have a reunion, and you're going to a dark-skinned country, like Africa. I also see you taking a suitcase across a border, and you might live there. The name Lillian means something. And you may lose something small today or tomorrow. You are creative and eventually you will start something to do with catering."

"Do you see anything about my current relationship. Jack?"

She shrugged and shook her head, a hint of disapproval in her expression.

Psychics can be wrong, I thought.

"Marriage will come much later," she said.

So not October then? And maybe not Jack? But later could mean anything. I did not— maybe because I was afraid of the answer—ask for more clarification.

The following day as I was leaving the house to meet Samantha at the pub, I looked for my brown leather gloves, but they were nowhere to be found. Maggie's words *You will lose something small today or tomorrow,* echoed in my mind. Uh-oh! If she was right about the gloves, was she also right about Jack?

On Friday, February 5, I woke feeling sick to my stomach. Too nauseous to go into the office, I picked up the phone next to my bed and dialled the office number. A loud, shrill, long flat tone sounded on the other end.

Hmm? Maybe this phone is faulty, I thought and got out of bed to go downstairs. In the living room I dialled the office again. I got the same tone. Why would the number of a major airline be out of service? Maybe it was *my* device that was faulty? As I stood there puzzled, the strident ring of my phone filled the living room. Nothing was wrong at my end then. I picked it up.

"Oh my god, Natasha!" Charlotte's upper crust voice moaned. "I'm *so-o-o* sorry!" Charlotte and I had flown together on Dan Air and had many laughs. Despite my switching airlines, we had remained good friends.

What?" Had someone died? Who could it be? "What?"

"Oh, my God!" Charlotte sounded devastated. "You haven't heard, have you?"

"Wha-a-a-at?" I demanded again.

Charlotte took a breath before saying, "Laker's gone down."

I sank onto the wooden chair by my telephone table. So that's why the number was dead. The airline was defunct.

Just like that.

"But . . .why?" I didn't understand. "Freddie got his make-or-break loan," I told Charlotte.

"I don't know," she responded, sounding as helpless as I felt.

Still in shock as if someone *had* died, I said simply, "Well, thank you for letting me know, Charlotte."

"Of course, darling. Of course. If you need anything. . .," she offered lamely before hanging up.

Just a job.

Then Maggie Cullen's words came to mind again. *Big change coming. Something ending.* This was big and it had ended. Right again, Maggie.

I don't know how long I sat there staring out of the window at the spindly, bare-leafed trees and yet another grey wintery day. Why did bad things always happen in February? It *did* feel like a death. Who should I call? Jack was in Taiwan on business. Victoria? Amy? And oh . . . Ellen was doing a night Tenerife! Would she make it back or get stranded?

And what about all the other 2,500 Laker people now suddenly out of work? Despite the pun, the flying business *was* up and down. We had all been witness to the sudden demise of other airlines and done a few "rescue" flights for passengers and crews stuck in other countries. After the carrier Courtline had ceased operations overnight in 1974, a few of their stewardesses were taken on by Dan Air, and we had worked side by side in our navy uniforms with them still in their beige Courtline outfits. And what of our own crews now stranded in LA, Miami, New York and Barbados? How would they get home? Then reality hit. I wouldn't be seeing any of those exciting places again. The high life was over. The end.

The irony was that I had just had serious thoughts about leaving Laker. Now Laker had left me, which was just a tad inconvenient. While I felt *mostly* ready for the end of my flying days, I felt sorrier for the many others who would be devastated, who may never find flying jobs again. So many of us had mortgages and families to support, and many of the captains had to pay alimony to more than one ex-wife. With the present recession and a glut of flying crews out of work, the pilots would be the hardest hit.

I sat frozen to my chair. What was I feeling? Shock? Yes. Devastation. Yes. Sadness. Yes. But it wasn't just sadness for myself.

Freddie Laker had fought so long and so hard for landing rights into New York and then LA and Miami, finally winning over the FAA in the States, while also standing up to the "old boys club" in England. Passengers had been so grateful to him for his drastically reduced fares, allowing them to finally fly farther afield and visit long-lost relatives on the other side of the world. He had even survived the six-week grounding in 1979 after the American Airlines DC-10 crash. We had all been proud to fly for this pioneer, grateful for what we considered the best job in the world. And even though we had been teetering on the edge between expansion or bankruptcy for a while, today's development was numbing, like knowing a loved one has a potentially fatal illness but still being in shock when the end comes. The finality of never doing another Laker flight was sinking in.

The phone rang again, breaking into my thoughts.

"Hello, old girl." Victoria whispered as though in a church attending a funeral. "Have you heard?"

"Yes."

We sat in silence for a while, sharing unspoken thoughts.

I asked Victoria the question I had expected Charlotte to answer. "I don't get it. Freddie had been given his loan. I was in the office when it happened. Everyone was over the moon. How could this have happened?"

"Those tossers at the bank reneged on the deal," she supplied. "Not sure why."

Another silence while the information sank in.

"Fuck!" Victoria said, expressing my emotion. "*Now* what are we going to do?" she pleaded, her tone bereft. Victoria was an IFD and had been with the airline for ten years. "I'm not exactly a spring chicken, old girl . . ."

My own thirtieth birthday was looming on the horizon, too. "I don't know." Suddenly gloomy, I thought about my last days in the

Laker office. Being tied to a desk job had been depressing, but apart from flying, that's maybe all I had to look forward to.

"We're not going to go without a fight," she said, suddenly reverting to her stiff- upper-lip tone.

"What do you mean?"

"You know Sandy Wilson, the head of the Flight Attendants Association?"

"Yes." Sandy had told me her Woof, Woof story.

"She's getting together with the pilots and they're organizing a protest in London. Next week. For all of us, every single Laker employee."

"Protest?"

"Yes, we're going to ask the British Government to help bail Freddie out. After all, they've just given £83,000 to bloody Delorean for his car business in Ireland. Why wouldn't they want to support us?"

"I-I don't know . . . How much does Freddie need?"

"Just a mere £66 million." She snickered. "That's only $300 million US."

"Oh, is that all?" I joked, not feeling funny at all. "When. . .?"

"Tuesday. We're going on coaches from Gatwick. Be outside Concorde House at 9.00 a.m. in full summer uniform."

"*Summer* uniform?" That meant donning the bright red dress and jacket, black bowler hat and white scarf. Hardly February attire for ye dampe olde Englande.

"More color for the media," Victoria explained. "Our black uniforms would make it look like a bleedin' funeral."

"By the way, are there any crews stranded down-route?" I asked, thinking mainly of Ellen.

"Yes, they're all over the place. It's messy." Victoria sighed. "Other airlines—Pan Am, United, Continental and the like—are bringing stranded passengers and crew home. A night Tenerife was ordered to turn back so the Spaniards couldn't impound the aircraft for landing fees! It's brutal."

"Oh my God, Ellen's on that flight!"

There was another pause before Victoria added, "You know, I wouldn't mind having a glass of wine . . . or two or three." She chuckled, instantly making me feel a little better. "Want to come over for dinner tonight?"

"Love to," I responded, relieved at being able to share this devastating loss with someone who understood and as a bonus, I would sample Victoria's sumptuous cooking.

As I hung up, I heard the front door open. Ellen appeared in the living room in her black winter uniform–our funeral attire as Jose had called it–and stood staring at me, her shoulders slouched, her large eyes watery.

"I know," I said. "I know."

The following Tuesday, for our protest, Ellen and I drove to Gatwick together. Miraculously, the sun was shining out of a cloudless blue February sky. We trekked from the staff car park toward the terminal in a crisp-but-not-freezing temperature, grateful that we wouldn't die of hyperthermia in our polyester summer garb. As Victoria had informed us, a long convoy of buses was waiting outside Concorde House and along the Perimeter Road ready to take us up to London. A lot of the pilots had opted to drive themselves up to the city.

We climbed aboard and took our seats close to the rear. Surprisingly, the mood was almost festive. Despite the sad occasion, everyone was laughing and giggling. Was the elation due to denial, hysteria or hope? Many of them were wearing small Laker stickers or buttons with "I'm Freddie. Fly me!" Some chanted "Long Live Laker!"

Freddie should be with us, I thought, and see how proud we are of his airline and how much we loved our jobs. What was he doing now? If I were him, I would be curled up in a foetal position utterly defeated and sucking my thumb. I was just one person who had lost a job, but he must be feeling terrible for the end of a dream in which he had provided so much employment and fulfilled so many people's hunger for travel, crew as well as passengers. But flying wasn't "just a job." It was a lifestyle, and we were a bonded family, having shared many adventures. He had fought so hard just to get landing rights into New York and then successfully adding LA and Miami to his Skytrain routes. And now for it to end so suddenly.

But he had taken a risk purchasing another 10 Airbuses during a recession while doing battle with the cartels of European airlines. Greatly reducing fares for 666 routes around Europe had not made him Mr. Popular with BA, Air France, Swiss Air, Lufthansa and others, and maybe, just as Mary-Ellen had commented, that number of routes was "bad juju."

Freddie was no stranger to adversity. Years earlier his son and heir had died in the sports car Freddie had given him for his seventeenth birthday. Just last week after he had received the news that his airline was finished, he had been interviewed on TV. When the reporter had asked him how he was feeling, he had responded with "Let's just say that when I wake up in the morning, I'm surprised that my legs aren't broken."

As we drove up through south London on our way to the Houses of Parliament, Irish Franny, one of our beloved IFDs, stood up at the front of the bus.

"Listen up, people," she yelled. "I'm just goin' to tell you what de plan is for de day. First of all, we'll be headed for de House of Commons where Iain Sproat, Under-Secretary for Trade and Minister of Aviation, and some other toffs have agreed to hear our case. De buses will drop us off a ways from Parliament, so we'll be walkin' along de Embankment for a good half mile. You can chant "Long Live Laker Airways" as loud as yer want. We're going to make people listen. Now who wants to take dese stickers?" She waved the familiar long white ribbons with Laker logos, NEW YORK SKYTRAIN and a picture of the Statue of Liberty on them.

Willing hands reached out. "Slap them on walls, cars, buses and trucks," Franny added. "We really want to make a helluva fuss today. We know de general public are on our side and love us. Hell, even British Airways crews tink we're de bees' knees. So, talk to everyone and get dem protestin' too."

Franny sat down and the coach buzzed with lively conversations.

"One more ting." Franny stood again and waved a hand for attention. "We've told the media dat we're going to be there today to meet with Mr. Scroat, I mean Sproat . . ." Low snickers rippled around the coach. ". . . so you might be interviewed on TV or quoted in the media, and while we want to make a to-do, remember dat you're still in uniform and representing de airline. So, behave. Now does anyone have any questions?"

"What happens if the protest doesn't work?" a steward at the front asked. "What's next?"

"To be honest," Franny said, grimacing, ". . .we don't know, but we'll stay in touch with you after today. Whatever happens. . .," she paused and took a deep breath, "I wish yer all good luck. It's been a real honour and pleasure flyin' with y'all."

Her teary last words had a sobering effect on the whole group, and we lapsed into silence.

"What will *you* do now?" I whispered to Ellen sitting staring out of the window.

"We-e-ell. . ." She beamed. "Greg proposed. Just like Maggie said he would."

"Oh, that's wonderful!" I said, happy for her. "So that means?"

"Yes. Sorry, Natasha. I'll be moving out at the end of the month and going back home until the wedding. Greg wants me to get a 9-to-5 job so we can spend more time together."

Back to ordinary life. How depressing! "Even though I don't see a lot of you, Ellen, I'm going to really miss you. Now I'll need to find *two* new flatmates to help with my mortgage ... Bloody hell, everything's changing," I blurted, suddenly feeling lost.

"What about you and Jack?" she enquired. "Seems like you two are getting along really well these days."

"Yes, we are. But we're going to his brother's wedding in a few weeks and ..."

"So?"

"Oh, I don't know. I just have a bad feeling. Sometimes I think he's on the edge of proposing ... and then he suddenly does an about-face. I just know people at the wedding will bug him about us getting married and that might just push him away for good. Maggie wasn't exactly encouraging about us getting married, was she? And she's been bang on so far."

"Psychics aren't right *all* of the time," Ellen offered a little lamely.

We retreated into our own thoughts as the coach driver negotiated South London suburbia. The future stretched out before me like a roll of blank carpet, but with a mortgage to pay, no flatmates, no job and with the country in a recession, that carpet was turning black. And what could Maggie have meant when she said I would be going to a dark-skinned country like Africa?

An hour later a hoard of men and women dressed in red and black with splashes of white were descending from the long line of coaches onto the Embankment. We were joined by more pilots coming from all directions. We all fell into a line, three- and four-abreast and marched toward Parliament and the House of Commons.

With Ellen and I walking together near the front, we soon became aware that pedestrians were stopping to look and shouting encouragingly, "We love Laker!" and "Freddie rocks!" We waved back, moved by their support. Cars, buses and trucks began honking. When the driver of a double-decker that was stopped in traffic yelled out of his window, "Freddie's the best!" one of the stewards plastered a Skytrain sticker across the front of his bus. More cabin crew were handing out stickers to pedestrians as well as slapping them on car bonnets. Traffic was always slow-moving in this part of London, but now drivers were slowing to a stop to see why thousands of flight attendants and Laker staff were clogging the streets. Helicopters whirred overhead. What did we look like from the air, I wondered? This long red and black snake of people weaving its way alongside the Thames? I felt comforted, as if the whole world was cheering for us to win.

More bobbies than usual were lining the streets. Did they expect trouble or were they just making sure the traffic kept moving? Maybe both. As we flirted with the police and took photos with them, it occurred to me that this might be the last time any of us would wear this red and black uniform.

When we arrived at the Houses of Parliament, waiting at the back entrance was a mob of newspaper reporters and TV cameramen from all over Europe and the US, shining their lenses and poking their microphones into our faces. Ellen and I hurried straight into the large hall and found seats about halfway down on the right. Ahead of us was a bare stage with just four empty wooden chairs. Not a fancy affair then? This really was a place for commoners.

I looked behind us. The room was already full, and some of our staff–some in uniform, some in civvies–were leaning against the back wall. Others were still trying to squeeze into the room. Then on the left side of the stage a door opened, and four men entered, three in business suits and another dressed in pinstripe trousers and tailed black jacket—presumably the Under-Secretary of Trade, Iain Sproat. They strutted onto the stage and took their seats. All four surveyed the room with irritated disdain as if we were a huge nuisance and had just interrupted their morning tea and chocolate biscuit ritual. I sensed that they intended to dispose of us as quickly as possible.

Ritch Kievers, our beloved senior captain and elected spokesman—seated at the front— stood up. He got straight to the point. "Mr. Sproat, if the British Government saw fit to bail out Delorean and his car-making company in Belfast, could they not see the value of supporting Laker Airways and two thousand, five hundred jobs through this recession?"

"Well, of course, you know," the undersecretary began—despite his Scottish heritage—in an upper-class *awfully-awfully* accent, "that we are supporting DeLorean because unemployment in Northern Ireland is so dastardly, and those jobs are *extremely* important to that economy. And as you may appreciate," he said, looking down his bulbous nose at our captain, "the political climate in Ireland is extremely sensitive. We felt it wise to-"

Ritch Kievers waved an arm at the room full of people behind him. "But there are twenty-five hundred jobs here, too, and aren't *we* important to *this* local economy?"

I must have tuned out at that point because underneath the sycophantic smiles from the politicians on stage and their placating words of commiseration, I sensed their agenda. They *wanted* Laker Airways to be out of business. Suddenly I realized that Freddie was a threat—not just to their precious British Airways and who knows which other European or American airlines they were in bed with— but also our government. It was over.

At the front of the room Ritch Kievers was still talking, almost pleading now.

Stop! I wanted to shout at him. *Stop!* Let's leave with our dignity intact. Let's just get out of here.

Maybe the men on stage heard my thoughts because Iain Scrotum–or whatever his name was–began his conclusions. He put his hands behind his back and paced across the stage and haw-hawed his way through apologies, tough times, calls for desperate measures and all that, and how he hoped we would all find new jobs. The British government were blah-blah-blah doing all they could to end the recession and bring in new opportunities. Blah, blah, blah.

Jolly good show, I thought sarcastically. I wanted to throw up.

Dejected, we all slowly stood and moved toward the exit. Outside the sun was still shining and passers-by were still yelling messages of love and support. Franny had told us that the coaches would be leaving at 3.00 p.m. so, still stunned and with an hour to spare, we wandered aimlessly around the Parliament Buildings, mingling with the media, flirting shamelessly with shy young bobbies and chatting with sympathetic pedestrians. We took more photographs of each other as it was now definite. This *was* the last time we would be wearing the Laker uniform.

"Natasha! Natasha!" I turned and saw one of my colleagues rushing toward me, closely followed by a man holding a massive camera on his shoulder. "You speak French, don't you?"

"Er . . . er . . .yes."

"He wants to interview you," she said, pointing to the man who was aiming the lens at my shocked face.

While my French was rated good conversational, my vocabulary was mostly limited to on-board lingo. I began to think of the words I would need; bankrupt, recession, glut of pilots, no bail out, unemployed. My memory of the French language and my mind suddenly went blank. "Laker *est fini*" probably wouldn't fill an interview. And maybe I was just too sad to think straight.

"*Je suis desolee,*" I'm sorry, I apologized and shrugged French-style. "*Mais je ne peux pas . . .*" I can't.

"*Zut alors . . .*" The reporter cursed and moved away, resuming his search.

Just then a woman stepped in front of me "Don't you worry, love," she said and then peered more closely at me. "'Ere, don't I know you? I fink you was on my Laker flight to LA last December. Such a shame. God bless Freddie! If it 'adn't been for 'im, I never would 'ave been able to see my sister in Australia after 30 years of separation."

She did look vaguely familiar, but how many faces did we see in a week on three transatlantic sectors? A thousand or more? "Yes, I think I do remember you," I said anyway.

She beamed. "Yeah, we love Freddie, but these things 'appen for a reason, ducks. Maybe it's time to move on?"

Who was she? Maggie Cullen's psychic sidekick?

"Yes, maybe you're right," I said.

That evening when Ellen and I finally arrived home, we both slumped onto the couch.

"Well, that was a bloody waste of time," she grumbled as she eased her tired feet out of the uniform black high-heeled shoes.

"I know we didn't win, but at least we didn't give up without a fight," I reminded her. "Seeing all the people who were cheering for us cos they love the airline was wonderful. *And* getting together at the end of an era was like a completion, a final airline party. I don't think it was a waste. Now we know without a doubt that the airline is done, and we have to look forward."

"To what?" Ellen frowned.

"Well, as Monty Python would say, 'something completely different!'"

19

AND NOW FOR SOMETHING COMPLETELY DIFFERENT

Not So Jolly Olde Englande
February – September 1982

On February 14th, six days after the Laker staff's attempt to save the airline, Ellen and I were sitting in the living room, drinking coffee. Now that neither of us were flying anywhere and had no jobs to go to, we had lots and lots of time to sit around and drink coffee. We were both poring over the Sunday newspapers and various magazine articles, still torturing ourselves with reports on the airline's demise.

Valentine's Day had fallen on Sunday that year, and unlike America which seemed to never close, nothing was open in England—except, that is, for churches, pubs and the odd corner shop where we could buy necessities like cigarettes, milk and baked beans. Outside a thin misty fog hung over the trees, adding an extra layer of misery to the day. The thought of Jack taking me out for dinner later was the only ray of light in my existence.

"Look at this!" I told Ellen, as I read the *New York Times*. "Iain Sproat says, quote, *"Sir Freddie is a very great man who has done wonderful things for passengers around the world, providing them with cheap air travel."*

"Ugh!" Ellen scoffed, remembering his performance in the House of Commons. "Too bad he didn't put his money where his mouth is. What a tosser!"

"We could always go back to Dan Air," I teased, glancing at Ellen for her reaction.

"Not in a million years!"

"You're right. We'd have to be desperate. Let's look for *great* jobs," I said, flicking through *The Sunday Telegraph*.

Ellen and I had both prepared job applications for various new positions and deposited them in the red post box in front of our house. As Horsham was located halfway between London and Brighton, we had extended our job search to include both cities and every town in between. We had also called other airlines, but the answer was always the same. "We're not hiring at the moment." With the recession, Laker had not been the only airline in trouble.

Ellen suddenly tilted her head to one side listening. "Someone's at the door!" she said, putting her cup down on the coffee table. "I'll get it," she offered, jumping up.

"Maybe Greg's come to surprise you!" I suggested as she hurried to the door. "Or it's a telegram from British Airways begging you to join them!"

"And pigs might fly!" she scoffed.

Ellen would be moving out in two weeks' time, and I would miss her. But as she was also now unemployed and engaged to her long-time boyfriend, it made sense for her to move back in with her parents until she got married. I should really be looking for a replacement flatmate, I thought, but I didn't have the gusto to begin the laborious process of putting ads in the paper and then interviewing all the idiosyncratic personalities that responded. And now I was home all the time and unemployed, the choice of a companiable renter would be even more critical.

My spacious maisonette seemed to have a lucky romantic charm . . . for others anyway, as all my lodgers had moved out after just one year of renting from me, always to get married. Maybe it would be my turn soon. Despite my psychic's lack of enthusiasm for a happy-ever-after with Jack, I was very content with him. Sometimes I caught him staring at me, grinning, pondering. He might be a commitment-phobe, but was he finally getting ready to propose? Now that I wasn't flying, our relationship would change, of course, but for better or worse? And though Jose was never far from my thoughts, it was clear now that we would never be together—not in this lifetime anyway.

Ellen burst into the living room, beaming and clutching the largest bouquet of flowers I had ever seen.

"Oh, how lovely!" I cooed, a little envious. "How did Greg manage to get those delivered on a Sunday?"

"No. They're for you, Ratbag!" Ellen laughed.

"*What!* Who from?" I asked as I took them from her. "They're so-o-o-o beautiful!"

"Is there a card?" Ellens' fingers fluttered over the flowers, just as excited as I was. "They *must* be from Jack."

"Not necessarily. I don't think Jack is a sending-flowers kind of man." I said. But Jose was. Or they could be from LA Roger who was still smitten despite my protestations of "Let's just be friends."

I poked around the flowers, searching. No card. There was, however, the name and address of the florist embossed on the red ribbon, which was–oh my god—in the village where Jack lived! The flowers *must* be from him. I smiled, happy. This gesture was unexpected—and quite the romantic breakthrough.

That evening when Jack picked me up and took me to my favourite restaurant, the Red Lion in Handcross—despite being unemployed and soon-to-be-lodger-less, I was blissfully happy. Even though I had often joked that always having to look up at his 6' 4" height gave me a pain in the neck, something about Jack's lean frame, blond hair and dynamic energy gave me butterflies. After he coyly admitted to sending me the flowers, we laughed and flirted all night. Contrary to Maggie's gloomy prediction, I thought, I *will* marry Jack, sell my house and we *will* live happily-ever-after.

"So, my brother's wedding is at 3.00 p.m. on Saturday two weeks from now," he reminded me. "I'll pick you up at 2.00. Okay?"

Ah yes. The wedding. The event might have either a positive or a negative impact on our relationship. His brother's romance might nudge him toward a proposal, or conversely, pressure from friends and family might also send him running for the hills. While he and I were getting closer, our harmony was still new.

"How on earth did your brother and Jane meet, anyway?" I enquired over coffee and liqueurs. "Hasn't he been living on some remote sheep station in Australia while she's been tucked away down a country lane in Sussex?"

Jack grinned. "Jane's the original girl-next-door. We've both known her since she was little, but she's been engaged to this other bloke, Mark, for the last seven years. Strange thing is whenever they arranged a wedding date, something drastic would happen, someone would die, and once he even got into a car accident. Then when my brother came back from Australia, he and Jane took one look at each other and fell madly in love."

"Poor Mark!" I knew how hard rejection was. "How's *he* doing?"

"Oh, he'll be okay," Jack waved a dismissive hand, never one to show empathy for people in messy emotional situations. "They probably didn't really want to marry each other anyway." Jack leaned in closer, grinning and peered deep into my eyes. "When it's right, it's right, don't you think?"

I beamed back at him. "Yes, I do."

Fortunately, I didn't have to look for a new flatmate. An ex-Laker friend introduced me to Martin, a social worker who worked primarily with children. He was a gentle soul with an ironic sense of humour. I liked him instantly.

Over the following week, though my relationship with Jack was making me happy, I was still concerned about finding a job. With a worldwide recession, I wasn't very hopeful that my numerous applications through agencies would bear fruit. And though we called each other frequently commiserating about our fruitless job searches, I was missing my flying colleagues. Just as I was giving up on employment in the UK and considering selling up and moving to another country, the phone rang.

"There's a company in Brighton," the woman from the agency said, her tone crisp but still tinged with warmth. ". . .who would like you to come for an interview."

Brighton! An hour's drive "Yes? Who are they?"

"Medamex is an international insurance administration corporation, and they urgently need an executive secretary."

I groaned inwardly at the thought of a boring office job, but after six weeks of no prospects, I wasn't in a position to be too picky.

"They're really interested in your language capabilities," she added.

More interesting.

"Can you go today?"

Who was I to say no? "Yes, I can. What time?"

Gertrude, the blonde woman in a bright red dress who interviewed me, had also been a flight attendant, but with Air France and she too spoke four languages. She was impressed when she tested me on my French, German, Italian and even my rudimentary Spanish. "Norwegian might come in handy, too," she told me, although she admitted she didn't speak it.

I got the job.

The daily hour-long drive to Brighton through the Sussex countryside was long and pleasant, but after eight years of the non-routine of flying, I would need time to adjust to the rigid structure of a 9-5 routine. An office job was proving expensive, too. As a flight attendant, uniforms and meals were provided as well as discounted dry cleaning, petrol and travel. I now had to buy new office clothes, pack or buy lunches and pay full price for petrol and dry cleaning. Nothing like coming down to earth with a bump.

Medamex was a new and rapidly growing enterprise. Jonathan, its Texan company president was courting Lloyds of London—one of the oldest and most respected institutions in the UK—to partner in new insurance administration programs. After just one week, I realized that insurance could be very interesting. Being able to use my languages on the phone, comforting stranded tourists in the mountains of Mexico, the jungles of Jakarta or villages in South Africa and offering information that helped them get out of precarious situations was rewarding.

Life was looking up.

When Jack collected me for his brother's wedding at the appointed time, he was a little tense. Being best man was probably causing him some stress, I decided. This would be my first big social event with his aristocratic family, so I was a tad nervous. And although he was usually very complimentary on my appearance, he simply scrutinized my outfit and didn't comment. Uh oh.

The day was sunny and surprisingly warm. The ceremony—planned in a hurry—was taking place in the garden of his family's rambling farmhouse. The event was a simple affair, and after the rituals were performed, everyone moved inside where large arrays of food were laid out on long farm tables. Already feeling a little out of place with Jack's circle of lords and ladies and his famous uncle, I was a little miffed when he abandoned me to a room full of strangers. I attempted superficial conversation with his father's business partner but being unfamiliar with Lord's cricket matches—though I had watched Jack play, hunting—which I found distasteful and clay-pigeon shooting—which I had a talent for, my middle-class insecurities reared their ugly heads. Did I really want to marry Jack and be a part of this upper crust world, often feeling "less than"? Although his family was considered nouveau riche with only three generations of wealth behind them, they often travelled with the aristocracy, some of whom I found arrogant. If I could remove Jack from this world, I thought, life could be perfect for us.

After the speeches, a tall elderly gentleman came over to me, nudged me heartily and said, "So-o-o-o, Natasha, what about you and young Jack then, what? When are you two tying the knot, eh? Not getting any younger, what ho?"

"W-well," I stuttered, "he . . .he has to ask me first."

Two more women approached and gave me the same interrogation. Oh, no! If they were saying these things to me, how were they pressuring Jack? Is that why he was keeping his distance? Every time I looked over at him on the other side of the room, he threw me cool, puzzled glances.

Driving home in the dark, he was eerily quiet. Still hurt at having been abandoned at the wedding reception, I was tempted to throw recriminations at him, but instead I chose silence as well.

Once he had parked his Land Rover just outside my maisonette, he clutched the steering wheel with both hands. "I think we should split up," he said and exhaled.

"Oh God," I moaned. Here we go. "Why? Because some people mentioned marriage?"

"Oh, Natasha." He sighed. "You're too good for me!"

Too good? "What does that mean?"

"You're such a good person . . ."

Was that a crime? "*I* thought it was the other way around," I sneered. "I'm not good enough for *you*." Angry and crying, I reached for the handle and pushed the door open. As I rushed toward the house, I heard Jack behind me open and close his car door. A gentleman to the last, he was following me to my flat. Just go, I thought as I ran up the stairs, crying.

Before I knew it, we were both sitting on the edge of my king-sized bed. While I sobbed in devastation, he was spouting all the reasons why our relationship wouldn't work and downplaying all the reasons why it could. After a year of ups and downs, I thought we had reached a deeper harmony, so his words cut like knives into my heart.

"But you just sent me flowers! Why?" I asked, stunned. The contrast between our flourishing romance two weeks ago and now this complete one-eighty did not make sense. Except if someone at the wedding had pushed too hard and scared him off. What had they said to make him turn away so quickly and completely?

"I wish I was dead!" I moaned. My flying job, my flat-mate and friend, and now my hoped-for marriage were all disappearing. With no family to speak of, I felt bereft.

"No, you don't." He reached over and tried to hold me.

"Oh, what do *you* know?" I snapped, pushing him away. "You know *nothing* about me." And then I realized that he really *did* know nothing about me because I hadn't told him. "Please leave!" I pleaded. There had been enough humiliation for one day. "Go! Just go!"

Slowly he pulled his tall frame off the bed. Before he disappeared through the door, he paused, turned to me and whispered, "I'm sorry."

The following morning when Ellen had handed the last of her cardboard boxes over to Greg as he helped her move out, we hugged and said our goodbyes.

"I hate to leave you today," she said. Seeing my puffy face, her large brown eyes oozing concern. But she didn't have time for tea and sympathy this morning. She had a reunion with her family and a future wedding to look forward to. As I closed the door after her, my home fell eerily silent.

And it was Sunday. Ever since leaving home and my formerly happy hectic family, I had hated the long void of Sundays. Like the restless ghost that I often sensed haunted my home, I roamed its emptiness, intermittently crying and sitting and staring out of the window. Like my ghost, I was also a lost soul. With nothing to do, nowhere to go and no one to talk to, my home felt like an even bigger vacuum. It wasn't until evening when at last I began emerging from the black hole of my self-pity that I reminded myself, at least I have a job!

While grieving for Jack, I threw myself into my work, often staying late and even going into the office on weekends. After just one month, Jonathan promoted me to Insurance Coordinator, which involved the preparation of an administration system and a protocol for the clients of each program. In the second month he tossed a computer print-out on my desk which I recognized as yet another new insurance administration program.

"I want you to go up to London," he said, "and talk to Lloyds about this."

"*Me?* But . . ." I glanced at the stack of paper. How would I be able to glean enough from this IBM print-out to talk to an esteemed Lloyds agent about the intricacies of a new offering?

"Deal with it. I'm going to Texas," Jonathan said, turning his back on me and leaving the office.

After my meeting with Lloyds where, despite profuse perspiring, I miraculously winged my way through the agent's intelligent questions, I was promoted yet again. "We'll give you your own office," Jonathan announced. "You'll need an assistant, and we'll double your salary."

Hmm? While romance obviously wasn't my forte, maybe a career in insurance would now be my *raison d'etre?*

For an assistant I immediately thought of Caroline, my friend and neighbor, also an ex-flight attendant who needed a job. It would be returning a favour. Just two months after my break-up with Jack, she had set me up—despite my protestations—with David, who owned a gorgeous, renovated millhouse in the Sussex countryside, drove a red Porsche and travelled internationally for a hi-tech company. Though he was attentive, he wasn't Jack or Jose, but maybe he would grow on me.

Life was a little brighter.

After working long hours for a month setting up my department with two assistants, including Caroline, I had established four functioning insurance programs.

That's when my ex-Dan Air buddy, Felicity Farmsworth, called and invited me to join her on a long spa weekend. When I asked Jonathan for the extra two days off, he replied cheerily, "Sure. As long as everything's covered. You've worked hard. Go for it. See you Tuesday."

I was just packing for the weekend when the phone rang.

"Hello, Natasha. It's Joy Poirrier."

Why was the ex-chief air stewardess of Laker calling me?

"After Laker went down, I started my own agency for temporary flying contracts," she explained. "And I'm looking for crew for a Haj based in Lagos. Are you interested?"

Lagos? The armpit of the world, at least according to the stories I'd heard from other flyers. But after hearing my colleagues talking about their amazing adventures in middle eastern and African countries on these Muslim pilgrimages to Mecca, I had always wanted to do a Haj. But now, this was an easy decision for me to make.

"I appreciate you thinking of me, Joy, but I've finally found an amazing job, so I'm going to say no. And anyway," I confessed, "when Laker went down, I was kind of ready to quit flying."

"Good for you. Well, if you know of anyone that might want a two-month Haj, let me know."

The massages, facials and body wraps at the health farm made both Felicity and I positively glow. But after two days of a super-healthy diet of 500 calories, on the third night we found ourselves at the nearest pub scarfing down fish and chips followed by chocolate cheesecake. Miraculously, I still managed to drop four pounds, which when I went to visit David at the Millhouse on the way home, he noticed with appreciation.

"You need to call Caroline," he told me. "It sounds urgent. You can call her from here."

I frowned. Uh oh.

"Ohmigod, Natasha!" Caroline's voice sounded distraught. Her devastation reminded me of Cheryl when she had told me of Laker's demise. As if there had been a death.

"I feel horrible being the one to tell you this but . . . oh, you won't believe it."

I waited. What the hell could it be?

"They've dismantled your office. It's all gone."

"*Wha-a-at?* Why?"

"I'm not sure, but I know it has something to do with Gertrude. Suddenly they were speaking really badly about you and . . . oh, it's horrible!"

Yes, that would make sense. Gertrude had been really welcoming at first, but her attitude had soon changed to covert cattiness, and over the last month she had frequently made snide comments to me. I wasn't sure why. But what had she been saying behind my back?

"What about *your* job?" I asked.

"I'm back out in the big office doing filing."

"Oh, no!" Poor Caroline.

"Do *I* still have a job?" I couldn't think why not. I hadn't done anything wrong.

"Yes, but Jonathan wants to see you first thing tomorrow morning. And there's some other guy from Texas there who's kind of taking over. He's walking around with a tape recorder, recording conversations. Like he's from the FBI or something. It's so-o-o weird."

The healthy relaxed being that I had become over the last few days suddenly vanished, and my body went rigid with stress. Was I feeling fear, rage or confusion? I began to tremble. What the hell was going on? Even though I was bracing myself for my entrance the next morning, no amount of psychic protection could have prepared me for the shock.

I walked down the corridor and encountered Simon, the accountant. I smiled at my friend and said, "Good Morning!" Formerly joking and friendly, he now scowled at me as though I had done something heinously disgusting. Julian, the computer tech who was usually pleasant, would not look me in the face either as if I was giving off a foul smell. In my absence I had turned from being highly respected and liked to being scum. What was I supposed to have done while I was away? Robbery, murder, pedophilia?

Jonathan was at his desk, head down. "I understand you want to speak with me?" I said, trying to hide my shaky nerves.

Barely acknowledging my presence, he grabbed a notebook and said, "Let's go into the conference room."

I followed his large physique as he moved across the massive open plan office. Everyone at their desks had their heads down, some peeking at me surreptitiously but all looking like frightened rabbits.

While Jonathan sank down on one end of the couch, I sat, two cushions away, at the other end. He placed a small tape recorder on the round glass table. "Do you mind if we tape this?" he enquired in his Texan drawl.

I almost laughed. "Of course not. I've got nothing to hide."

"We have a problem . . . with you." He sat staring straight ahead, not able or willing to look me in the face. "Do you know that in three months you've learned what it would have taken anyone else three years to learn?" He made it sound like the crime of the century. "How'd yer do that?" He glared at me, suspicion in his eyes.

"I was interested in the work . . ." I shrugged. Learning and doing a good job was part of my upbringing. But he seemed to be spooked by my diligence. Or, and I smiled at the thought, did he think I was a corporate spy?

"And I got an earful from the Lloyds people about how *wonderful* you are," Jonathan continued, raising his hands in the air, and then shaking his head as if that conversation was a painful memory.

Oh my god, was he *afraid* of my ability? Strange. While my own family had made me think I was not too bright, since I had left home, employers had always praised my intellect.

"Well, I'm sorry," I said, "but isn't that what you wanted?" I was so confused. "You gave me programs to deal with, you promoted me, you gave me the department, you sent me to Germany to set up an office, I just wanted to do a good job, and you–"

He put up a hand to stop me. "Yes, but the problem is that Gertrude has been here much longer than you and her nose is out of joint. Seems you both want to be Queen Bees and there's only room for one."

I shook my head, shell-shocked. It was true. I did not like Gertrude and her manipulative ways, so I had minimized my contact with her. "I have no interest in being a Queen Bee, Jonathan," I told him. "I just want to do my work and do a good job." Work had always been my salvation, but now doing well was apparently a crime.

"Yeah, too good," he mumbled, peering out of the window at the blue summer sky.

The words "too good" again. Was it my curse? According to my family, I had never been good enough. I was confused.

"Well, Natasha, it ain't going to work. Someone has to go, and it won't be Gertrude. She's put a lot into this company."

And I haven't? Wow. So, I was being fired for doing *too* good of a job! I had only been gone four days. What had happened so quickly to turn it all around? I had sensed Gertrude's competition with me, but what had she told Jonathan and everyone else to make them treat me with so much disdain?

"What I *can* offer you," Jonathan continued, "is Toronto."

"Toronto?"

"Yes, we're opening an office there. You already opened one in Germany so you could do the same in Toronto. Don't you have brothers there or something?"

Toronto. I had seriously considered moving to Canada but not to the east side of the country. I didn't know a soul in that city and Vancouver and Calgary where my brothers lived were three thousand miles away to the West.

"No, thanks." I wanted nothing more to do with this nasty, hokey company.

Trembling with the rage of injustice, I cleared out my desk, nodded at Caroline, who was hunched over at her station pumping out dynamo tape, and walked out of the office and the company without saying goodbye to anyone. Whatever Gertrude had told them had turned all their previous bonhomie and camaraderie into some unfounded hatred. What hurt the most is that they had been so willing to believe whatever it was she had told them. And I couldn't imagine what "it" was.

Later that evening Caroline and I went to The Lamb at Lamb's Green to drown our sorrows and work through our confusion.

"I'll leave Medamex, too, if you want me to," she offered.

"No, you don't have to do that on my behalf," I said, touched by her loyalty and fully aware of how hard it was to get any job in the current recession. "But I'd really like to know what the hell Gertrude said about me. That's the worst part of it—being treated like a criminal and not knowing my supposed crime."

Caroline bowed her head. "That Gertrude's a *bitch!* Whatever she said, you know it's not true. You did so much for that company!" I suspected Caroline knew *exactly* what Gertrude had said, but she wanted to avoid adding to my pain. "What are you goin' to do now?" she asked, concerned.

"Damned if I know." I stared into my red wine. "Nothing's working. I feel like the universe is trying to give me a big fat message, but I'm not getting it."

"What about David? He really likes you, you know. He could propose."

"Ugh." Romance was the last thing on my mind. "Sorry, Caroline. David's sweet, but he's not doing anything for me. I might call Joy Poirrier back and ask her if she's got any more Hajes."

"You'd go to Lagos?"

I nodded.

"Bloody hell! Aren't there easier ways to pay your mortgage?" She exclaimed, slamming down her wine glass. "You could get killed there!"

"So?" I shrugged. "Right now, they'd be doing me a favor."

The next morning right after 9.00 a.m. I picked up the phone and rang Joy Poirrier. After having bragged about my great job just days earlier and claiming that I didn't want to fly again, this about-face would mean I had to eat a little crow.

I got straight to the point. "Good morning, Joy. It's Natasha Rosewood. My situation has changed since we spoke. Do you have any more of those Hajes going?"

"Well, actually, yes. Lagos is full but we've got one based in Libya."

"Libya!" Now that's something completely different. I remembered the *Reader's Digest* article I had recently read. Situated on the northern edge of the Sahara, this country looked cleaner than Nigeria, but was it more dangerous?

"You'd be based in Tripoli for two months. Although we do already have a full complement of 20 girls, there may be some dropouts. Shall I put your name on the standby list just in case?"

"Yes, please."

"If you make the list," Joy continued, "is there anyone who would object to you going? Remember you won't have flight deck to protect you. You girls will be on your own."

Libya! She was, of course, implying that Libya was a dangerous place for 20 young, undefended and attractive women. But what did I have to lose? I thought about my ex, Jack, my disturbed mother who harassed me constantly with abusive phone calls, my absent siblings and my luke-warm relationship with David.

"No. No, there's no one," I reassured her.

As I hung up, I remembered Maggie Cullen's words. *You will have a reunion with people, and you will go to a dark-skinned country like Africa.* If I made the list, I *would* be reuniting with my Laker colleagues after six months, and Libya *was* in North Africa. Including my break-up with Jack, the palmist had been bang on with all her predictions . . . so far.

The next day Joy called back. "We've had five dropouts," she announced.

Quelle surprise! Had these girls chickened out, or did they have people who loved them so much that they would not allow them to risk their lives just to pay their mortgage?

". . . So you're on for Libya," Joy continued. "You'll have to attend an interview at Libyan Arab Airlines in London. Take your passport. And I'll send a list of items you will need to take like plugs and saucepans. There's also a list of what you *aren't* allowed to take into the country. And you'll want to take a suitcase of food. There are rules of behaviour for western women living in a strict Islamic culture so, for your own safety, follow them precisely. You'll get paid in cash at Heathrow before you depart. Any questions?"

"Who else is going?" I asked. If I was going to be in a strange place, I wanted to know who was going to be with me.

Joy reeled off some names, some of whom I recognized but no one especially close to me.

"Do you need more people?" I asked.

"Actually, yes, I need two more."

"Victoria Bainbridge and Amy McDervish were still available the last time I talked to them, and they're always up for an adventure."

"Thank you, Natasha," Joy said, sounding grateful.

"No, thank *you*, Joy!" I couldn't wait to leave my home, my life and all the emotional disasters of the last six months behind me.

As I hung up, just for a split second I wondered about my sanity. Libya! Was I doing the right thing? Ach, what's the worst they could do? Kill me? Oh, well.

20

IT'S TOO LATE NOW!

London, England – Tripoli, Libya
September 1982

Our strange interview at the London office of Libyan Arab Airlines should have been our first clue about Libya and what was in store for us.

While double-deckers rushed along Piccadilly behind us, Victoria, Hannah, Lillian and I—all ex-Laker flight attendants—stood on the pavement in front of the nothing-but-glass façade of Libyan Arab's office, its name and a green-arrowed logo splayed across the frontage. From the outside, the classy London premises appeared to represent a flourishing Middle Eastern airline.

I pulled on the heavy door and we stepped inside. The expansive, clean, white interior with its deluxe round glass desks and several maps of the world adorning the walls was, I thought, how a first-class, international airline should look. Except that the office appeared to be entirely empty of occupants.

"Yes?" The man's voice startled us until we realized he was sitting all the way at the back of the room with yet another map of the world behind him as his backdrop. His head was down as he stared at some paperwork. Dark-haired and swarthy, he was presumably Libyan.

Lillian stepped forward and we followed, approaching his massive desk. The man did not look up, still intent on writing something.

"Ahem." Lillian coughed politely in an attempt to get his attention.

When he finally raised his head, he waved us closer impatiently, as if we had been keeping *him* waiting. "Yes! Yes!" he ordered.

We soon realized, that his "Yes" was his way of asking the question; What do you want?

"Well," Victoria started, sounding extra posh, and with her slightly amused Princess Anne smirk on her face, "we're here for our interview with Libyan Arab Airlines." She paused, waiting for signs of intelligence in the gentleman's face but he continued to stare at us. She then asked in an oh-for-God's-sake tone, "Are we in the right place?"

"What are your names?" the man snapped in a heavy Libyan accent, giving Victoria an angry look. Determined to avoid eye contact with us, he searched his paper-laden desk for something that he couldn't seem to find. Giving up, he pushed a pen and pad at Lillian. "Write down your names," he snapped.

We complied.

"Yes, yes!" he said, accepting the pad again, and not even glancing at our writing. He held out a hand. "Passports!"

After we handed them over, he flicked through the pages of our well-used documents, sometimes stopping to inspect the stamps. Did he want to ensure that we had not set foot in Israel, the country that was just one of Libya's sworn enemies? Although I had often flown to the Israeli resort of Eilat with Dan Air, I had never entered the airport, so there was no stamp in my passport to give me away. Satisfied, he opened a drawer, pulled out several green slips of paper and placed one in each passport.

"Tickets!" he said, handing them back to Lillian in one pile. "You fly to Tripoli next Monday on our airline. In Libi, you fly 707s." He finally looked up, not directly at us but at some point over our shoulders. "You know 707," he said more as a statement than a question.

While I was checked out on four aircraft, the 707—one of the oldest Boeing planes—was not one of them. But before any of us could speak, he waved a dismissive hand and said, "*Mafeesh*. It doesn't matter. You train in Libi. Go now."

Stunned that the "interview" was over, we turned and left. Outside the glass door, we stood in a cluster, shocked, and exchanged looks, half-smiling, half-frowning.

"What the hell was *that*?" Hannah asked, chuckling.

"Hardly a British Airways-type interrogation, was it?" Victoria said and snickered.

"It means we're *really* going now," Lillian said, almost gulping. "We're committed."

"Anyone else need a drink, cos I do?" I asked. "Let's find a pub."

Fifteen minutes later, as the four of us sat with drinks in hand around a small table in what felt like a 16th century establishment while we waited for the lunches we had ordered, no one spoke.

Hannah finally broke the silence. "Do you think we're crazy?" she asked.

"Of course!" Victoria said, smiling. "We're stark raving mad!"

Hannah nodded. "You know, I've come to think that airline people are always running away from something."

"Or toward something," I said. "Like adventure."

"Maybe both." Lillian shrugged.

"Well, whatever we are running away from, it has to be better in Libya," I commented. None of us had jobs or boyfriends, and Victoria and I both had mortgages and no family to rely on.

"At least it'll be dry and sunny in Tripoli . . ." Lillian cast a glance out of the window at the cloudy sky. "So we won't have to put up with a miserable winter here."

"Well, that's *one* good thing then," Victoria said, standing up to collect our lunches from the bar.

"But I wonder if that very strange so-called interview we just had is a sign of things to come?" I took a large gulp of wine.

All three women nodded absently, apprehension written on their faces.

"Well, old girls," Victoria said, picking up her wine glass, "here's to whatever happens cos it's too late now. We're going."

As we all clinked our glasses, I saw that behind the smiling eyes, the question remained: What the hell are we doing?

After lunch we walked back to Piccadilly Circus and our tube station.

"See you in a week then!" Hannah called as she and Lillian headed toward the shops.

Having left our cars at the airport, Victoria and I boarded our train to Gatwick. We were both silent, staring vacantly out of the window at the Sussex countryside, the almost-bare trees shedding their last brown leaves as the autumn took its toll. A kind of death, I thought, and Libya could be the death of us. But what choice did we have? Do or die.

Not taking my eyes off the rows and rows of cloned suburban houses as the train jostled us rhythmically through the town of Redhill, I asked Victoria, "Did I tell you that I went to see a psychic in Brighton recently?"

"No! Really?" Victoria surveyed me with interest. "When?"

"The day before Laker went bankrupt."

"What did she tell you?"

"She warned me that there would be a big change and that something would end very soon."

"Really?" Victoria's interest was piqued. "Well, she got that right, didn't she, old girl? This is a big fucking change all right!"

Laker's demise had been much harder on Victoria. Unlike me, she still enjoyed flying. Otherwise, we had a lot in common including failed romances, broken families and both being Taurus. People in our zodiac sign weren't supposed to like change, and change seemed to be the only constant in both our lives.

"She also told me that I would lose something small that day."

"And did you?"

"Yes, my brown leather gloves."

"Bloody hell! And I suppose she told you that you'd be going to Libya, too." Victoria chortled, thinking she was being funny.

"Actually, she did!"

"Wha-at?"

"Well, her actual words were that I would be going to a dark country, like Africa, that I would be having a reunion with some people, and that the name Lillian would mean something."

"Fuck me!" Victoria stared at me, gobsmacked.

I laughed at the way she said the "f" word.. She paused before asking, "But the question is, dear, did she tell you that you would come back alive?"

"Not directly. But she did tell me that eventually I would be crossing a border into Canada, and obviously I won't be doing that before Libya."

"Jolly good. Well, if *you* have a future in Africa, I'm going to stick close to you, old girl. Then all should be well, shouldn't it?" She looked at me, hoping for reassurance.

I shrugged. "Theoretically."

"Hey," she said veering the conversation away from our potentially imminent deaths, "have you seen the list of stuff that Joy told us to take?"

"It came in the post this morning," I told her, pulling the papers out of my handbag. "Makes you wonder why we need to take a saucepan, a bathroom plug *and* a suitcase full of canned tuna. Are we camping out in the Sahara or what?"

"Oh, I don't mind that." She waved a dismissive hand. "The list was far longer on our Lagos Haj. But what about this business of no bikinis?"

"Well, we are going to a Muslim country . . ."

"If they think I'm going to cover up in hot weather, they can sod that for a game of marbles. I'm bloody well going to wear mine."

It is written that the seeds of the future are in the present. The Libyan "interview" that day and my conversation with the rebellious Victoria were glaring embryonic signs of things to come. Yet I was still willing to go where angels feared to tread.

A week later Victoria and I were sitting in the second to last row of seats on a half-empty Boeing 727 winging our way to Tripoli. The other eighteen ex-Laker crew, including Hannah and Lillian, were scattered throughout the cabin, no doubt also sitting there asking themselves if they were in their right minds. At Heathrow we had been met by Joy Poirrier's assistant who had handed out cheques, advance payment for our two-month contract. We had all discussed whether we should ask for danger pay, but it was too late now. The contracts had been signed. While the money was still good—and before my account was completely empty—I had deposited the cheque straight into my bank.

After take-off and once we had levelled out, a portly middle-aged man seated in the aisle seat of our row struck up a conversation with Victoria sitting in the middle.

"Are you sure you ladies want to be working in Tripoli?"

"Oh, how did you know we were going there to work?" Victoria asked.

He gave her an incredulous look as if she was out to lunch. "Well, no one goes there on holiday, love. Don't tell me," he added, before

Victoria could respond, "you're going to fly for Qu'adafi and Libyan Arab?"

"As it happens, yes," Victoria responded, a little surprised. "But just the airline. Not Qu'adafi."

"He *is* the airline, and he is everything else in Libya," the man responded. "How long's your contract. The usual two years?"

"Good Lord, no!" Victoria scoffed. "We're just doing a Haj. Two months."

"Ah. Well, okay, you might last that long."

"Is it that bad?"

"I've been there on and off for three years, working in the oil business. Libya's a . . ." he searched for a word, "a unique place."

"Oh?" She peered at him more closely. "Why do you say that?"

Victoria was not known for reading the news, and therefore she was not up-to date on current affairs and obviously hadn't learned anything about Libya before agreeing to go, except that it might be dangerous.

I sat forward and listened. Even though I had only read the *Reader's Digest*'s version of Qu'adafi's rise to power and the dynamic changes he had made to the Libyan economy, I wanted to hear this man's own experiences of the country.

"Libya's no picnic, especially for Western women. Don't take this personally, but they'll treat you all like whores."

I gulped. They didn't write about *that* in *Readers Digest*. "What . . .what do you mean?" I asked, fearing rape and pillage.

He sat forward and looked at me. "Oh, don't worry, love. They won't touch you. They'd get hanged, beheaded or imprisoned for going anywhere near a non-Muslim woman. No, they'll probably just spit and swear at you."

Lovely!

"All the Libyan women," the man continued, "walk around covered in sheets. Then they cover their faces and hold the sheet in their mouth, so you can only see one eye." He smiled and then curled a finger around his eye for added effect. "At first, seeing just one-eyed women everywhere gave me the creeps, but you get used to it."

"What else can you tell us?" Victoria enquired. It was unusual to see my shy friend so chatty with a strange man.

"Be careful. Don't be saying anything bad about Qu'adafi, especially in front of secret police."

"Secret police!" I repeated, louder than I meant to. Scary memories of going through East Germany and then into Russia years earlier and being watched by the Stazi came to mind.

"Yup. They'll follow you. And if you're unmarried and found in a room with a man unchaperoned, they'll make you get married, ship you off to Malta or put you in their jail, and that's just a rat hole in the middle of a field, complete with rats. Not many come out of there alive."

"Alrightee, then." Victoria turned to me and made one of her crossed eyes and sucked-in-cheeks faces.

I grinned, grateful for her humor.

"Well, thanks for that," she muttered to the man before he put his head back, ready for a nap.

After our inflight dinner, Victoria also nodded off, but my mind was racing, and I was unable to sleep. Before leaving, had I remembered to do everything? If not, it was too late now. Joy had told us that while in Libya, we would have little or no contact with home but sometimes by booking a line ahead, we could call out. Posting letters was an iffy proposition. No phone calls into Libya were possible either. That meant that although friends could not contact me, nor could my mother—my nemesis, psycho stalker and worst nightmare. Despite the unpleasant picture our neighbouring passenger had painted about the Libyan culture, I wondered if two months of mother-free peace might turn out to be the best thing about our time here.

I also understood the reality of what Joy Poirrier had told us. Unlike our trips with Laker, we would have no flight deck to protect us. Even if sometimes they hadn't all behaved exactly like gentlemen, they had been at least male companions and, as such, acted as deterrents to other unwanted lusty men. Now twenty of us nubile girls, all between 27 and 35 were going to be on our own in a strange country. Ah well, I thought, we will just have to protect each other.

Mentally I revisited my "to do" list again. The money was in the bank, so the mortgage was covered. And my ex-boyfriend-now-friend, Julian, had accepted power of attorney so he would make sure the rent was collected from my two tenants. If anything should happen to me, he had my solicitor's instructions.

And if I didn't come back, who was I really leaving? Even though Jack had been happy to take me out for a goodbye dinner, that romance was well and truly over—for him anyway. And family? Maybe they all took my adventurous spirit for granted, but only one relative seemed to even care that I was risking my life to stay financially afloat, and that was my awfully-awfully proper Auntie Jane. At least, she had taken the time to ring me. I smiled, remembering our conversation.

"Natasha? Your father told me that you are going to Libya for two months. Is that true?"

"Yes, Auntie Jane. That's right."

"Oe-er." The upper crust way she said "Oh" always made me smile. I imagined the look of shock and horror on her sweet face. "But . . . are you sure?" she continued. "I was so happy when your father told me that you were done with all that." Auntie Jane loved to travel but due to her terror of flying, she would never step inside an aircraft.

"I thought I was done with it too, but—"

"I mean . . .wouldn't you prefer to have a nice, steady 9 to 5 job instead of . . . I mean . . . Libya!"

"God, no! Been there, done that!" I told her, thinking of Medamex and cringing. But bless Auntie Jane and her steady, predictable and boring English upbringing. "I tried being normal, Auntie Jane. I really did," I told her, hoping to appease her, "but it didn't work."

"Well, all right then," she said, finally giving up on changing my mind. "Please be careful."

"Don't worry," I said, having no idea whether she should worry or not. "But thank you for caring."

After four hours and thirty-five minutes of flying time, the aircraft began its descent. Looking out into the dark night, there were no lights visible on the ground and nothing to see of Tripoli, our home base for the next two months. Maybe, I wondered, we were flying in from the south over the Sahara. The Sahara! Images of Peter O'Toole riding his camel across the desert in the film *Lawrence of Arabia* came to mind, and I could see the wind and the flying sand making his Arabic garb billow. A shiver of excitement ran through me. I inhaled. A new adventure was about to begin.

"Wake up, Victoria!" I whispered as I gently nudged my friend. "We're about to land in Tripoli."

She stirred and sat up.

"Look," I pointed outside into the pitch blackness. "That's Libya down there."

She peered sleepily out of the window. "Natasha, what the *hell* are we doing?"

"I don't know, but even if we wanted to turn back, it's too late now."

ABOUT THE AUTHOR

Natasha Rosewood, who was born in England, has always been fascinated with people, travel, languages, storytelling and the mystery of metaphysics. At 22, with three European languages under her belt, Natasha began a career as an air hostess on short haul routes, followed later by long haul flying, while at the same time studying palmistry and reading willing victims. In 1983, after eight years of operating on international routes, including a contract in Libya—and having acquired conversational proficiency in three more languages—Natasha emigrated to BC, Canada where she evolved into a master metaphysician and prolific write of books and films. Her first four published books—*Aaagh! I Think I'm Psychic (And You Can Be Too)*, *Aaagh! I Thought You Were Dead (And Other Psychic Adventures)*, *Mostly True GHOSTLY Stories* and more recently, *Flight of Your Life (Confessions of a 1970s Air Hostess)*—continue to elicit the highest accolades for her can't-put-it-down writing style, humor and teaching skills. Her intention in her Quantum Healing practice is to heal and empower the spirit while her goal for her writing of inspirational and funny stories is to reconnect humanity with its greatest potential and sense of humor! Let's bring laughter back into fashion!

MORE BOOKS BY
NATASHA J. ROSEWOOD

All books are available on Amazon in Print, Kindle, additional e-stores and soon to be in Audible format. Please refer to natasharosewood.com for a list of bookstores or visit Amazon.com.

In *Flight of Your Life,* Natasha, a multilingual British air hostess recounts her uproarious adventures in the 70s flying short haul all over Europe for a notoriously unsafe airline while dealing with the idiosyncrasies of numerous nationalities –and survives to tell the tales. Not only do drunken exit-removing Scottish football supporters, naughty captains, haunted aircraft and flying on old, defective planes threaten her safety, she must also navigate the eccentricities of outrageous passengers and crew. Even on the ground, friends' "emergencies" and her own romantic escapades threaten to derail her. But through it all, Natasha shows us the best, the worst and the funniest sides of humanity and how imperfect and lovable we all are!

Aaagh! I Think I'm Psychic (And You Can Be Too) is a sometimes humorous, sometimes heartbreaking account of Natasha's reluctant psychic awakening. Her story is accompanied by metaphysical endnotes to help the reader recognize and develop his or her own inherent intuitive ability, and to offer a deeper understanding of the psychic forces that were at play when Natasha magnetized these events to her. Prepare for a sense of déja vu. Aaagh!

Aaagh! I Thought You Were Dead (And Other Psychic Adventures) …"Do you see dead people?" a potential psychic client once asked me. "Oh, yes. All the time," I responded. "And so can you …if you are open." But seeing spirits is only a small element of Natasha Rosewood's life as a psychic development coach, spiritual healer and writer.

Join Natasha in ***Aaagh! I Thought You Were Dead (And Other Psychic Adventures)*** as she shares just some of the fun and fascinating-true life experiences from her personal and professional life as a psychic. Her fast- paced, light-hearted storytelling entertains as it empowers us all to explore our greatest mind potential. The "Dear Natasha" responses that follow each out-of-this-world tale answer the questions that many of us would all love to ask a psychic.

Mostly True GHOSTLY Stories is a collection of ten spooky, fictionalized tales inspired by the real-life experiences of ex-flight attendant, psychic and author, Natasha J. Rosewood. Whether set in a haunted youth hostel in France, a ghost town in Death Valley, California, over the Alps at 35,000 feet or in the alien-invaded English countryside, every story will have you teetering on the edge of the abyss between reality and illusion.